Costume Society of America series

Phyllis A. Specht, *Series Editor*

Forbidden Fashions

Forbidden Fashions

Invisible Luxuries in
Early Venetian Convents

Isabella Campagnol

Texas Tech University Press

This book is typeset in Minion Pro. The paper used in this book meets the minimum requirements of ANSI/NISO Z39.48-1992 (R1997). ∞

Designed by Kasey McBeath
Cover Design by Laura Jones Martinez
On the cover: F. Guardi, *Il parlatorio di San Zaccaria*, Venice, Ca' Rezzonico, ca. 1755. Reprinted by permission of Biblioteca del Museo Correr, Venice.

Library of Congress Control Number: 2014930499
ISBN (cloth): 978-0-89672-829-5
ISBN (e-book): 978-0-89672-830-1

14 15 16 17 18 19 20 21 22 / 9 8 7 6 5 4 3 2 1

Texas Tech University Press
Box 41037 | Lubbock, Texas 79409-1037 USA
800.832.4042 | ttup@ttu.edu | www.ttupress.org

This book is dedicated to my daughter
Camilla
and to our adventure together

New Orleans, May 2008

Contents

Chapter 4

Chapter 5

Illustrations

Acknowledgments

A lthough the job of a researcher is mostly a solitary one, it would have been impossible for me to work on this book without the help, suggestions, and support of many colleagues, friends, and family members.

I spent long, fascinating hours in the archives of the Istituzioni di Ricovero e di Educazione and the Patriarcato of Venice, where I benefited from the assistance of Giuseppe Ellero, Agata Brusegan, Manuela Barausse, and Davide Trivellato. I am very grateful to them for the kind and professional support they offered and for the passion they put in preserving those gold mines of historical information. I also owe a debt of gratitude to many other Venetian institutions that, in one way or another, allowed me to use images of the artwork they preserve or gave me access to libraries and archives. I would like to acknowledge don Gianmatteo Caputo and Irene Galifi from the Ufficio Beni Culturali of the Patriarcato of Venice, Marigusta Lazzari and Elisabetta Dal Carlo from the Fondazione Querini Stampalia, and the personnel of the Archivio di Stato of Venice, the Library of San Francesco della Vigna, and the Correr and Palazzo Mocenigo libraries.

I feel honored to have been a student of Doretta Davanzo Poli. She has been a constant and encouraging presence throughout my career, and I wish to express my most heartfelt thanks to her and my admiration for an amazing teacher who ceaselessly continues to spread knowledge about the history of textiles.

Jane Bridgeman made valuable suggestions after reading the first draft of the manuscript: her intellectual generosity and the warmth of her hospitality is a gift that I treasure deeply.

This book would not have been born without Judith Keeling of Texas Tech University Press. I still remember the excitement I felt when she told me, after my presentation at the Costume Society of America symposium in New Orleans, that she had been fascinated by the research and that this was "a story that needed to be told!" Thank you Judith, for believing in the value of my work, and thank you Kellyanne Ure for all the work you have done on the manuscript in these past months.

Family members and scores of friends have also been of great encouragement during the long time it took to write this book, which I began working on at a very dark moment of my life. I could not have found the mental energy for it without, first of all, my sister, Beatrice, my parents, Renzo and Fernanda, and my Lorenzano.

Last, but definitely not least, a huge thank you goes to my daughter Camilla. She has been my biggest supporter during the years of research, always ready to come with me in photographic expeditions around the city to take pictures of surviving convents and artworks, always so interested in the progress of the writing. I loved her intelligent questions about the story I was so caught up in and her witty comments and "suggestions."

Finally, thank you Cami, for giving up so many bedtime stories to let me go write!

Venezia, January 2013

Abbreviations

a.   *anno*: year

ASG   Archivio di Stato, Genoa

ASPV   Archivio Storico del Patriarcato, Venice

ASR   Archivio di Stato, Rome

ASV   Archivio di Stato, Venice

b.   *busta*: envelope

BMC   Biblioteca Museo Correr, Venice

BNM   Biblioteca Nazionale Marciana, Venice

c.   *carta*: page

col.   *colonna*: column

fasc.   *fascicolo*: file

IRE   Archivio delle Istituzioni di Ricovero e Educazione, Venice

no.   number

pt.   *parte*: part; or page

r.   *registro*: volume

t.   *tomo*: volume

Forbidden Fashions

Introduction

There is in Venice a large number of nuns, usually of noble origin, since all the noblemen that have daughters destine them to the cloister from a very young age and they force them to become nuns in order to save their dowries. . . . Therefore (the nuns) publicly declare that having been forced to take the veil, they can behave as badly as they want . . . living without religious spirit or devotion. Some of them also dress very dishonestly, wearing curled hair and low necklines just as laywomen do.

From the "Relazione del Stato, Costumi, Disordini et Remediis de Venetia," a seventeenth-century manuscript cited in Molmenti, *Storia di Venezia nella vita privata*[1]

Around 1564 there were in Venice over thirty convents and monasteries, inhabited by 2,107 nuns.[2] However, a true inclination toward a withdrawn life of prayer was not as common among Venetian women as these figures suggest. As explained above in the "Relazione," these nuns were actually born within the most important families of the city, and only rarely had chosen of their own accord to profess the three self-denying vows of poverty, chastity, and obedience.

From the late fifteenth century until the fall of the Serenissima, in 1797, the destiny of thousands of "involuntary" nuns was systematically sealed by their very own parents. The expense of a proper aristocratic marriage usually allowed only one out of three daughters to marry; the remaining daughters were more or less "sentenced" to the cloister.[3]

Thus, far from reflecting religious fervor or devotion, the population of nuns reveals much about the demographic, social, and moral dynamics of the city.

Through carefully orchestrated marriages, Venetian aristocratic fathers sought to promote and improve their families' standing and to forge useful political and economic connections, while at the same time striving to close ranks and preserve the body politic of the Most Serene Republic. This marriage system became the very foundation of the exceptional political and social stability enjoyed by Venice for centuries, in light of which it becomes easy to understand how a single magnificent and well-connected marriage could seem to a patrician father far more prudent than three or four of lesser note. Concentrating one's resources in the interest of securing one most lucrative match was simply good business sense.

Yet as marriage of one sort or another was nonetheless requisite to preserving a family's good name, whenever the costs of an additional secular wedding seemed prohibitive, a divine marriage provided the perfect solution: it offered to "unmarriageable" young women a socially decorous role, while maintaining the honor and wealth of their families and contributing in preserving the timeless, almost miraculous social solidity of the Most Serene Republic. Patrician-women-turned-nuns became the axis of the entire system as convents achieved primary civic significance and even religious authorities praised such sacrifice as patriotic.

The Catholic hierarchies of the Serenissima were, indeed, very well aware of the situation. In a letter to the Senate dated 1619, Patriarch Giovanni Tiepolo, head of the Venetian dioceses, acknowledged the needs and frustrations of the over "two thousand patrician women" who "live in this city locked up in convents as if in public warehouses," essentially because of the "impulse of their parents." Out of compassion for their unfortunate situation, he therefore decided to allow them some latitude "in everyday life, in respect of the rules and in their habits" granting them permission to enjoy a few "honest comforts" in order to, at least partially, console them for their unfortunate condition. He stated that he needed to take into consideration the fact that they were "noblewomen, raised and nurtured with the highest delicacy and respect so that if they were of the other sex, they would command and govern the world," whereas instead "they have confined themselves within those walls, not out of piety, but obedience to their families, making of their own liberty . . . a gift not only to God, but to the fatherland, the world, and their closest relatives."[4] The enclosure and integrity of a distinct and powerful class endowed with political powers and special privileges found, then, a living embodiment in these noblewomen "stored" in the convents, who became, rather literally, incarnations of "virginal" Venice.[5]

In exchange, maybe even out of some sort of guilt, the government of the Serenissima constantly maintained over the centuries very close relationships with its nuns. The doge himself accompanied by the highest officials of the government periodically and ceremoniously went to visit "aristocratic" convents such as Santa Giustina, San Zaccaria, or San Lorenzo.

The most spectacular proof of the deep connections between the republic and the monasteries was, however, its association with the monastery of Santa Maria delle Vergini. Mirroring the annual marriage to the sea on the day of the Sensa,[6] the doge, in fact, "married" the Abbess of Le Vergini on the day of her investiture, thus establishing a direct link between the two institutions, one political, the other religious.

In addition, the relations between the Venetian government and the local monasteries included the right of government itself to exercise control over the nuns. In 1521 the specific office of the Provveditori sopra Monasteri was created, composed of three noblemen charged with overseeing all affairs connected with the city's convents.[7]

For their part, the nuns were more than eager to keep up any sort of interaction with the outside world and to preserve some degree of secular comfort in their daily lives. Although they were supposed to lead modest, contemplative lives, free from mundane preoccupations, in reality many aristocratic and "involuntary" nuns actually continued a rather lavish secular routine inside the convents. They entertained guests in the parlors, and not just their parents and close relations, as prescribed by conventual regulations, but also friends and occasionally foreign visitors transformed the parlors into stages for plays or concerts; and the nuns considered their cells as private apartments inside which they received other nuns. Many of them dressed elegantly for these social gatherings, wearing not the required habits of their order, but secular, fashionable, and rather audacious clothes.

This behavior constituted not only an infraction against the vow of poverty, but also a dangerous sin. It could potentially expose the nuns to the gaze of outsiders in parlors, or even stir undesirable emotions among the nuns themselves. The evocative powers and symbolic and subversive meanings of these "forbidden" monastic fashions highlights at the same time the significant role played by clothing in ancien regime societies, and in Venice in particular, where specific colors and shapes were regulated by law.

Dress represents a distinctive peculiarity of human existence.[8] "Invented" out of necessity, in order to protect and shelter the body from the inclemency of the weather, it soon became layered with much more elaborate meanings. Clothes evolved into class-defining status symbols, developing as a means of communicating an image of the self, signaling status, class, and group affiliations and/or a way to modify the aesthetic perception of the body.[9] Dress is what made the human body culturally visible, revealed the economic means of a person, and crucially facilitated the characterization of his or her social and professional role. Clothing could also help in defining the morality or religion of an individual: prostitutes, convicts, and other "pariah" of society were, for instance, mandated to wear either certain symbols on their clothing or specific colors or patterns, such as the yellow "O" worn by Venetian Jews, or the striped patterns reserved for buffoons, heretics, and lepers.[10]

The act of dressing became therefore a language that performed a strategic function in the construction of the personal identity of the individual.[11] It was a "sociologic" act, an element of a formal and normative structure consecrated by society itself.[12] As an exquisitely societal aspect, dress became a privileged channel through which lifestyles and cultural models, ways of thinking and acting, rules and values of a society were passed on, in a process that was not only cognitive but behavioral and symbolic.[13]

Thus dress used as a symbolic language is common in any human society: this was even more true for Venetian society between the fifteenth and the eighteenth century. The Serenissima consistently relied on a strict dressing code and a complex corpus of sumptuary laws in her attempts to distinguish and regulate social classes. Francesco Sansovino, sixteenth-century author of *Venetia città nobilissima et singulare*, specifically states that he aims in his work to describe, among other things, the city's "ancient customs, clothes, magistrates,"[14] thus acknowledging the importance of clothes in the definition of Venetian culture.

The opinion of Sansovino was shared by Cesare Vecellio, who, in several of his engravings, associated the political myth of Venice with her fashions.[15] For instance, the dress of the "Doge antico" is said to "truly represent the felicitous and well-founded greatness of this most Christian Republic, founded on the firm rock of the Holy Faith . . . as can be seen clearly [from the fact] that up until today she has preserved herself as an intact Virgin. The coat above is of great decorum and [attests to the] greatness of this Most Serene Republic."[16]

Regulation of dress was the responsibility of another very peculiar public office, the Magistrato alle Pompe,[17] which for centuries strenuously, if pointlessly, strove to impose on the citizens the respect of a predetermined dress code meant to consolidate the Venetian social hierarchies.[18] Such an intense effort to regulate the clothing style of the Venetians,[19] with specific attention to women's fashions, reveals the sensitivity of the topic in the republic. Without a doubt, in Renaissance Venice, more than anywhere else in Europe, the place of an individual was announced by his dress; this was even truer in the case of women's clothes because a woman's clothing identified her visually and socially, even for those who did not know her family of origin.

Cut off from any sort of political role, women in Venice expressed themselves, and the power and wealth of their families, through their clothing. "While she expressed her individuality, . . . a woman also expressed her husband's status. This represents the main reason why governments everywhere were so concerned with sumptuary regulations: clothes represented a metaphor of the social distinctions and a means to structure social relations."[20] A perfect example of this system is offered by the promulgation in Genoa of sumptuary laws that regulated female dress on the basis of dotal levels, allowing different styles according to the amount of the dowry.[21]

In reading the clothes as linguistic elements, it is essential to consider not just the shapes, but also the eye-catching function of the colors. Colors, in fact, "attract the gaze of the people, as a magnet attracts the iron"[22] and can "offer a reading frame that needs to be crossed with the notions of heraldry and religious and romantic poetics."[23] Similar to what happened in Catholic liturgy that provided for a well-defined and significant chromatic code,[24] colors contributed to the definition of the complex Venetian social and political stratification, since it was through the use of certain colors that specific positions, ranks, and appointments were recognized.[25] "Venetian insistence on specific dress for a particular official may be compared to the use of religious habits or liturgical garments and colors":[26] the *procuratori*, for instance, the most important public officials, were the only one allowed to wear crimson *veste*, imposing robes with wide sleeves.

Having established the importance of the "dress" issue in Venice, the almost obsessive attention given to clothes even by the city's nuns becomes more understandable. The symbolic meaning of clothes, fabrics, and colors was not lost on or forgotten by the "prisoners" inside the convents. Forbidden fabrics, audacious dress styles, precious embroideries, and elegant laces became the "weapons" of choice to be used in the quiet rebellion against the rules and prescriptions of conventual life by the vast majority of "involuntary" nuns. Conscious of the value of appearance in the outside world, aristocratic nuns began to use clothes as a way to define roles and social status inside the monastic "society" as well.[27]

In numerous circumstances did the clothes used by the nuns play an essential part in the life of Venetian convents. From the fashionable white silk dress worn during the ceremony of presentation of the novices, to the scandalously secular (and often tantalizingly masculine) costumes used while performing plays during Carnival; from the modest habits in which many lay noblewomen requested to be buried, hoping to reacquire an at least ideal virginity, to the "dishonest" dresses seen by Patriarch Querini during a visit to the Celestia monastery in 1426, clothes and luxury accessories such as silk hoses, jewellery, furs, and watches always played a controversial role inside Venetian monasteries.

Thus it is essential to understand the anthropological, psychological, and social meanings of the use of prohibited or immodest clothing inside these peculiar all-female communities. These dresses conferred identities to the individual nuns as they communicated their positions within the cloistral social structure; they spoke a symbolic language, a language valued and understood both inside and outside the monasteries, and constituted a subtle, yet effective, way to ignore the impositions of monastic life. They were also intrinsically dangerous because they suggested, or even showed, the bodies of the nuns, bodies that were denied, since the nuns were supposedly angelic beings.

The analysis of the "forbidden fashions" of Venetian nuns can therefore offer crucial help not only to the study of dress in these peculiar communities, but also to the definition of a not so small, and anyway essential, cross-section of the female population of the Serenissima and represents a precious, although often neglected, way to read and get to know Venetian society and culture.

The scandalized reports describing the dress infractions of these nuns expose the turmoil inside these women's souls and help us understand their frustrations and their desperate attempts to preserve the fleeting images of a life that was to be for them forever forbidden.

One

Maridar o Monacar, To Marry or to Become a Nun? Nuptial Strategies in the Venetian Aristocracy

. . . Simple little girls

Innocent, or silly and very young

Have been made Nuns

With flattery and deceits

They dressed us as Nuns

. . .

Fathers and mothers drove us away

As their mortal enemies

. . .

This fate that rules the world

Blind, deaf, hard, and fallacious

Mother to some, stepmother to others

She takes away and gives as she likes

If there are sisters

One is lucky

The others are sent away

Little imprisoned Nuns

One sister is among pain and tears

The other among games and parties

One wears jewels and rich dresses

The other is veiled in black.[1]

*f*rom their birth, the women of Venice had just two life prospects: either they got married or they entered a convent. And the choice was not theirs: the families chose their destiny, whether they liked it or not.

When, on December 17, 1680, Francesco Tiepolo wrote his will, he appeared rather concerned about his daughters' future, strongly urging them to embrace monastic life, a choice he considered much wiser than a marriage, "in consideration of how expensive and risky for the families weddings could be."[2] In other words, he was not apprehensive about their personal happiness, but rather about the negative effects their marriages could have on the family's patrimony. Financial concerns played a key role also in the final dispositions of other fathers, who explicitly gave their bad financial luck as the main reason for why their female offspring could not marry.

Zuane Falier, for instance, writes in his will: "I wish that my daughters Bianca and Cecilia be placed in a monastery when their time comes and if they so desire, but I beg them to go, because they will have a better life than if they married (and also because I do not have enough means to marry them) . . . and I urge and beg them to become nuns and to serve God that they will never have a better master."[3]

Decades later, Zuane Badoer followed the same line of reasoning, stating that "since his family has been hit by numerous disasters," his daughters will be much better off in a monastery.[4]

Badoer, Tiepolo, Falier: these last names belong to some of the most prestigious Venetian houses, and yet, in their last wishes, all of these fathers clearly point their daughters toward a cloistered life for what were essentially economic and "practical" considerations. The opinions, wishes, and desires of the girls do not appear to be taken much into account, and, even when they were, they seem suspiciously manipulated. In Francesco Contarini's will, dated August 2, 1647, it emerges that he was leaving "to my three girls at home a convenient dowry to enter a monastery, as by the grace of God, I see them inclined."[5] It certainly seems strange, if not unlikely, that three out of three daughters dreamed of a monastic life!

Finding suitable spouses for his daughters was at the top of the must-do list of every Venetian father: a parent unable to provide suitable dowries (and therefore proper husbands within their own social class!) would in fact suffer dishonor, blame, and embarrassment. Given the skyrocketing cost of dowries from the fifteenth century onward,[6] the practice developed of shipping off to religious destinies "superfluous" young women who, for economic reasons, could not get married.

The same marriage strategy that aimed to preserve the wealth of the families also shaped the lives of the sons of the aristocracy. Nearly half of male nobles who reached adulthood in the fifteenth century appear to have remained bachelors: "to be precise, of 952 men from sixteen clans whose entry into adulthood can be documented, 412 apparently never married."[7] From the thorough studies of Davis on the Donà family, it emerges that, customarily, only the oldest son got married,[8] while the other brothers usually remained to live in the family's palace, sometimes creating strange, mostly male households, while occasionally enjoying the female companionship of the famous courtesans for which Venice was known all over Europe.[9] This rather unusual lifestyle prompted the creation of such literary works as De Coelibatu, written by Ermolao Barbaro around 1485. In it, male unmarried life was exalted and praised because of the freedom offered, a freedom that, according to the author, should have been purposefully devoted to humanistic or other types of studies.

These bachelors mostly worked in the family business, but also constituted a key presence in the government. "Their function as government officials may have been an extension of their role within the family:

the function, namely, of holding government jobs and casting electoral votes in line with the family interests supervised by their fathers and married brothers."[10]

Venice was most certainly not the only Italian city to apply these social strategies, but because it was a republic that prided itself on the freedom of its citizens, the moral issues raised by these questionable practices were discussed and, occasionally, challenged more openly than elsewhere, as in the literary works of "involuntary" nun Arcangela Tarabotti.

A key role in the actuation of these policies was, from the early Renaissance and until the end of the Republic, played by Venetian convents that stood in as boarding schools for girls and "warehouses" for women who could not marry. According to Antonio Ottoboni, a gentleman who lived in the seventeenth century, this custom was absolutely necessary, being the only way to effectively safeguard the innocence of the girls whom, he thought, needed "to be locked in exemplary monasteries as soon as they enter adolescence because women are a merchandise that needs to be jealously guarded since they are so easily ruined."[11] In keeping with this belief, local patrician families for centuries routinely sent their daughters of about ten years of age within the safe cloistral walls of one of the many convents of the city. The purpose was to "polish" their education by having them learn the essentials of sewing, embroidery, lace-making, singing, and music and to keep them in a protected environment until their future was decided, usually between the age of fourteen and twenty.

There were two life options open to them, simply expressed in Venetian dialect as "maridar or monacar," to marry or to enter a convent. The third option, continuing to lead an unmarried life in the paternal house, was a rare exception, only reluctantly accepted by the families because of the risks involved with the presence of an adult single woman in the house.

Only one daughter was usually selected for marriage: she was either the youngest, in order to allow the family to keep profiting from the monetary part of her dowry for as long as it was possible, or the most beautiful or talented. The other sisters were destined for a religious future, and, according to a realistic estimate, more than a third of them were locked in the cloister without any sort of divine calling.[12]

The girls themselves were acutely aware of the real motivations behind the choices of their families:

> "My mom wants me to become a nun
>
> To save for my sister's dowry,
>
> And to obey my mom,
>
> I am cutting my hair and will become a nun."[13]

Should the parents decide against the secular marriage of a girl, the transition from "figlia a spese" (boarding girl) to novice was frighteningly easy:[14] the girl was simply never "retrieved" from the convent where she was being educated. She just remained in the familiar environment she knew, where she had friends and, most often, close relatives, such as aunts and cousins or even sisters, ready to offer an essential support system, extremely valuable in the new nun's adaptation to religious life and with the help of which she could start to build her own "family" inside the convent.

The fact that we do not find a lot of public documentation regarding the protests of the involuntary nuns against this imposed life is not surprising. To them, initially at least, what was probably more worrying was the thought of leaving the world they had known since childhood to live with a complete stranger who was often ten to twenty years older than his bride.

The "lucky" girls destined for marriage did not have, in fact, any say in the selection of their future husbands: the arrangements were made by their fathers and, occasionally, brothers who aimed to conscript their nubile kinswomen into strengthening their family's position, with little or no regard for the woman's wishes. "The needs of the family were the dominant consideration, and . . . the inclinations of a teenage potential bride were of little account."[15] What really mattered was the union between the two families and the strengthening of political and economic alliances.[16]

Furthermore, a patrician marriage was undoubtedly a very complex event that did not involve just the families of the bride and groom, but rather the Venetian aristocratic class as a whole, up to the doge himself, to whom, until 1501, patrician brides were routinely introduced and who acted as "public testimonial" of the union.[17]

These "bridal shows" were so impressive that part of the reputation of the city rested on them. In the celebration of aristocratic weddings there were expectations to be fulfilled and rituals to be followed: "The display of wealth and the observance of ritual in the binding of two patrician families reflected in microcosm the wealth and civic rituals of the city, as well as reciprocal arrangements between potential allies which formed the bedrock of the Venetian political system. For this reason every aspect of the process was viewed critically for its larger political and propagandistic implications."[18] Public and private interests were intricately interwoven, and, if marriage constituted the hinge connecting government and elite families, dowries represented the crucial indicator of a family's position within the political and social environment.[19] As they used to say, "while arranging a marriage it is necessary to consider the amount of the dowry first, and the woman after, because her virtues do not enrich the house of the husband as much as her dowry."[20]

Patrician women, instrumental in the realization of this policy, therefore played at the same time two very different social roles: excluded from their own lineage, which they left upon marriage, they played through marriage a key role in defining their families' social strategies at the center of which were their own dowries.

The dowry represented the daughter's share of her father's patrimony. "Unlike her brothers, who were forced to await their father's death to collect their inheritance, a Venetian woman received her share when she married or entered a convent."[21] At the signing of the wedding contract she, in fact, would give up any sort of claim on the rest of the paternal patrimony: the dowry was then conveyed to her husband as the bride's contribution toward the maintenance of the new household. Only a widow could reclaim her dowry from her acquired family, to pass it on to her own daughter or dispose of it as she saw fit.[22]

In the second half of the fourteenth century the average dowry was about one thousand ducats,[23] but, from the fifteenth century onward, despite the best efforts of the government to stop the spiraling process, the figure appears constantly on the rise. A law dated August 22, 1420, set the limit for the dowries at an official maximum of sixteen hundred ducats. The only possible exception was for a plebeian wife marrying a noble; in that case, in order to help the shaky finances of aristocratic, but impoverished, families, the limit was raised to two thousand ducats. The imposition of a threshold was deemed necessary because many fathers, having insufficient funds to provide for the dowries, resorted to sending their desperately crying daughters to monasteries in order to offer them a decorous position in society.[24]

The efforts of the legislators were therefore clearly aimed at protecting the families' properties and honor by facilitating the marriage of young women while, at the same time, diminishing the recourse to forced monacations. The rationale behind the law was very realistic: since "there was no hope that fathers would stop in competing for the dowries, it was necessary that such corruption be corrected by our regime."[25] However, since "a Venetian law lasts but a week,"[26] this one was also widely ignored, and, on November 4, 1505, the legal limit for the dowries was once again raised by the Senate to three thousand ducats.[27] In 1551 a new, and not the last, adjustment was made, with dowries allowed up to five thousand ducats.[28]

The point is that the amount of the dowry of an aristocratic bride was known all over the city.[29] "Dowries were more than private exchanges of assets. They were meant for public display and were actually exhibited in a demonstration of wealth which served the self-satisfaction of the city and its propaganda."[30] Marin Sanudo, the gossipy chronicler who in the pages of his *Diarii* recounts an infinite number of interesting episodes of Venetian life, describes the presentation of a rich dowry this way: "at the dinner hour, when I was present, about 4000 ducats, part of the bride's dowry, were brought in six basins. The first one contained gold (coins), the rest (silver) coins. Well done, for those who can afford it."[31]

The dowry constituted only a portion of the unavoidable wedding expenses. There was, for instance, the trousseau or *corredo* that consisted of clothing, jewels, furniture, sometimes paintings, and other items that were given to the bride for her personal use.[32] Moreover, the expenses for a proper aristocratic wedding entailed numerous parties to be organized and banquets to be paid for, during which elaborate, even gilded food was served in an orderly fashion,[33] framed by elegantly clothed and bejeweled women, and brightened by music, song, and entertainment.

During all these events brides were exhibited as iconic symbols of their families' wealth. These young women, who before their engagements were "so strictly looked after and watched over in their paternal homes, that often not even the closest relatives could see them until their wedding,"[34] starred in the many social functions that composed the multistaged process of a patrician marriage. The luxury of these wedding extravaganzas was known all over Europe and played a not negligible diplomatic value: foreign dignitaries were often invited to aristocratic weddings in order to impress them with the exotic and costly foods served at bridal banquets, the richness of the dowries and of the bridal trousseaux, and the number of beautiful and magnificently dressed noblewomen who accompanied the bride. Here again is Marin Sanudo describing a feast to celebrate the Nani-Badoer betrothal in 1506 at which the Turkish ambassador was invited "to see the women,"[35] while, at the wedding between ser Ferigo Foscari and the daughter of ser Zuan Venier, granddaughter of the doge, were present no less than the three ambassadors, of the pope, of Spain, and of Hungary, besides the prior of the Knights of St. John of the Temple and a knight of Rhodes.[36]

In comparison with the splendor and the extreme expenses of a secular wedding, the more reasonably priced divine "marriage" provided a decent and permanent accommodation for the ever-increasing number of "excess" women in the society.

The "benefits" of monastic life were praised and exalted to make it more attractive to the nuns-to-be. On several occasions Carlo Goldoni, eighteenth-century Venetian playwright, favorably commented on the possibilities offered by life in the cloister. In his "Song for the Monacation of Angela Maria Venier," who was going to be clothed in the monastery of Santa Caterina, he describes the carefree life led by choir nuns, remarking that they did not work much—just a little needlework if they wanted to—were free to pursue their literary and musical inclinations, and could have more fun than in their own homes. They were also spared the trouble of dressing up three or four times every day and the torture of the hairdresser for three hours every morning.[37]

There were other compensations. Inside their communities, nuns benefited from considerable political liberty, being free to cast their vote during the regularly scheduled chapter elections; when elected, they had the power to hire personnel, act as landowners, and administer the monastery finances. They were also exempt from the dangers of continual childbearing, and, finally, seemed to have been less likely to contract the plague or other dangerous infectious diseases.[38]

These "advantages" offered but a small recompense for the loss of freedom suffered by the "involuntary" nuns. Their desperation at having been victims of the strategy of "marrying off one or two daughters with large marriage portions rather than a large number with mediocre ones" was, however, seldom publicly expressed.[39]

Although the vast majority of them did not put up much of a struggle, having being subdued by their families' strength, clear evidence of their wrestling against these decisions remains in a number of folk songs and poems.

In one of these a mother begs her daughter:

> "Dear daughter do become a nun
> Do not get married
> I will have a habit made for you
> So you can wear it,
> Without any worry
> You will participate in liturgies and masses
> And you will always
> Be with the Abbess"

The daughter replies:

> "Dear Mom, do not send me to the monastery
>
> Do not prepare the habit
>
> Because I do not want to wear it
>
> Participating every day
>
> In vespers and in Mass
>
> And also because the Abbess
>
> Does not do anything but yell."[40]

Occasionally, subtler means of persuasion were employed, as is bitterly recalled, for instance, by Arcangela Tarabotti in her literary works.[41]

Tarabotti's voice was that of an insider. Elena Cassandra Tarabotti was the eldest of nine children of a Venetian merchant family. She had four younger sisters, of whom the two youngest married, while the others remained at home. When she was twelve years old, she was sent as a boarding girl to the Benedictine monastery of Sant'Anna, a "convent so ancient that it has been almost completely deprived of beautiful objects: it is, however, a venerable institution because of the pious nuns that reside there and for its remarkable location."[42] At sixteen she became a member of that community, taking the name of Arcangela; three years later she was solemnly consecrated, thus becoming an "involuntary" nun.

In her writings she repeatedly indicates that she entered the monastery not by choice, but rather under the coercion of her family, and she begs parents not to sentence their daughters to the cloister, not to bend to economic reasoning in deciding their future.[43] She presented her objections about forced monacations not as much as personal complaints, but rather as a defense of those who had not been allowed to freely choose their future: "If you would not accompany your daughters to wealthy and noble wedding rites with high-ranking and wealthy spouses, as your vainglory requires, then join them at least in more modest marriages. Divide up your estates and wealth among them without preference, for that is the will of God. Do not aim at raising one of them to the summit of worldly pomp by casting the others down into a chaos of wretchedness and damnation's abyss. Temper the wealth of your sons, and remember that your daughters are also your flesh and blood; do not wish to constrain the feelings that God has left free to all His creatures."

She also describes how her own father maliciously convinced her to enter the convent, while other parents deceived their daughters by pointing to sugar confections hanging from the convent's trees and describing the balls, parties, and dinners they would enjoy in the monastery.[44] Venetian religious authorities tried to impose a period during which the novices could try conventual life and verify if it was suitable for them, in order to avoid future complaints, but they encountered the opposition of the families that considered mere admission to the convent definitive detachment from the world.[45]

The erudite Tommaso Garzoni expressed his opposition against this policy, harshly criticizing those fathers who "in order to give a large dowry to one daughter, place the others into nunhood . . . and when they are in the monastery . . . they curse the day and hour of when they entered the cloister, and become bitter, instead of blessed."[46]

Actually, in fact, nuns were supposed to serve and support the state through their piety, purity, and prayers; less than proper behaviors were equated with sacrilege, or lèse-majesté against God, and could have disastrous consequences for Venice.[47]

Understandably, the presence of hundreds of "involuntary" nuns in Venetian monasteries could only increase the possibility of improper behaviors, and, in fact, many of these religious institutions, and the women who lived in them, had a rather scandalous reputation. As a consequence, preachers and historians who endorsed the religious and moral status of the city as the best defense and protection from her enemies and who considered the purity and virginity of the nuns as metaphoric of the immaculate body of the virtuous city of Venice, quickly began blaming on the nuns totally unrelated events and asking for strong reformation of

the monasteries. One such example is in the homily given by Fra Timoteo Casoli da Lucca during the Christmas Mass of 1495 in the church of
San Francesco della Vigna. He held the sins of the nuns responsible for a
plague outbreak and suggested to the doge: "If you want a remedy to the
plague you have to stop these horrible sins. . . . Whenever a foreign dig-
nitary comes to Venice, they give him a tour of the city's convents, which
in reality are not convents but public bordellos. Most Serene Prince! I
know that you are aware of the situation much more than I am. Take steps
against this and you will stop the plague."[48] Gerolamo Priuli[49] made a
similar point when he blamed "the most grave sins of the whoring nuns"
for no less than the military defeat in the battle of Agnadello![50]

The unruly behavior of many of the involuntary nuns was simply the
logical consequence of forced monacations: whose fault was it if some of
the monasteries were not the immaculate heavens they were supposed
to be?[51]

The mother superior of the monastery of San Daniele had no doubts.
In 1604, during the trial of Suor Serafica Balbi, accused of having had a
relationship with a man, she strongly defended the nun, declaring that
she was "a good girl, but may God forgive those who force their daughters into convents." Serafica herself desperately cried during her own in-
terrogation, expressing the wish to rather having been born "the daughter of a porter," because she would not have been imprisoned against her
will.[52] Similarly, Suor Deodata from the monastery of San Giuseppe was
also very angry against the relatives who forced her into the convent. Her
sisters in religion testified that they "heard her cursing her father, and
mother and everybody else in the family who sent her to the monastery,
and she also cursed her brother in law, Zorzi, saying that he never did
anything good and he ruined her own family."[53]

Forced monacation represented therefore only a temporary fix to the
social dilemma of the destinies of women; actually, it soon revealed itself
as a double-edged sword. If, on the one hand, it saved aristocratic families
from huge monetary disbursements, on the other hand it could, according to the thinking of the time, cause terrible damages to the Republic

herself because of the unspeakable behaviors and sins of the conventual "prisoners," sins that often had something to do with the nun's "fashions," such as forbidden clothes and accessories that found their way inside the conventual walls in a worldly display of elegance that began with the ceremonies that welcomed the nun-to-be in the cloister.

Two
Weddings and Clothings: A Comparison

*W*hat kinds of preparations were made for a patrician wedding and for a monastic ceremony? And what styles and colors of dresses were Venetian brides and nuns-to-be to wear? Numerous, and sometimes strikingly similar, were the steps and ceremonies that transformed a young noblewoman into either a resplendent bride, the icon of her family's fortunes and social status, or a demure nun, who was supposed to follow the example of Saint Catherine of Alexandria, the most iconic bride ever thanks to her mystical marriage to Baby Jesus.

Brides

Venetian brides wore robes of white.

Centuries before the proclamation, in 1854, of the dogma of the Immaculate Conception that made white the customary color for wedding dresses,[1] the *novizie*, or novices, as brides-to-be were called in a curious analogy with their religious counterparts, paraded themselves on their wedding day in "an immaculate white tight-fitting dress, suitable to the candor and innocence of a well-brought-up maiden."[2]

In the sixteenth century, according to the symbolic language of colors, white alluded to the virginity and chastity of women;[3] it also marked their transition into a new status, as it did in classical times, when young Romans wore an immaculate toga upon entering adulthood, thus indicating

Giovanni Grevembroch, *Donzella*, from *Gli abiti de' Veneziani di quasi ogni età . . .* , vol. I, 1754.

both their willingness to accept the rights and duties that came with their roles as citizens and the pure soul with which they approached their new position.[4] In Christian times the newly baptized were given a white tunic as well, symbolizing their new life and their liberation from original sin.

Easily soiled, white represented in Venice the color of luxury, and it was therefore reserved for the most important political and iconic figure of the government of the Republic, the doge. His white and gold robe expressed the sacrality of his role and followed a custom that had been imported from Byzantium, with which Venice consistently maintained key trading and political relationships, and where the emperor always appeared dressed in magnificent white capes, occasionally brightened by the precious shimmering of incorruptible gold threads. White was also considered equivalent to gold both in heraldry and in liturgical vestments.[5]

Venetian women in general were hardly ever seen around the city, their place being in the protected domestic environment, with the routine exceptions of religious ceremonies. This was even more true in the

Gabriel Bella, *The Wedding of a Venetian Noblewoman*, last quarter of the eighteenth century, Venice, Querini Stampalia Museum. Courtesy of Fondazione Querini Stampalia Onlus, Venice.

case of young women, "both Patrician and Citizens": if they were not already in a convent to be educated, "when they, rarely, ventured out of the house, they used to cover their heads with an ample White silk veil called *fazzuolo*, and with it they hide their faces and chest. They do not wear but few jewels with pearls, and some simple gold necklaces. The outer dresses are for the most part *rovano*[6] or black, made of light wool cloth, or *ciambellotto*[7] or other similarly inexpensive fabrics, although underneath they wear colored gowns, and silk sashes called *poste*."[8]

Given the social and diplomatic importance of patrician weddings, any single detail was carefully planned and executed. The display of luxurious clothes constituted such an essential key element of the ceremonies that, although sumptuary laws forbade the use of white clothing, temporary exemptions were routinely made for aristocratic brides, in the choice of colors and shapes and in the fabrics.[9] Marin Sanudo offers us several confirmations of these exceptions. In 1517 a bride from the Grimani family, having obtained an *ad personam* permission for the day of the wedding, wore an "illegal" dress made "half of cloth of gold and half of white fabric."[10] Similarly, in October 1519, a bride from the Pisani family sported a "white and gold dress,"[11] prompting the matter-of-fact comment of Sanudo that "everybody does whatever they want, even if it is against the law."[12] A few months later, in fact, Sanudo reports again that a bride from the Foscari family was married wearing a "chequered white and gold dress, forbidden by the law, a gold chain necklace and many big pearls."[13] Showy jewels, in the form of necklaces, coronets, and earrings or precious belts, were indeed characteristic accessories of bridal outfits.

In the second half of the sixteenth century, the pointed waistline typical of the period was marked by the heavy *colana in sbara* or *paternostro*,[14] a gold and pearl chain-belt, the extremity of which reached the hem of the dress and that symbolized the love bond and the solidity of the marital knot; often the large metal beads that finished the belt were hollow and filled with a scented paste.[15] A precious pearl necklace, usually matched by pearl earrings, was another classic jewel worn by brides. It was donated by the future mother-in-law, its maximum value could have been up to four hundred ducats, and it could be worn only for ten years, starting from the day of the wedding.

The characteristic Venetian-blonde hair of the brides was left loose for a year after the wedding ceremony and was enhanced by thin gold threads mixed within the hair, held in place by a small coronet. Grevembroch remembers that, on the occasion of the coronation of dogaressa Cecilia Dandolo in 1557, among the over two hundred noblewoman who composed her following were "six Brides with loose hair enriched by gold threads."[16]

The opulence and style of the bridal attire was matched by the preciousness of the wedding trousseau. It could include dozens of gowns, lengths and lengths of laces, personal and house linens, but also jewels, furniture, and paintings that accompanied the bride to her future home. Because of their material value and the key role they played in the ne-

Cesare Vecellio, *Sposa sposata*, from *De gli habiti antichi et moderni di diverse parti del mondo* . . . Venice, 1590, c. 126.

Giacomo Franco, *Novizza col ballerino*, from *Habiti delle donne venetiane,* Venice, 1628.

gotiation of the marriage, trousseaux were always meticulously detailed in the marriage contracts, and many of these lists are still preserved in Venetian archives.

One example is offered by the trousseau inventory of Paulina Provisina Vignon, in which was included, besides over twenty dresses made with precious fabrics and decorated by needle-made laces and the usual linens, such valuable items as paintings in gilded frames, gilt stools, flounces of the expensive type of Venetian needle lace called *punto in aria*, a bureau desk, a spinet, precious zibeline, marten and ermine furs, and twenty rugs.[17]

The actual wedding consisted of a sequence of rites and ceremonies that occurred mostly during the long Carnival season, from St. Stephen's Day through Mardi Gras. Marriages were usually arranged through a third party and were preceded by the formal commitment of the father to concede the hand of the daughter to the fiancé. The matrimonial edict (*de futuro*) was then posted in the courtyard of Palazzo Ducale, where the groom would receive the congratulations of relatives and friends. The following act was the official proclamation of the mutual consent of the betrothed couple to the wedding (*de praesenti*) and, later, the giving of the ring to the bride. At this point the nuptial contracts were prepared, and the amounts of the dowry and the trousseau, "le cosse per el vestir della sposa," were minutely described. On the day of the signing the groom, dressed with the patrician *vesta*,[18] went to the house of the bride accompanied by his male relatives. They were introduced in the *portego*, the large longitudinal hall that in Venetian palaces served as the banquet and music hall or ballroom. There, the magnificently dressed bride would make her appearance, accompanied by the dance master, and "after having greeted the groom and thanked the guests, she moved a few dance steps, then she danced a little more, and finally, with a nice curtsey, she left."[19] The same ritual was repeated the following day for the female members of the families; afterward, the bride would enter the gondola "outside of the *felze*,[20] and sat on a rather raised seat entirely covered with rugs (and this is called 'andare in trasto'). She is followed by a large

Giacomo Franco, *A questo modo vanno le novizze in gondola*, from *Habiti delle donne venetiane*, Venezia, 1628.

number of other gondolas, and she goes to visit the nunneries where her sisters or other relatives are."[21] These customary visits were originally conceived to somehow include the nuns, still considered part of the family, in the wedding festivities. However, these visits could be rather depressing for the nuns, faced with the glamour and luxury of a lifestyle they could only dream about. It is not by chance that Patriarch Lorenzo Priuli, in his "Orders for Those Who Have to Talk with Nuns," prescribes that "women need to avoid bringing *novizze* accompanied by other well-dressed women [to convents] because they cause great sins [probably of jealousy and envy!] and upset the souls of the nuns."[22] During these visits brides usually received a present from their cloistered relatives; Tarabotti tells us that it happened that these embroidered gifts, on which the nuns had worked day and night, and sometimes even indebted themselves for, were superficially received, and this unenthusiastic reception was a cause of great humiliation and pain for them.[23]

At daybreak of the day of the religious ceremony (*subarratio* or *desponsatio*) the future couple set off from their respective homes and moved toward the church, followed by their guests. The impressive welcome committee that received the bride at her arrival at the church has been well captured in the eighteenth-century painting by Gabriel Bella titled *The Wedding of a Venetian Noblewoman*.[24] In front of the basilica of the Madonna della Salute noblemen and ladies are lined on either side on the steps, waiting for the white-clothed bride, who is being accompanied by a magnificent procession of gondolas with the liveried gondoliers. After the religious rites, a banquet, sometimes for hundreds of guests, was held in the bride's house, followed by many more on subsequent days. Finally, after all the festivities and banquets, the groom would take the bride to his house and married life would begin.

Mystical Bride, Ideal Nun: Saint Catherine of Alexandria

The walls of numerous Venetian convent churches, were, regardless of the order to which they belonged, usually decorated with inspiring works of art that were supposed to motivate the nuns and point them to the right path to follow in their lives. Most suitably, many of these paintings depicted the life of Saint Catherine of Alexandria and, specifically, her mystical marriage to Baby Jesus.[25] Saint Catherine of Alexandria was considered a Christian female model of virginity and culture, her cult reaching a peak during the fifteenth century. According to the legend this noble young woman fought the order of Emperor Maxentius in 305 AD to sacrifice to the idols. She bravely went to the temple and publicly attacked the emperor with remarkable eloquence, even converting the fifty orators that had been called to dispute her thesis. Eventually she suffered the torture of the dentate wheel, which became her symbolic emblem, was beheaded, and while her body was transported to Mount Sinai by some angels, she was accepted into heaven by a voice that addressed her as "my beloved bride."[26] The spiritual event was narrated in the *Conversio*, a hagiographic text that developed into the prototype of the ceremonies of the consecration of the virgins and of monastic "marriages," where

Matteo Ponzone, *Mystical Marriage of Saint Catherine*, sixteenth century, Church of St. Catherine Island of Mazzorbo, Venice. Courtesy of Patriarcato di Venezia, Ufficio Beni Culturali.

the specific iconographic theme became an easily readable parallel with Clothing ceremonies.

In these paintings the beautiful and noble young woman is almost invariably represented as an elegant and attractive Venetian bride or religious postulant, resplendent in a luxurious white silk dress. One such example, known by the informal title of "The Mystical Marriage of Saint Catherine," is offered by the canvas that still hangs on the left wall of the presbytery of the church of the now-demolished monastery dedicated to Saint Catherine of Alexandria Virgin and Martyr on the island of Mazzorbo, in the north lagoon.

The work of art, painted around the second half of the sixteenth century by Matteo Ponzone, portrays the saint kneeling in front of Baby Jesus, accepting the ring that is in his hands. As a proper aristocratic Venetian bride, she wears a white satin dress with the fashionable pointed waist of the period, the traditional bridal pearl necklace, and leaves the lush blond hair loose. Her noble origin is indicated by the small jeweled crown, an ornament that, as confirmed by Grevembroch,[27] was also typically used by Venetian brides. The entire outfit perfectly matches the one worn by Vecellio's *Sposa sposata* and the one visible in Golzius's *Venetian Wedding.*[28]

Almost identical in style, but more luxurious still, is the dress worn by Saint Catherine in another contemporary painting, similarly destined for the Venetian convent named after her. In Paolo Veronese's *Mystical Marriage of Saint Catherine*, painted around 1575 for the main altar of the convent church,[29] the saint is placed at the center of the composition in an innovative diagonal arrangement that focuses the attention of the viewer on her magnificent dress, made of brocaded white and blue silk. It was a fitting choice of colors since light blue, considered to represent "the sky, and among the four elements, the air,"[30] was most suitable to symbolize the divine nature of the union. There are further references to bridal attire in the magnificent jewel around her neckline that is matched by the precious coronet on her head, the ritual pearl necklace, and, again, her long, loose blonde hair.

Catherine's dress plays a key role in yet another cycle of paintings depicting episodes of her life that used to decorate the same church. In the set of paintings by Jacopo Tintoretto and his *bottega,* Catherine's gown is essential in highlighting her patrician status and her "social" role of divine bride.[31] Made of white fabric brocaded in gold—a favorite combination, as we have seen, of Venetian brides—it takes center stage, worn by the saint while she pleads her case and making her shine against the darker figures around her. Even later, when Catherine has already fallen prey to her tormentors, it is still prominently placed in the foreground, as a symbolic attribute, side by side with her small crown: both objects are used to visually reinforce the emblematic references to her nobility, marriage, and martyrdom.

Three paintings, three examples of how a mystical bride should look.

Saint Catherine became an inspiration and a role model for the nuns of the convents, and, even before that, for the would-be nuns, who could identify with her thanks to the almost matching elegant clothes worn during their own "divine" marriages, in their own rite of passage that was the Clothing.

Political and Symbolic Marriages: The Doge and the Abbesses of the Monastero delle Vergini

> June 14, 1506, Sunday. The Doge went with ceremonial galleys to wed
> the Abbess of the Verzene. She is of the Badoer family and the Doge
> [always] comes to marry the Abbess in the year of her installation since
> the church is under his patronage.
>
> Marin Sanudo, *Diarii*, VI, col. 353[32]

A very peculiar monastic wedding ceremony took place in the Venetian monastery of Santa Maria delle Vergini after every new abbess's election.[33]

It was one of the most ancient monasteries of the city, dating back to 1117, when it was founded by Doge Sebastiano Ziani, Emperor Federico Barbarossa, and Pope Alexander III, during the historic meeting in which the pope began the tradition of the "marriage to the sea," a ceremony that later became a part of the Venetian myth.

The Emperor's daughter, Giulia, was made abbess of the monastery and was clothed and consecrated immediately. The doge gave her possession of the convent and "married" her twice: first with a ring with the seal of St. Mark, and again with a gold and sapphire ring, starting a ritual tradition.

The lavish wedding ceremony between the doge and the abbess is repeatedly illustrated in the Cronica, a fifteenth-century manuscript that narrates the history of the monastery.[34] One miniature plays a particularly meaningful role in the study of Venetian dress because of how the colors identify the different characters involved in the ritual. At the center of the scene is the gold-clothed doge, seated on a throne behind which is also a precious cloth of gold; he offers the "wedding" ring to the kneeled abbess, who is covered in the characteristic and imposing white mantle of the Vergini, as are two other canonesses placed on a lower level: their

Marriage of the prioress and the doge with senators, in *Cronica del Monisterio delle Vergini* (fol. 46), Ms. Gradenigo. Reprinted by permission of Biblioteca del Museo Correr, Venice.

heads are completely covered by a matching white coif. Around the doge, and witnesses to the scene, are seven male figures, identifiable in their specific roles thanks to the colors of the patrician vesta they are wearing. In 1485, in fact, the Maggior Consiglio elaborated a precise chromatic code in order to define which colors were suitable for which occasions and public offices;[35] senators, *cavalieri*, and *avogadori* were allowed to wear a crimson robe accessorized by a gold stole.[36] The doge's *consiglieri* wore a purple vesta, while bright red was reserved for members of the feared Council of Ten, the magistrates overseeing homeland security. Finally, the different shades of *pavonazzo*, from purple to peacock blue to dark blue, allowed it to be used on the most diverse occasions.[37]

In light of this it is easy to identify the male figures as, respectively, two senators or *avogadori* in crimson, three *consiglieri* in purple and two other nobles dressed in two different shades of *pavonazzo*.

As the miniature shows, the accessories of the vesta were the *bareta da vesta*, a hat shaped like an upside-down pot made of black cloth and lined in black silk,[38] and the *becho* or *bechetto*, a totally Venetian accessory, descendent of a much older headwear that evolved into a long strip of fabric, generally worn on the left shoulder and called, elsewhere, *stola*.[39]

The doge also used to visit the Vergini annually, on May 1. He first participated in a solemn Mass in the conventual church; then he went on to the parlor, where the abbess waited for him with all of the other nuns dressed in the traditional white mantle, their heads covered with the two veils reaching the waist. The abbess addressed the doge with a welcome speech and offered him a bouquet of fresh flowers with a gold handle and encased in precious Venetian laces. Other, less expensive presents were offered by the nuns to the other dignitaries.[40]

Sponsa Christi

I went to Mazorbo with Ser Pandolfo Morexini, the councilor, and some other relatives of ours to see three young daughters of Ser Ferigo Morexini, who is his brother and my cousin, take the veil in the convent of Santa Catarina. Their names are Lodovica, Catarina, and Vitoria. Six other girls also took the veil: two from the Badoer family, a Quirini, a

Zorzi, a Barozzi, and a Michiel. It was very lovely to see the ceremonies in which they were given their habits; I saw all of it, something I have never seen before.

Marin Sanudo, *Diarii*, 50: col. 336, May 17, 1529

The "lovely" ceremony described by Sanudo was the Clothing. It was the first step in the definitive parting of the nun from the outside world, a process that, at its most essential, consisted of two separate liturgies: the Clothing, when the girl would, for the first time, wear the religious habit of the order she was entering, and, few years later, the Profession, or the pronunciation of the perpetual vows. According to the customs of the convents, however, these steps could easily double, including such ceremonies as the acceptance into the monastery and the Consecration, also called Sagra in Venetian dialect, when the nun was given the black veil and granted the right to participate in the chapter. The path toward the celestial Groom was, therefore, marked by a sequence of events, in a cumulative process that mirrored the many steps of secular weddings. Nuns-to-be were, in fact, regarded as brides, actually future brides, of Christ, an assimilation that went back to the third century, and was in common use by the fourth century, when Saint Ambrose was already reporting similarities between the ceremonies of consecration of nuns and secular weddings.[41]

The first and most obvious equivalence between the two ceremonies lay in the fact that a woman was "entrusted" to a man to be protected by him. Inside a community a woman could achieve standing only through marriage; she needed to "belong" to a man in order to hold a respectable place in society. In monacations "the actual presence of the husband was a formality that could be dispensed with, but the notion of a husband could not."[42] In either ceremony, the consent of the woman was considered crucial: both brides and nuns were, in theory, supposed to agree to embrace their new lives, but, since the decisions were in both cases made by the respective families, the concept of individual assent clearly was not a major issue.

The alteration in the identity and status of the married woman was marked by the change in her name and appellative, "her identity subsumed in her marital role."[43] Then again, while wives were styled "madonna" and kept their Christian names, adding their husband's to their father's, nuns, instead, since they were dissolving their connections with the families of origin, were supposed to relinquish their last names and were styled "suora."

In the transition from the lay world to the cloister, nuns-to-be were also requested to renounce all secular clothing, accessories, readings, and pastimes, affectations considered inappropriate for a bride of Christ. Understandably, however, novices were rather reluctant to part with these comforts and tended to bring with them a number of forbidden or unsuitable items and habits.

This quite secular attitude toward religious life was at least partially justified by the planning and festivities organized by their families for their entrance into the monastery. The families of the future nuns, in fact, stressed the equivalence between secular weddings and Clothing ceremonies, preparing their trousseaux "as if they were getting married."[44] Parties, banquets, and gifts were exploited by the families as a way to transform these fatal rites into something the girls could somehow look forward to; they also constituted an opportunity to display the power of the aristocracy, thus revealing the subtle balance between the individuals, their families, the conventual institutions, and the government of the Venetian Republic. The patrician clans involved wished to publicly display their affiliations with specific institutions and to share their merits. In this light, the secular elements of the conventual dowries, and of the banquets and receptions that were customarily held right after the religious liturgies, were not considered superfluous or useless. For the families concerned and for the nuns-to-be they were as important as the rites themselves because "the status of the family had to be upheld in exactly the same way as it would have been at a secular wedding."[45]

Consequently, despite the fact that "divine" marriages were a more economical life-solution than secular nuptials, they did not come free of costs. Money was needed for the dowry, the food, the music, and the floral decorations, which, over the centuries, tended to become more and more magnificent, in line with the solemnity of the ceremonies.

There were also the expenses for the customary trousseau, even if strictly limited to the basics, which included the fabrics for the habit and the linens and furniture needed to furnish the cell of the future nun.[46]

A nun's dowry, the so-called *elemosina dotale* (dotal alms), was intended as a lifetime income, sufficient to provide, modestly but regularly, for the food and clothes of one person;[47] after the passing of a nun, whatever remained was for the convent's use. An annual pension of sixty ducats was considered sufficient: fifty for the food and ten for the dress. It was estimated that this amount would have enabled even the more modest convent to be self-sufficient: an additional four hundred ducats was allowed to be spent for monocation ceremonies.

Around the late sixteenth century conventual dowries begin to increase significantly, as, at the same time, did secular dowries. Since November 24, 1593, Patriarch Lorenzo Priuli had attempted to stop the "excessive and vain expenses that up to this point had been made in banquets, presents or other that has been done for some nuns at their Clothing."[48] The position of the patriarch was supported by the action of the government that, once again, tried to prevent the increase of the dowries with a Senate decree dated July 26, 1602. The decree stated that "the expenses for the monacation ceremonies, for the conventual dowries, for the trousseaux, and for useless and completely superfluous ceremonies have become so high that it is absolutely necessary to stop these abuses and bad habits, in order to allow the families of this city to send their daughters to serve God without having to spend more than is universally considered necessary and proper."[49] Nuns-to-be could not receive more than 800–1000 ducats in cash, and not more than 200–300 ducats for the chest and the trousseau; excessive decorations were forbidden, and it was permissable to spend only up to one hundred ducats for decorations and musicians for the religious liturgies.[50]

The concept was once again stressed by the Senate on April 15, 1610: a law was passed that defined the conventual dowry as the lifelong usufruct of sixty ducats, plus two hundred for the festivities, one hundred for the nun's trousseau, and two hundred for the additional expenses that the convent might have to bear.[51]

As usual, all of these laws and promulgations did not seem to have much effect. At the beginning of the sixteenth century the nunnery chest of a wealthy novice could easily have contained such items as "a gold jewel, an embroidered veil for the hair . . . six lengths of satin for hose,"[52] while in an unspecified year of the seventeenth century the expenses for the Clothing of Suor Laura Molin amounted to no less than one thousand ducats, of which one hundred were spent for "the first habit" alone.[53] Even Carlo Goldoni in his "Canzone" for the Clothing of Maria Lippomano writes: "I hear that they send a mass of things to a novice."[54]

Many archival documents confirm the custom of sending the girls into nunhood with lots of opulent goods. Some papers belonging to the corporation of the *marzeri* (haberdashers) testify to the fact that on the occasion of Clothing ceremonies expensive laces were sold in great quantities just outside the monasteries.[55]

These excessive luxuries are not substantiated, however, in the impressions and feelings recorded by Arcangela Tarabotti on the same subject.[56] In the *Inferno monacale* she compares the disturbingly different provisions made for two sisters, one destined for marriage, the other for the cloister. For the bride, shirts made of fine Dutch linen have been prepared, trimmed by needle laces so precious that just two of them are worth the entire trousseau of her cloistered sister, whose shirts of "the coarser and rougher fabrics" available were neither long enough, nor had sleeves of matching fabrics.[57] Instead of the magnificent silk gowns of her luckiest sister, the cloistered young woman would wear a humble woolen habit, cover her legs with coarse *rassa*,[58] and walk in wooden clogs poorly covered in leather. This more than modest apparel, a generic list for which was usually provided by the convents themselves, arrived in "two of the most worm-eaten chests"[59] that Arcangela had ever seen. Despite the shabbiness of this and similar nuns' trousseaus, Arcangela noted that the families nonetheless often resented the cost, behaving "as if they [the nuns] should cover themselves with hair, as did the loving disciple [Mary Magdalene]."[60]

The stinginess of the families in providing for daughters entering religious life was a source of recurring complaints from the nuns-to-be and caused great distress. If, on the one hand, aristocratic families were bent on outdoing each other in the luxuriousness of their Clothing ceremonies, on the other hand more modest, middle-class, families tended to "forget" to provide for even the most basic needs for ceremonies following the Clothing, such as the Profession. A particularly poignant example comes from documents detailing the monacation of Laura Acerbi dated July 1715.[61] In a very moving letter from Laura herself to her parents living in Calle della Testa, in the area of San Giovanni e Paolo, she begs her father piteously to provide her with the very basic items she needs for the Profession ceremony. Writes Laura:

> The moment of my church Profession is nearing and I am without any sort of cell furnishings or linens and in great need of these things: I also need everything from the list I already sent you for the Profession ceremony. Dear father (I pray) that you get me these things, because I feel humiliated being among the other novices and the nuns who already have everything they need, both for them and for the cell. Now that it is possible to find it at cheaper prices, please do go buy me these things, such as the walnut wood chests and also the copper things and the linens. I have found some fabric to make a pair of *boccassini* [veils],[62] which is of good quality; that which is sold in stores for more money is of an inferior quality: So if you would ask to see it at home and buy it, I would have the *boccassini* made; it is necessary to hurry dear Father, because I have just two months left before my Profession and after you have provided me with these things I will not bother you anymore. It will also be a good thing for our family, because otherwise it would seem that we are tramps, since my cell is in a far worse condition that the one of the last *conversa* [convent servant], despite the fact that she is so poor. You can only imagine how ashamed I am because I can-

not appear alongside the other nuns. I then beg you Dear Father to be good to me, and if you cannot spare some time to do this, leave it to my brother Piero. . . . I cannot bring myself to believe that you no longer come to visit me; maybe it is because I keep asking you to provide me with my necessities . . . but if you get me what I need, then you can come and visit me, because I really wish you would come, and I will not say anything about that. I also recommend you to remember the nine and a half ducats that have been lent to me and I beg you to forgive me and I kiss you, your most devout [daughter].[63]

The file contains also lists of things needed for the various festivities, of the presents that were customary for the different important positions inside the monastery, and the receipts for the items eventually received by the convent: flour, used to bake cookies (*bussolà*), marzipans, sugarloafs, candles, and rolled-up wicks (*magioli*).[64]

Even the more modest institutions stipulated specific requirements to close the "deal" successfully. The documents detailing the expenses for the monacation of Anna Toniuti in the convent of Santi Andrea e Mauro on the island of Murano include a list stipulating that the family provide no less than fifty *brazza* of fabrics to be used for the veils and wimples, three black dresses with their corsets and sleeves, three pairs of stockings, three pairs of shoes, two combs, and more fabrics for the winter habit. The convent also asked for one hundred ducats after the end of the first "trial" year that could be returned if, after two years, the girl decided not to take the veil. After the Clothing, the convent asked for two hundred more ducats and, again, presents for all the nuns, along with more flour and sugar to bake the traditional sweet treats offered during Clothing receptions. A large piece of veal, four doves, and four capons were required for the ritual lunch that followed the rites.[65] Food was traditionally also dispensed to the families who lived in proximity to the convents; when the custom was not met, the neighbors were utterly disappointed: "After three days of trials finally the Ladies of the Vergini have elected their Prioress and the election was in favor of poor Sister Mora; therefore they will need to diminish their expenses and they already began to do so yesterday, while the people who did not have anything to drink did not rejoice."[66]

The basic clothing necessities mentioned in both the Acerbi and in the Toniuti files, veils and black habits, played a key and highly symbolic role in the Clothing ceremony itself, symbolizing the severity of the nuns' daily life to come. However, oddly enough, the celebration of the "celestial" marriages of the future nuns, which should have marked their farewell to the luxuries and allurements of the world, began instead with

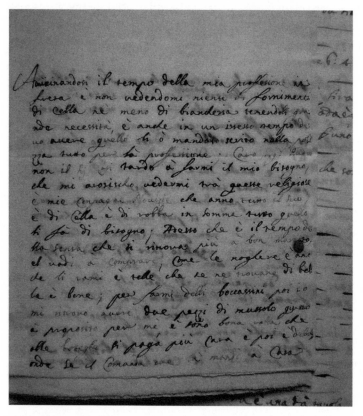

Letter of Laura Acerbi, DER E 3, 1726. Courtesy of IRE, Istituzioni di Ricovero e di Educazione Venezia, Venice.

a rather worldly and often decidedly glamorous outfit. The postulants appeared for the Clothing ceremony, starring in a procession that was visible to the public, resplendently clothed in elegant white silk dresses, the long hair loose on their shoulders; while advancing toward the altar, they sang the psalm "Quemadmodum desiderat cervus,"[67] accompanied by solemn music that was considered an essential part of the ritual and, not incidentally, constituted another close link with secular weddings.[68] The lavish procession became such a worldly show that Patriarch Grimani felt the need to forbid the girls from "enter[ing] with great pomp, [wearing] silk dresses, jewelry, and pearls,"[69] considering it scandalous that this "sacred and pious act" could actually be transformed into nothing more than "a vain performance."[70]

The churches themselves were usually prepared in a rather ostentatious fashion;[71] so pretentious and rich, really, that the Provveditori sopra Monasteri intervened, sternly reproving the excessive and theatrical decorations of the churches and forbidding the building of ad hoc choir stalls and stages for the ceremonies and the excessive use of candles.[72]

In a fifteenth-century manuscript that belonged to the rich Benedictine monastery of San Lorenzo is a miniature illuminated by Venetian artist Cristoforo Cortese representing the *Benediction and Consecration of Virgins*.[73] It depicts the ideal vision the Catholic hierarchies had of the Clothing ceremony: the complete absence of the secular public and a simple tone results in a very sober and religious event. Two postulants wearing Benedictine habits and veils are kneeling in front of a bishop, who is giving one of them a ring, while a haloed figure, maybe Christ himself, is placing a crown over both of the nuns' heads. As with secular brides, crowns and rings indicated the completion of the marriage with Christ, solemnly proclaimed by the bishop: "Receive the sign of Christ over your head so he will be your husband."[74]

A similar simplicity shines through a miniature in the Benedictine ritual handbook *(rituale)* commissioned by the nuns of the monastery on the island of San Servolo.[75] The miniature represents a Clothing ceremony taking place at the grille of the convent: the postulant is again shown

Gabriel Bella, *The Clothing of a Nun in San Lorenzo*, last quarter of the eighteenth century, Venice, Querini Stampalia Museum. Courtesy of Fondazione Querini Stampalia Onlus, Venice.

on her knees in front of a priest and flanked by two women in secular dress. The habit has been passed through the bars of the grille for the ritual blessing by a nun wearing the white headdress of a Benedictine novice.[76] A crowd of nuns waits to welcome the new novice, and the tone of the liturgy appears to be very sober and spiritual.

Two centuries later the atmosphere during the investiture ceremonies developed into a much more secular, even casual style. In *Clothing of a Nun in San Lorenzo*, an eighteenth-century painting by Gabriel Bella, the ceremony is represented as some sort of theatrical event. The large church, divided by the gilded grilles that separated the part dedicated to the nuns from that where the general public was admitted, is filled by scores of fashionably dressed noblemen gathered in small groups and busily chatting together, as are the ladies comfortably seated in gilded chairs. Entertainment is provided by numerous musicians, and almost nobody seems to take notice of the actual ceremony that is going on at the main altar. The novice, placed at the center of the painting, but who is clearly not at the center of the thoughts of the participants in the ritual, is already wearing the black habit and is receiving the white veil of the novice from the officiant.

As the three representations document, the ritual was officiated by a bishop. The postulants were introduced to him by a priest, and then, lying facing down and entirely covered with a black veil, they pronounced their three solemn vows, affirming their wish to be chaste, poor, and to be consecrated. Embracing the altar they gravely proclaimed: "I offer myself in sacrifice as a living host."[77]

What did they really think during the ceremony? Arcangela recalls that she "did not know what that really meant,"[78] but she notes that the fact of lying down covered by the black cloth among "tears and sobs"[79] gave her the feeling of participating in her own funeral.

The bishop would then bless the habits, veils, and belts, highlighting their role as signs of contempt of the world—"spretis omnibus vanitatitubus huius mundi"[80]—and ended the ceremony with the exhortation: "Get up my daughters and light your lamps, your spouse is coming, go and meet him."[81]

Relatives and friends would then accompany the postulants in procession to the convent's door, where they were received by the abbess and the entire monastic community. At that point, the abbess asked the expected questions, waited for the standard replies, blessed the novices, and welcomed them to the monastery: the first act was over.

The effect on the postulants, now novices, was often shocking. Tarabotti remembers that she was horrified by the dark habits worn by the nuns and noticed that their sad faces made them look like they "were already dead."[82]

In consideration of the highly symbolic value of dress in ancient society, the act of disrobing from the secular luxurious dress during the Clothing and donning the black tunic marked a dramatic change in the life of the novices: it signaled their renunciation and contempt for their old condition and the beginning of a new life, with a new identity and a new name. An excellent parallel is found in the story of Saint Francis of Assisi, who publicly renounced worldly riches by abandoning the refined clothes of his rich merchant family for a humble habit.

In recognition of their sacrifice, novices were, in the eighteenth century, often praised and exalted in the poetic compositions dedicated to them on the day of their Clothing. For the Profession of Chiara Milesi, afterward known as Suor Giovanna, Carlo Goldoni wrote:

> She has changed her name
>
> (changed) the gold and silk with wool cloth.
>
> Last year I saw her dressed
>
> With a skirt made of fourteen *brazzi* (of fabric).[83]
>
> Now she covers herself head to toe
>
> with a tunic identical (to that of the other nuns).[84]

Cornelia Barbaro Gritti, a Venetian noblewoman who used the nom de plume of Aurisbe Tarsense, also praised the contempt of future nun Angela Maria Renier for the vanity of worldly goods:

> Jewels, laces, and rich gowns
>
> She does not want them anymore;
>
> She wore them for a short time,
>
> and left them to us . . .
>
> How better is the wimple
>
> Instead of the toupee!
>
> How much more worthy is the tunic
>
> In comparison with hoops and *andriennes*![85]
>
> . . .
>
> Nuns do not worry about
>
> What they wear.
>
> . . .
>
> Where did she leave her embroidered shoes,

. . .

She exchanged them for clogs,

big, comfortable, and good for all seasons.

Bonnets and lace cuffs, where did they go?

She despised them and put them aside.

She gave up everything . . .

(she who was) rich, noble and born in a gold dress,

She could, as many others do,

With ribbons, laces, and jewels ornate her hair.

. . .

But Angiola scorns the luxuries, and under her feet

She puts gold and silver, and in humble wool

You see her cover her body.[86]

The Clothing was so charged with spiritual and psychological meaning that it was continually identified as a key moment in the life of female
saints. In the frescoes of the private chapel of the Suardi family, for instance, Lorenzo Lotto represented Saint Bridget kneeling face down in
front of the altar wearing a yellow dress.[87] Her secular gown has been
cast aside and she is waiting for the bishop to cover her head with the
just-blessed white veil. The frescoes also show the secular point of view of
the Suardi family, portrayed in their lavish outfits, who probably wished
to acquire piety through their visual associations with sanctity.

The plainness of the monastic habit prepared the nuns for the renunciation of private property, a characteristic trait of religious life, while
its uniformity expressed equality of identity among the nuns; the rules
prescribed that no nun should keep secular dresses or even consider her
own the tunic and other accessories she received at the Clothing. Even
these, in theory, were simply entrusted to her by the nun in charge of the
wardrobe and linens, as recommended by the patriarch: "May poverty
be always with her, and she never has to have, give, or receive anything
without the abbess's permission, never considering anything as her own,

always being ready to deprive herself if the abbess so decides; otherwise she would be guilty of a mortal sin and considered unworthy of a holy burial."[88]

Every element of their new religious "uniform" had a very specific symbolic meaning, carefully defined during the Clothing ceremony itself. According to Saint Bernard, the habit was to be worn by "the female sex . . . as a sign of subjection, humility, and honesty."[89] The belt, or *cingolo*, described by Tarabotti as made of "coarse leather"[90] and also mentioned in the Acerbi file, indicated temperance and chastity, so that "the Lord may gird the loins of my body and circumscribe the vices of my heart."[91]

The tonsure, or the cutting of the hair, pointed to their renunciation of the allurements of vanity.[92] Each nun of the community would take turns in cutting off a strand of the novices' hair, a sacrifice made out of love for their Groom, as enunciated by the officiant, who prayed "for these servants of his, who hurry to discard their hair out of love for Him." In the anonymous painting representing the Clothing of Saint Clare it is instead her brother in religion, Saint Francis, who cuts her hair.[93] Once again the cast-aside secular dress is prominently displayed, as are the precious jewels on the floor near the knees of the saint. Among them is clearly visible the bridal pearl necklace.

Head and neck were covered by a severe wimple signaling "modesty, sobriety, and continence."[94] The abbess would then place the white veil on their heads, a veil that surrounded their bodies and protected them by hiding their charms. It was a helmet of salvation and sign of widowhood, to be worn "in memory of the disgraceful death of your sweet groom."[95]

Finally, at the end of the investiture, the abbess would sew three stitches on the wimple itself, indicating the three days of meditation and silence prescribed for the new nuns.[96]

The ceremonies were, at this point, still far from over. Following the religious rites were several receptions offered by the families of the new members of the community. The tradition mirrored the custom of giving numerous parties after secular weddings, and the generosity and largesse displayed during these banquets were especially meaningful: they offered the new nuns the opportunity to introduce themselves and show their economic power, supporting them in claiming their proper status inside the monastic "society."

The patriarchs tried many times to provide general guidelines and to condemn excessive luxuries during these feasts, to no avail. In 1742 Alvise Foscari condemned "the too expensive and common luxury of refreshments, drinks, and illuminations," stressing again the prohibition "to offer any sort of refreshments and drinks from the grilles of the parlors," such as "waters, sorbets, coffee, chocolate."[97]

Among the forbidden luxuries were the gifts that new nuns, in their role of new brides, used to receive from the guests. From the fifteenth century onward, for instance, in the convent of San Zaccaria, one of the richest of the city, it was customary to place a bowl on a carpet just outside the grilles of the parlor to gather donations from the public on the day that nuns were consecrated.[98] Even between abbesses it was usual to exchange presents on the occasion of a Clothing ceremony or other important days for their monasteries.[99]

Finally, once all the pomp and luxuries of these prolonged liturgies and festivities were over, the new nun officially entered in the monastic community. Her family could, at long last, sigh with relief since, as they used to say, once the girl was clothed, "everything was fine."[100]

Three
Nuns and Fashion

*L*aces, wide décolletages, high-heeled shoes, makeup: Venetian nuns were famous all over Europe for their elegance and their relaxed, quasi-secular lifestyle. Starting from the description of the ideal demure habits prescribed for the nuns of different orders, we will slowly reveal the reality of the far more luxurious and sensual gowns these nuns wore, peering into some of the most prestigious convents of the Serenissima. Extravagant Carnival parties, elegant accessories, and beauty secrets will be uncovered and compared to the more austere styles worn by the foreign nuns who lived in the city and by other "categories" of encloistered women.

Religious Habits . . .

A round marble bas-relief dated to the late fifteenth century and placed on a pilaster of the side portal of the church of the monastery of Santa Maria dei Miracoli offered contemporaries an idealized representation of the perfect nun.[1] Modestly covered from head to toe by her habit and mantle, the face severely framed by the rigorous coif and wimple and by the long veil, this creature no longer looks like a woman, but rather a genderless, almost angelic being, dedicated only to spiritual life, as highlighted by the small prayer book she held in her right hand.

In definitively detaching from the customs and worries of secular

The Ideal Nun, marble roundel, fifteenth century Venice, Church
of Santa Maria dei Miracoli.

life, the nun passed through the necessary step of the rejection of worldly clothes and vanities that constituted the main focus of the Clothing
ceremony. The concealing and austere monastic outfits that the novices
received in that solemn occasion, and would have been required to wear
after, were a visual indication of their new condition, signifying their separate position from the outside society and desexualizing them. The role
of the habits was to support them in this transition, to forever hide their
bodies, even from their own sight,[2] to express their new moral and religious values, at the same time shielding them from any sort of dangerous
exposure to the influences of the outside world.[3]

The key characteristic of the religious habits was not their uniformity,
which was a common trait of the clothes of other professional categories
or devotional congregations, but their intrinsic poverty and humility, an
evident feature, especially if compared with the precious and brightly col-

ored outfits worn by the upper and middle classes from which the vast majority of the nuns came.

Poverty was practiced by using for the monastic outfits the humblest materials available. Usually the fabrics of choice were coarse wool cloths in a range of indistinct shades,[4] from light gray to dark brown, named, for instance, *griso, beretino, morello,* and, of course, *monachino* (from the word *monaca,* nun): "the habit is gray, both in the summer and in the winter, and we are allowed a suitable habit . . . and a tunic in the winter and a mantle each in the summer; everything else, collars, veils, and *facioleti* is held in common among the nuns."[5] The use of white, the color of prestige and of luxury, was only rarely and in few select cases permitted, or, to be more precise, tolerated:[6] it was used for instance by the secular canonesses of Le Vergini, a very exclusive institution under the patronage of the pope himself.

The adoption of particular shades for the habits or of certain accessories often helped identify the members of an order or congregation. In the sixteenth century, for instance, the so-called *zoccolanti* were so christened because they chose to wear modest wooden clogs, or *zoccoli,* and, analogously, it was the total rejection of any kind of footwear that prompted the definition of *carmelitani scalzi* (Discalced Carmelites) for the congregation founded by Teresa de Avila. In the Veneto region, striped dresses were traditionally worn as a symbol of humility by the Clarisse (Poor Clares). For instance, the prioress of the Clarisse of Treviso is represented in her seal with a striped dress.[7]

Even the visual identification of such important religious figures as Saint Jerome relied on the introduction of emblematic clothing accessories. Being a cardinal, his biretta constituted his standard symbolic attribute and was usually placed beside him.

The prescribed shapelessness and muted colors of the habits approved by the religious orders made them very similar to the clothes worn by the lowest classes. However, this did not establish a social equivalence between the nuns of those classes. Quite the contrary: their humble religious outfits carried with them a deeply symbolic value of dignity, similar to that of the liturgical vestments, and a social status appreciated even outside the convent. It was not uncommon, in fact, for married lay noblewomen to request in their wills to be buried wearing the habit of one of the many Venetian convents in the hope of reacquiring an at least ideal "virginity." For instance, in 1601, Lucrezia Corner requested in her will to be dressed in the habit of the nuns of Santa Croce. An identical choice was later made by Franceschina Littegato, who also named two *converse* of the same convent whom she wished to dress her body: they were to be paid one ducat each besides the cost of the habit.[8]

Unfortunately, despite the constant surveillance by ecclesiastical authorities, the increasing affectation of the religious habits and accessories prompted in the first half of the eighteenth century the publication of several "catalogs" in which the different religious uniforms were meticulously illustrated by engravings, accompanied by a detailed description of the characteristics of each habit.

Two especially interesting works, focused on the habits of all monastic and equestrian orders, both male and female, were published in Rome, almost contemporaneously. Between 1706 and 1710 appeared the three volumes (the second specifically dedicated to the habits of the "virgins dedicated to God") of the *Catalogo degli ordini religiosi della chiesa militante*, compiled by Jesuit Filippo Bonanni and illustrated by 319 engravings. A few years later, between 1707 and 1715, Bonanni's *Catalogus* was followed by the almost identical effort of Franciscan monk Vincenzo Coronelli, *Ordinum religiosorum in ecclesia militanti catalogus, eorumque indumenta, iconibus expressa, auctus*, which similarly offered a panorama of the habits of all the different European monastic orders, giving an even more in-depth look at those of the Venetian nuns that Coronelli knew well, having resided in the city for a long time.[9]

The clothes usually worn by many of these nuns were not the severe habits hoped for by religious authorities and sought after by pious noblewomen. While the prescribed habits were usually worn during the semi-public religious ceremonies, during their private everyday life nuns often wore fancier, almost secular, dresses. In a desperate effort to preserve a fragment of their past identities and to assert their individuality and status inside the convent itself, most aristocratic nuns refused, in fact, to wear the simple tunics of their orders and had their clothes tailor-made with fabrics far less simple than those offered by the conventual wardrobe. According to the patriarchal ordinances, every monastery was to have a communal wardrobe stocked with all that was needed to outfit the nuns. The nun in charge of it was also responsible for supervising the style of the habits themselves as prescribed by Patriarch Priuli: "It is necessary that in every Monastery there is a communal wardrobe where are preserved all the communal properties needed to dress the nuns: and since in our monastery the nuns have the permission of the abbess to privately keep their own clothes and linens, this wardrobe will at least be used to keep the properties of deceased nuns, which will be later distributed to the nuns in need according to the dispositions of the abbess. In the wardrobe will also be cut and sawn the new habits following a univocal pattern. . . . The teacher (the nun in charge of the wardrobe) is not allowed to cut habits that do not comply with the custom and religion in fabric, colour, and shape. . . . It is especially important that the head-covers do not let the skin show, as has occurred with great scandal."[10]

Some monasteries were rigorous in respecting the vow of poverty. In the monastery of Corpus Domini, according to the chronicle that narrates the life in the convent, "they had nothing but a blanket, a single tunic, and a single scapular: when they needed to change, they went to the wardrobe mistress and were satisfied with whatever she gave them. The wardrobe mistress routinely changed all their tunics and scapulars four times a year; no one recognized her own things."[11]

A very interesting document preserved in the archive of the monastery of San Zaccaria, the "Libro del vestiario," shows how the wardrobe of the monastery was managed. The first entry in the parchment-bound book, dated July 19, 1775, records the amounts of fabric given each year from the conventual wardrobe to every nun or *conversa* present inside the institution. The orders of Prioress Rosalia Zorzi specified the different dress allowances, ranging from the twenty-one *brazza* of *scotto* for the prioress herself to the sixteen for each of the professed choir nuns, to the eleven but less expensive *sarza* for the *converse* with more than twelve years of seniority. Special directives took care of particular situations: Should a nun inherit from a relative in the convent, in that year she did not receive her allowance: "No dress allowance is given to the Rev. ma: D.a : M:a Dolfina Dolfin Priora and A D.M:a Teresa Dolfin following the death of their sister D:a M:a Giovanna Dolfin on May 22, 1776." For the Clothing or Profession ceremonies the allowances were, respectively, twelve and twenty-eight *brazza*. D. Cecilia M. Gritti, who was professed on May 26, 1784, received the prescribed 28 *brazza*, each costing 4 *soldi* for a total amount of *soldi* 112.[12]

In spite of the rules, thanks to the regular allowances paid to the nuns by their families or to other sources of personal income, such as inheritances[13] or the profits of their own work,[14] nuns were able to purchase fine fabrics and elaborate trimmings. In apparent respect of the vow of poverty, the money was entrusted to the prioress of the convent, but, while technically not in their possession, it was readily available for the "necessities" of the nuns, and, from what it is possible to gather from the detailed accounts of the patriarchal visits from the late fifteenth to the eighteenth century, most of them spent their money on clothing.

The task to regulate and control female religious dress, therefore, was from the very beginning rather complicated, and the endless, and invariably useless, recommendations of modesty that appear in the records of the patriarchal visitations, paired with the reports of infractions and the long lists of names of the "guilty" nuns show the tension between rules and reality.

The habits that should have symbolized the beginning of spiritual renewal became instead the focus of the struggle between nuns and ecclesiastical authorities: the former strenuously trying to elaborate on their present lifestyles and to emulate the luxury of their secular relatives, the latter untiringly seeking to erase the nuns' worldly memories and set them on a more spiritual path.

. . . And Forbidden Fashions

Ne dilettate in vestimenti o veli

E meno in apparenza corporale

Ma ne' costumi pensate valere . . .

E che nessuna ispecial suggello tenga,

né anel da suggellare.

. . .

Non dipingete le mani e la gola . . .

Né ricevete giojelli da gente . . .

lassar convengono i lor veli e drappi

tutta leggiadria e vana vista al mondo.

Francesco da Barberino[15]

After having celebrated their mystical marriage to Christ much like secular brides did, it was time for the novices to adjust to life within the cloister. They needed to get used to new routines and life rhythms such as choir duty, daily masses, and the other rituals that constituted religious life, and that often included the use of a specific habit: more solemn and imposing for the choir, simpler and more modest for everyday life. Frequently, however, the boundaries between the world and the cloister appeared rather undefined, particularly given the presence of both girls about to get married and about to pronounce their vows inside the enclosure, in a confusing medley of roles that shaded the already blurred distinctions between inside and outside, angels and women, the sacred and the profane.

Permeable Boundaries: The *Putte*

A disturbing secular presence brought within the enclosure was the *putte a spese*, or boarding girls. Despite the income deriving from the conventual dowries and by the properties owned by many convents both in the city and on the mainland, the profits from the education of the daughters of the upper classes was often needed to supplement the finances of most Venetian convents. In some cases, the money coming from the families of the girls was absolutely essential for the very survival of the institutions. The presence of these girls, who ranged in age from as young as five to older teens, however necessary, was often an inconvenient one. Although, according to the rules of most convents, they were not supposed to have any contact with the nuns, with the exception of their *maestre*, or teachers and caretakers,[16] it was rather common to find them practically living in the cells of some nuns, and particularly nuns from their own families. They also used to "run around in the dormitory and wherever they wish without any rule, and they play cards late at night causing great scandal,"[17] thus disturbing the monastic discipline, disrupting the established routine of the convent, and especially introducing unwelcome distractions during the celebration of the liturgies, particularly when older *putte*, engaged to be married, appeared at the ceremonies lavishly dressed in secular clothes and precious jewellery,[18] setting off an array of malicious comments and envious gossip among the nuns.

Consequently, in order to limit the pomp of these girls and, at the same time, limit their contact with the nuns and thus the possible disturbances caused by their ostentation, Patriarch Federico Cornaro established that "boarding girls should not be vainly dressed, and especially should not wear silk, or forbidden colors, or wear vain and elaborate hairstyles decorated with pearls or any type of jewellery, not on the neck, or at the arms, or other worldly vanities . . . and their collars will have to be well closed in the front in order to hide their décolletage."[19]

The situation became so critical that Patriarch Francesco Contarini, in 1554, recommended that "novices [i.e., secular brides] before their matrimony, or transferal, should not appear in the parlors or elsewhere in the convent in bridal attire."[20] Since the *putte* insisted on wearing these luxurious outfits while still in the enclosure, Patriarch Trevisan ordered that "weddings should not be celebrated in convent churches, that marriage contracts should not be negotiated in convent parlors or at church windows and that the *novizze* should not be shown for contracting those matrimonies" (i.e., should not be exhibited in the parlors lavishly dressed to show the wealth of the family while the marriage contract was written).[21]

Eventually, because these recommendations continued to be widely ignored, Patriarch Vendramin ordered that girls engaged to be married were to leave the convent immediately, so that they would not "dress up as brides and receive their fiancés at the windows with great scandal."[22]

Lay Boarders

A further secular presence inside the monasteries, certainly not encouraged and barely tolerated by ecclesiastical authorities, was that of aristocratic laywomen, who, for a number of possible reasons (i.e., widowhood, conflicts with the husband or the family of origin), used the convents as temporary residences or visited them as guests for extended periods of time. Their age could vary significantly according to the different reasons that brought them to the cloister, but a common trait was that they mostly continued to wear their customary secular dresses, thus often becoming the cause of great scandal (and envy!) among the nuns. Occasionally, their clothes could even be called outrageous, such as those worn, for instance, by Betta Bianchi. Betta used to retire within the convent of San Mauro di Burano every time her brother, with whom she lived, was out of town on business. At some point the nuns, irritated by her unbecoming behavior and offensive clothes (or, possibly, just plain jealous of them!), refused to readmit her, declaring that "never again shall this type of woman be among us." Betta reacted furiously, publicly denouncing many others, such as Marietta, another "scandalous" lay boarder who was "constantly in the parlor, pompously dressed."[23]

Parlors or Salons?

Parlor use and habitual visiting patterns were, in fact, a critical issue, and carefully considered by both religious and civic authorities. Venetian convents had a sort of osmotic relationship with the city, and the parlors

Communion window, seventeenth century, Venice, Church of S. Alvise. Courtesy of Patriarcato di Venezia, Ufficio Beni Culturali.

constituted a key space, a borderland where the boundaries between the lives of the encloistered women and those of the people of the outside world could be, at the same time, highlighted and blurred. The "short, modest, and devout" conversations that were supposed to take place behind the protective screen of the curtains covering the grilles of parlor windows and overheard by the *ascoltatrici*[24] could frequently become worldly confidences or even romantic tête-à-têtes that encouraged the nuns' minds to roam outside the walls of the cloister.

The curtains should have played a double protective role: to shield the nuns from the sight of the visitors and, conversely, the visitors from the sight of the nuns. However, most of the times, the curtains remained completely open during the visits, entirely thwarting their defensive role and in open infraction of the proscriptions of the religious hierarchies.[25] In blatant disregard of the prohibitions—"Nobody will be ever allowed to eat, drink, play instruments, sing, dance or play (in the parlors) or behave irreverently"[26]—many parlors became places where forbidden dinners, concerts, or other secular entertainments, even balls, took place. Visitors flocked to the most popular convents to see the elegant nuns shamelessly exhibiting themselves. In 1678 patrician Niccolò Contarini wrote to his Roman friend nicknamed "Marforio," recommending that during his stay in Venice he visit some conventual parlors, real "terrestrial paradises of celestial beauties" filled with scores of beautiful and charming ladies.[27] Contarini's tip was, some time later, followed by the comment of another foreign visitor to the city, Baron de Poellnitz, who, around the middle of the eighteenth century, still equated parlors with worldly salons where the nuns appeared "with the hair braided . . . , their dresses so short that you can see their ankles, they wear jackets with short yokes, most suited to a slender figure; the neck is bare."[28] Sometimes the dresses were not only short, but nonexistent: a particularly indecent nun from the monastery of Santa Maria dell'Orazione in Malamocco was reported having naughtily received a lay male visitor dressed only in her chemise.[29]

Just from these few examples, it appears clear that parlors could be morally dangerous places for the nuns. The possibility to see and to be seen wearing improper outfits was deeply satisfying for the inmates' self-esteem, but worrying for the patriarchs because: "It is without a doubt that from immodest habits and too refined accessories are born indecent thoughts in proper nuns, thoughts that turn his Brides away from the Love of God, and from his Holy service; besides, this also causes great scandal to the people of the outside world, and gives rise to negative prejudices."[30]

Novices and Nuns

Between the spoiled *putte*, the magnificently dressed *novizze*, the pompous lay boarders, and the secular atmosphere of the parlors, it is easy to understand how confused the novices must have been about the proper dressing style inside the cloister. The often audacious fashions sported by some of the nuns themselves did not help either.

According to the description of Suor Arcangela Tarabotti they too used to wear "abiti vani," vain clothes,[31] instead of the humble tunic they were given during the Clothing ceremony. Often, newly arrived novices were bewildered by the worldly elegance of the habits of some of the professed nuns, who even encouraged them to "wear lascivious clothes."[32] Needless to say, soon novices "formed in their heart the dishonest desire to imitate or even outdo their fashionable outfits."[33]

Arcangela states that she herself was a "nun only in the name, not in the dress or habits, this crazily vain, those vainly crazy,"[34] as many others of her sisters were religious women only in their name, being "secular both in their hearts and in the actions."[35] In 1298 Pope Boniface VIII's *Periculoso* decree required the strict enclosure of all professed nuns of whatever order in Western Christendom. However, the decree was not implemented in Venice until 1519, when full enclosure was finally enforced in Venetian monasteries. Before that date the city's nuns were actually free to go about the city and only rarely wore the monastic habit, eventually inducing local religious authorities to convey strict orders to the prioresses: they were to no longer allow the nuns to go "around the city, secularly dressed."[36]

The well-preserved records of the patriarchal visitations gathered in the archive of the dioceses of Venice are undoubtedly the best and most exhaustive sources on these invisible luxuries and forbidden fashions. From scandalous décolletages to high-heeled footwear, from precious silks to the use of showy makeup, the list of fashion indulgences of the Venetian nuns is quite intriguing and definitely revealing of the determination of at least a significant number of them to maintain a secular identity and to carve out a role within the conventual "society."

The counsel for nuns "to live in the monastery with the modesty requested by their state, not wearing unsuitable dresses, or any kind of ornament, covering the head with the veils, and keeping the hair cut according to the customs of proper nuns" was repeated during every patriarchal visit. Nevertheless, the nuns' passion for wearing secular clothes and baring their décolletages in order to affirm their patrician status and their frustrated femininity, and the conflicting determination of the patriarchs to forbid these unbecoming attires, fill the pages of the docu-ments of the pastoral visits for centuries. Every time the patriarchs tried to reform the customs of the nuns, remarking that bare shoulders and wide necklines were not appropriate for them, they faced the stern oppo-sition of the cloistral inmates who saw forbidden clothing as their only way to express their individuality.

Monastic modesty should have begun with the underwear, the *camise* or shirts worn under the religious habit. Since the early Renaissance, in Venice, and elsewhere in Italy, the *camisa* played a key role in defining the aristocratic dress. Immaculate linen smocks, sometimes embroidered or trimmed with lace and discreetly emerging from the necklines, the cuffs, and the lacings of the sleeves, demonstrated the personal clean-liness of the higher social classes. The number of *camise* mentioned in inventories is really surprising, but justified by the fact that, at the time, laundry was done only twice, maybe three times a year, usually in spring and fall, when the climate was favorable. Francesco Sansovino admiring-ly describes the elegant lingerie of Venetian ladies: "And really it cannot be said what is the richness of the dresses and of the underwear of Vene-tian gentlewomen. Because every piece of clothing, both in silk or linen, is embroidered, decorated, and in any other way made beautiful with the needle, the silk, silver and gold threads . . . authentic symbol of immacu-late and clean soul and clear wisdom."[37]

Noblewomen turned nuns did not easily give up the luxuries that they had brought with them to the convent as boarding girls.[38] A large number of shirts in the conventual trousseau were the first indication of the status of the novices, particularly if these included such unsuitable, and for-bidden, items as embroidered or lace-trimmed linen *camise*, which dis-regarded the directions of the monastic orders that generally prescribed simple, if not coarse, woollen shirts.[39]

Another banned kind of undergarment borrowed from the wardrobe of secular women was the corset. Worldly dresses required the use of this very constricting garment in order to achieve a modish silhouette, espe-cially since the second half of the sixteenth century. Called in Venice *cassi* or *busti*, they were worn by aristocratic laywomen over the chemise and under the dress and were usually made with a wood or metallic structure lined with linen or even hemp inside and more refined fabrics on the outside.

In a decree dated May 16, 1547, the Venetian Senate forbade the *cassi* out of concern for the possible physical damages caused by this "harmful and dangerous fashion" that had sometimes caused "pregnant women to miscarry, many others to die, and their children to be born weak and crippled":[40] it was a serious problem because the death of unborn, and not yet baptized, children represented an offense to God. It was therefore established that no woman could wear the dangerous "long and pointed corsets"; though a less stiff version of them was considered acceptable.[41]

Choosing a "soft" version of the corset was not a feasible option for the nuns; to them corsets were strictly, but theoretically, forbidden. As always, however, they persevered in wearing them, as is documented by the continual prohibitions for over two hundred years, from the first mentions of the corsets inside the cloisters in the sixteenth century to the eighteenth.[42] In fact, fashionably pointed corsets were still worn in the 1714, when Patriarch Barbarigo, during a visit to the monastery of San Gerolamo, found out, once again, that some of the nuns were using the prohibited undergarments. In his "investigation" he was helped by a se-cret denunciation from an anonymous nun who, declaring her intention to contribute to the reestablishment of the internal order of the convent, sent him a note, still preserved in the visitation file, in which she con-firmed that many of her sisters were wearing "long and pointed corsets, hidden watches and *fichus* over the shoulders as noblewomen do. . . . But I beg you, after reading this, please immediately destroy it!"[43]

Venetian lay noblewomen were also known all over Italy for their almost indecently low-necked gowns. Milanese friar Pietro Casola, for instance, who visited Venice in 1494, was astonished to observe that the ladies' necklines were sometimes so wide, he was afraid the dresses would slide off their shoulders.[44] In their continuing efforts to imitate secular styles, fashionable nuns had no qualms about adopting even this characteristic detail of noblewomen's dress, and indecent décolletages apparently were already rather common inside Venetian monasteries by the late fifteenth century.

A portrait dated to between 1485 and 1495 of a nun of the Benedictine monastery of San Secondo, painted by Jacometto Veneziano[45] and once in the collection of Michele Contarini,[46] offers a good example of an unbecoming monastic outfit. In fact, it is striking for the quiet immodesty with which the nun, who wears a dark habit that leaves a white undergarment or chemise visible at the neckline and sleeve, exhibits a neckline so wide as to show not only her décolletage, but her shoulders. The "secularity" of the nun's outfit is even more evident when compared with the contemporary portrait of an unidentified woman, possibly a courtesan, painted by Vittore Carpaccio around 1495 characterized by a similarly wide neckline.

Despite all the threats of punishment, even of excommunication, generous décolletages were there to stay. About a hundred years later, in 1592, Patriarch Lorenzo Priuli was still admonishing the nuns in Sant'Andrea de la Zirada "to wear honest and modest clothes, underneath as well as on top so that neither the breast nor any other body part should be exposed. . . . [The nuns] should not show their hair but wear their head bands low over their foreheads." On September 12, 1597, the same patriarch addressing all the nuns of his dioceses expressed yet again his extreme disappointment in observing that they were still accustomed to "wear silk veils that leave the curled hair visible and generous necklines with great scandal." He then recommended them to go back to the original purity of the ancient habits with short hairs, simple veils, and covered breasts, at the same time warning them that he, or his emissaries, "will seek justice on those who will not comply with our ordinances."[47]

A century later no significant improvement had been made. In 1692 the nuns of San Giuseppe di Castello were reprimanded because of their "reprehensible abuse . . . of wearing very small veils over the shoulders and fashioned in a way that it would seem to lay people that the habits of the nuns were all different from one another; we therefore order the reformation of all the nuns, and that they go back to more modest and religious veils to cover the shoulders and breasts."[48] Among those guilty of this "fashionable" sin was Arcangela Tarabotti, who was accused by the writer monk Angelico Aprosio of following the regrettable styles of the time, wearing "her bonnet untied and maliciously leaving visible her breasts that were only scarcely covered by a thin veil."[49]

Not only were the décolletages scandalous, the habits too did not follow the rules. Made either with forbidden silk or colored fabrics,[50] too tight-fitting, sleeveless, or even transparent,[51] they satisfied the frustrated feminine vanity of the involuntary nuns and constituted a point of pride and social distinction inside the convent. However, they were available only to richer nuns who could afford to buy more refined fabrics, trimmings, and textile furnishings for the cell or who received them as presents. Ursia Condulmer, sister of the famous courtesan Elisabetta and nun in the convent of Santa Caterina, received from her sister a number of precious and highly monastically unsuitable items: among them "four door curtains of scarlet cloth decorated with arms and foliage; a green and yellow striped satin cape lined with squirrel skins; a ten-piece bed ensemble of green and orange *ormesino* silk . . . and five figured *spallieri* wall hangings, decorated with arms."[52] It is likely that these refined objects helped Ursia maintain her social status within the convent.

The inconsistent policy of the patriarchs allowed for the customization of the habits by a tailor[53] while, at the same time, prohibiting the alteration of the habit, "vainly transforming it into a tight fitting dress."[54] Always excluded was any garment, both visible and invisible, made of silk and of any other material not prescribed by the rule of the order, cuffs made with fine fabrics "forbidden as not appropriate for nuns," along with similarly elegant sleeves.[55]

In secular clothes the sleeves were often a detachable part of the dress and, because they were frequently decorated with intricate embroideries, sometimes representing coats of arms, heraldic symbols, or animals, and even enriched with pearls and jewels, were coveted accessories. Noblewomen and nuns alike used to decorate their own sleeves with precious embroideries. When Regina Donà from the Santa Anna monastery died, her sister Andriana Malipiero immediately wrote to Arcangela Tarabotti, who lived in the same monastery, requesting she be allowed to retrieve the sleeves that had belonged to the nun. Unfortunately, Arcangela replied, it was the custom of the monastery to seal off the cells of the nuns for at least a month after their death. Therefore Andriana had to wait a while before being able to show off the elaborate needlework created by her dead sister.[56] Anyway, according to the rules, another nun could not "inherit" the precious sleeves or any other article of clothing. The personal items of deceased nuns were to be preserved in the communal wardrobe and distributed to the nuns according to their needs.

The use and types of veils, essential accessories of the monastic habit, was another deeply controversial issue. The purpose of the veil was to protect the nuns by hiding their femininity. Yet they were used by the vast majority of secular noblewomen in the city, to the point that Casola exclaimed that when he walked around the city or prayed in a church, "It seemed to me as if I was seeing Benedictine nuns all over the place."[57] According to Vecellio, the black veils added a sense of mystery to these women and made every one of them more charming because it did not allow one to distinguish the young from the old and the beautiful from the unattractive! Similarly, the black but transparent silk veils of Venetian nuns were more likely to attract, rather than deflect, the gaze of male desire. These sheer symbols of the recalcitrant will of the involuntary nuns tantalizingly reminded viewers of the beauty of the nuns and embodied the dilemma of the perfect seclusion: "how permeable the convent walls, grilles, and doors could become from time to time . . . seemed to be captured emblematically by those veils."[58]

To enhance their seductive role, nuns who could afford it wore colored or preciously embroidered veils, sometimes decorating them with gold and silver needleworks.[59] They also fashionably starched and embellished them with gold or silver *agucchie da pomella*, or pins, used to secure them: precious pins were obviously forbidden, but nevertheless widely popular.[60]

Occasionally, some nuns refused to wear the veils, however elegant. In 1579 Patriarch Trevisan took the drastic measure of excommunicating the nuns of Santa Lucia because they refused to wear the prescribed black veils.[61]

The footwear of the nuns too could often have quite a worldly look. Very popular among stylish nuns for instance were the unlawful *calcagnini*, or *calcagnetti*. Described by Pietro Casola as "so high indeed that when they wear them, women do appear like giants,"[62] they were the exaggerated evolution of the *pianelle*; they did not cover the heels and were characterized by a very tall wedge formed by overlapping layers of cork covered in leather. Created initially for the utilitarian purpose of protecting the feet from the mud and the garbage in the not yet paved streets, they soon became an extravagant accessory. In Venice they could sometimes be decorated with mother-of-pearl inlay, and be as high as fifty centimeters.[63]

These unsafe "heights" were severely prohibited by sumptuary magistrates, concerned about falls that, not infrequently, could cause abortions or other accidents, but, conversely, were appreciated by Venetian fathers and husbands who saw this strange and uncomfortable fashion as potentially useful: a woman wearing these "platforms" could not go around the city alone, but needed an escort of at least one, if not two, servants, thus minimizing the risks of clandestine outings.[64]

Tarabotti strongly supported the use of the *calcagnetti* on almost philosophical grounds: for her they were like pedestals for women who deserved to be admired and protected from the "ordinary baseness" of the world.[65] Many of her encloistered sisters shared her point of view and rejected the prescribed wooden clogs, preferring instead sandals, or "Roman shoes," *scarpe alla romana* with silk laces,[66] so elegant and pretty "that not even an Arcadian Nymph" wore anything like that,[67] and that were occasionally even decorated with gold or silver leaf. In 1595, Suor Dorothea Sforza, Suor Mansueta Pase, and Suor Marietta Dolfin were identified as the source of disturbances in the monastery of Sant'Iseppo because of their proudly showing off "ornaments and high-heeled clogs, silk stockings with gilt lace"[68] as well as the *borzacchini*, leather ankle boots, another type of forbidden monastic footwear.[69]

The list of secular luxury items worn by patrician nuns is long and varied: in the collection of the "Ordini generali per le monache" are recorded numerous forbidden indulgences of the elegant inmates, which included the use of furs,[70] earrings, silk hoses or sashes, rings,[71] fans, and watches.[72]

Rather common was also the use of embroidered and lace-trimmed handkerchiefs, the *fazzoletti da portare in mano*,[73] once again in imitation of the habits of lay patrician women, the hands of whom were often kept busy by these rather large fine linen squares decorated by embroideries, small lace trimmings, or fringes. Because to be really elegant the handkerchief had to be immaculate. Many of these accessories are mentioned in inventories, wedding and conventual trousseaux, and they are occasionally very expensive, such as the "silk and gold" handkerchief mentioned in the wedding trousseau of Lucrezia Gradenigo and valued at two *ducati*, the price of twenty ordinary handkerchiefs. The custom of trimming these accessories with needle-made *punto in aria* lace is so common that in Milan, in 1584, even sumptuary laws allowed the use of this pricey decoration, as long as it was not wider than a twentieth of a *brazzo* (meaning "arm," an ancient unit of length) of silk.

Also borrowed from their secular counterparts was the use of gloves, *guanti da secolari*.[74] The role played since the Renaissance by gloves is extremely meaningful. They protected the hands of the aristocracy and were an essential complement of any elegant outfit. Gloves could be made of silk, linen, or, mostly, very fine leather, if not of the unusual *feltro di pesce*, or fishskin, and often decorated with intricate embroideries and lined with furs such as squirrel, marten, or sable. The most appreciated were made in Milan and Padua, and in many Renaissance portraits they are worn on just one hand and appear *stratagliati*, or slashed, on the knuckles in order to let the precious stones of the rings show. Characteristic were also perfumed gloves, scented with flowery or aromatic essences. Eleonora of Toledo received a pair of gloves of crimson silk perfumed by perfumer Ciano on December 20, 1549. Isabella d'Este Gonzaga was herself very skilled in preparing scented gloves, which she often gave as presents; on one occasion she sent them to the Queen of France, who reserved them for special events. Scented gloves made in Italy, writes Cesare Vecellio in 1590, were also worn by Neapolitan ladies, as an alternative to Spanish gloves made in Valencia.

Other luxurious items found in monastic cells were rugs, upholstered walls, sumptuously made beds with silk coverlets, and embroidered linens,[75] again all of them forbidden by monastic regulations that advised that, in preparing the trousseaux for the nuns, "all the vanità degli ornamenti" be abandoned in favor of "useful things, necessary for the lives of the Nuns."[76]

But how did nuns keep themselves current with the latest fashions? As we will see, their conventual servants, or *converse*, were often sent "into the world" to gather information on the new dress styles, but sometimes fashions infiltrated the convents through the presence in the parlors of peddlers who acted as salesmen for the latest fashions. In her letters, Arcangela Tarabotti shows she is perfectly up-to-date on the latest lace designs, although she did not use them to decorate her own habit. Also probably present inside the monastery were "fashion dolls" called *pupe* or *puve*. These dolls were carefully dressed with miniaturized versions of the latest dress styles and were circulated in the courts, both in Italy and abroad since the early Renaissance. In Venice, from the late seventeenth century, the so-called Piavola de Franza was one of the attractions of the Ascension celebrations in St. Mark's Square: during the fair a fashionably dressed mannequin exhibited in the square launched the latest styles, coming mostly from France.[77]

The punishments for the fashion sins of the nuns were potentially harsh, but, at the same time, inconsistent. The penalties ranged from one to six months of imprisonment to two years of deprivation of their electoral vote, of access to the parlors[78] or to the windows that looked from the convent into the church, or "even more severe punishments."[79] Should the prioresses be found guilty of laxity in carrying out these punishments, they could be immediately removed from office; confessors were ordered to exclude the guilty nuns from the sacraments until they asked forgiveness for their sins.[80] However, these measures were very rarely put into effect: when Patriarch Querini decided to incarcerate two unlawfully dressed nuns of La Celestia, he was stopped by the violent protest of all the other nuns: "all of the other nuns began to cry and hurl themselves in front of the door so that it was impossible to incarcerate the two guilty nuns."[81] Another common reason why the "sins" of the nuns were rarely, or not effectively, punished is to be found in the political connections of the nuns: being aristocratic by birth, they could count on their family's network to rally to their side, as they often did—for instance, during the internal elections in order to support their kinswomen.[82] Just how stubborn Venetian noblewomen could be in protecting their fashionable ways is proved by a petition sent to none other than the pope.

Patriarch Lorenzo Giustinian, concerned about the money lavished on fashionable clothing, had in fact tried to forbid them, and threatened excommunication. Venetian ladies reacted defiantly, appealing to the pope for permission to keep wearing their magnificent dresses "for the honor of their families." The pope granted his permission upon payment of a tax.[83]

The Fashionable Canonesses of Le Vergini

The Vergini held a special place among the numerous Venetian religious institutions: not only was the monastery under the patronage of the doge, it was also a very peculiar female community composed of *canonicae saeculares*, according to a definition that dates to the fourteenth century, who later became *canonissae*.

This form of female religious aggregation originally began in the German Empire, and particularly in the Lorraine and Bourgogne regions, around the end of the Middle Ages. The canonesses were essentially noblewomen who lived in a monastery but were not required to follow the enclosure rule.[84]

In fact, the canonesses of the Venetian monastery of Le Vergini did

Bas-relief and inscription from an arch once part of the monastery of Santa Maria delle Vergini, now incorporated in the Arsenale. Venice, May 2, 1557.

not take the solemn vows of poverty, chastity, and obedience, did not change their names when they entered the convent, and were addressed as "Madonna," like their secular counterparts, thereby emphasizing their unusual monastic status and signaling an identity that encompassed both the secular and the religious sphere.[85]

The Vergini could dispose of their private patrimony as they pleased, and even of the income they derived from the activities practiced inside the convent, such as embroidery and weaving. And although they lived within the institution, they had their own lavish quarters, staffed with private servants. They were granted the right to leave the cloister from time to time, to go to St. Mark's Square, or to visit their families and stay with them, sometimes for months at end; conversely, often members from their families came to visit them in the monastery, frequently prolonging their visits for weeks. Finally, the canonesses could even reverse their decision and leave the monastery to get married.[86]

Their religious duties were limited to choir practices, and in addition to their refined education, which included the study of Greek and Latin, they were known for their heavenly singing: their musical fame transformed the convent into one of the must-see places for the visitors to the city. In August 1505, even Queen Anne of Hungary asked to be brought to listen to the nuns' singing.[87]

Their secular lifestyle was matched by the secular habit they wore, as was the custom in other orders of canonesses.[88] Pietro Casola describes them, in fact, as "vainly dressed in white,"[89] and they were known for their fashionable and immaculate outfits, the use of white being a "vain" luxury in itself.

This rather lax attitude toward religious life sometimes did not match the expectations of the very few that entered the monastery to follow an authentic religious calling. For instance, Contarina Contarini, Eufemia Loredan, and Adriana Contarini, on May 10, 1488, were granted by Pope Innocenzo VIII permission to leave the Vergini to enter the nearby monastery of San Daniele where they could adopt a much stricter habit and rule.[90]

As a matter of fact, the canonesses were required to wear the habit only when in the choir or otherwise engaged in official duty, but, even then, the habit was uniquely different from that of other Venetian nuns. Much evidence about what the Vergini habit looked like has been preserved in the Cronica del Monistero delle Vergini in Venetia, an illuminated manuscript dated to the late fifteenth century and almost certainly the work of one of the canonesses, probably Madonna Franceschina Giustiniani.

The manuscript was written during the reformation process promoted since 1519 by the patriarch of Venice, who wanted to make the Vergini like the rest of the Venetian convents and prevent the reprehensible behaviors that had led to no fewer than fifteen fornication trials between 1381 and 1486.[91] The miniatures of the manuscript illustrate numerous times the characteristic white habit of the canonesses, the use of which, in those same years, was at the center of a power struggle between the nuns and the Venetian religious hierarchies.

The method chosen by the patriarch to reform the monastery was relatively simple: he decided to introduce some Observant nuns, that is, nuns following a much stricter rule, alongside the Conventuals, or choir nuns. In this case he arranged for a group of Observant nuns from Santa Giustina to move to Le Vergini.[92]

These nuns, according to their rule, wore a modest gray tunic. Soon after their arrival, however, the newcomers expressed their intention to take up the white habit of Le Vergini, encountering the stern opposition of the canonesses, who saw this as an illegal appropriation of their privileged status.

In their dispute the nuns were supported by their families, who even appealed to the Vatican. And on November 2, 1541, the pope, through Cardinal Antonio, Bishop of Albano, ordered that all the nuns at the Vergini wear a black tunic, reflecting that this "would set a very useful example for other Monasteries, where the ambition of the *converse* to imitate the habit of the choir nuns causes ostentation and originates disagreements and uneasiness among them."[93] The *querelle* eventually died down, and the Vergini were able to continue to wear their traditional habit.

But what did this much coveted dress look like? The somewhat stiff representations of the "marriages" of the abbesses in the Cronica consistently show a total-white, rather bulky habit flowing in folds around the feet of the women that completely hides the shape of their bodies. A white veil covers the heads, in contrast with other representations where the veil appears to be black. Several hypotheses have been made about the alternate use of white and black veils, among them the possibility that the white veil and total-white outfit were reserved for use during solemn liturgies, while the black veil was worn for more ordinary occasions.

Similar to the dresses illustrated in the manuscript is the one represented in the life-sized portrait on the tomb slab of Francesca Zorzi.[94]
The bas-relief, once placed at the entrance of the convent church, where
it would have been visible to visitors, shows the fine facial features of
the abbess modestly framed by the veil and wimple, while the body is
covered by the voluminous folds of the habit that lends dignity and highlights the hierarchic status of the abbess who governed the monastery for
over twenty-three years.[95]

Not a portrait, but rather a stenographic reference to a Vergini abbess, appears in *The Magdalene Transported by Angels*, a fifteenth-century
painting by Antonio Vivarini,[96] probably commissioned for the altar of
St. Mary Magdalene in the convent church. In it the habit becomes pre-
dominant in defining the abbess, who, because of her miniaturized size,
appears to be completely overwhelmed by the white folds of her habit.
Her veil is black, as are those of the two abbesses portrayed on the imposing marble hand basin, dated 1531, and once placed against the western
wall of the refectory at Le Vergini.[97]

Executed in the style of Tullio Lombardo and made of different types
of colored marble, it includes a bas-relief at the top containing a devotional image of the Virgin and Child flanked by the two canonesses identified, thanks to the initials carved on the basin itself, as Sofia Pisani and
Marina Barbaro. The abbesses are portrayed in very proper white monastic outfits, the very image of sobriety, continence, and devotion.

A much different message is conveyed by eighteenth-century representations of a canoness of le Vergini produced around the same time
by Francesco Bonanni[98] and Vincenzo Coronelli,[99] and later by Pierre
Hélyot.[100] In all three engravings the cumbersome and dignified habit of
the past centuries has dramatically evolved into a much more fashionable outfit: "A low-cut, white, tight-fitting dress with large flowing sleeves
secured by frivolous bows at the shoulders, shaped suggestively as if to
mock a nun's tunic and mantle. Their face is framed by a wimple and
shrouded by a black, transparent veil, short in the front and rather long
in the back." This example of conventual elegance has a lot in common
with contemporary worldly fashions: the bodice of the habit highlights

the shape of the body, and the transparency of the veil, paired with the small size of the wimple, rather than inspiring meditation, appears coquettishly attractive. The Vergini of the eighteenth century were just as stylish as their secular contemporaries.

Elegance at San Zaccaria

> Since I had heard a lot about female monasteries, I was accompanied on a visit to some of them, and the first one was that of San Zaccaria. There are many women there, both young and old, and they were very willing to be seen. . . . They say they are very rich and they are not concerned about being seen.[101]

The Benedectine monastery of San Zaccaria, founded in 982 by the Partecipazio family, was the first convent to be established in the city.[102] Together with Le Vergini and San Lorenzo, the three institutions constituted the elite of Venetian convents.[103]

San Zaccaria was honored every year on Easter Day by a visit of the doge, who participated in the solemn celebration of the Mass and was later received by the prioress, who presented him with a new *corno dogale*,[104] the characteristic headgear worn by the Venetian doges.

The surprised remarks of Casola about nuns who, against all monastic rules,[105] openly showed themselves to the visitors in the parlors introduces us to the very worldly customs of this convent where the nuns were known more for their erudition and the elegance of their outfits than for their religiosity.[106]

Emperor Frederick III, who visited the monastery on February 8, 1469, described the abbess as a "very elegant woman,"[107] an impression confirmed, centuries later, by Cosimo III of Tuscany, who, during his own visit in 1664, found the nuns "very gracefully dressed with a French style white habit. The bodice, which leaves the breasts halfway visible, is covered by pleated linen trimmed by black lace." Under the small veil that was tied round the front was visible "the curled and neatly styled hair,"[108] and this despite the fact that, numerous times, religious authorities had ordered that the nuns' veils be arranged "so that one sees nothing of the hair." In 1609 Patriarch Vendramin further specified that "the veils of the

T. VI. P. 314.
Fig. II.

Benedictine du Monastere de S.t
Zacharie a Venise en habit de choeur 78.

Choir Habit of the Nuns of San Zaccaria. Pierre Helyot, Histoire des Ordres Monastiques, Religieux et Militaires, vol. VI, p. 314, fig. II, Paris, 1743, Courtesy of Biblioteca San Francesco della Vigna, Venice.

shoulders be wide and ample so that they cover the flesh entirely, (and that they could be) thin, but not transparent."[109]

In contrast to this order, the veil that covers the head of the choir nun of San Zaccaria in the engraving by Hélyot dated 1737–1739[110] appears to be very transparent and the wimple so skimpy that the hair is well in evidence. The habit is black and not too form-fitting, with large *ducale* sleeves,[111] but the décolletage is quite generous and only partially covered by the white chemise worn underneath the habit.

More modest appears to be the attire of the prioress welcoming the doge at the grilles of the parlor in the painting by Antonio Zonca dated

Antonio Zonca, *The Doge's Visit to the Nuns of San Zaccaria*, 1688, Venice, Church of San Zaccaria. Courtesy of Patriarcato di Venezia, Ufficio Beni Culturali.

around 1690 and located in the upper portion of the right aisle of the church of the convent.[112]

Behind the not-too-thick grilles it is possible to notice that her décolletage, on this solemn and official occasion, is completely covered, the wimple ampler, and the veil seems to be made of a heavier fabric; even the downcast eyes of the prioress are more modest than the proud and direct gaze of the nun of Hélyot's engraving. The impression is of composed sobriety, in open contrast with the ceremonial magnificence of the outfit of the Doge, which is made entirely of gold cloth and ermine fur.

Bonanni offers yet another, humbler version of the dress of the nuns of San Zaccaria: the simple habit worn "in cubiculo," while praying inside their cells, is a modest tunic covered on the front by a *traversa*, a sort of apron, an accessory that is mentioned over and over in conventual trousseau lists.[113] Even in this secluded environment, however, a tiny bit of vanity emerges in the hairstyle, only partially covered by the coif. Very proper accessories are the rosary and the prayer book held in the hand of the nun.

Benedictina Monaftery S. Zacchariæ
Venetiarum, dum in Cubiculo degit

Vincenzo Maria Coronelli, *Nun of San Zaccaria in Cubiculo*, from *Ordinum religiosorum in ecclesia militanti catalogus*, Venice, 1707. Reprinted by permission of Biblioteca del Museo Correr, Venice.

The ordinary dress represented by Hélyot has a very different and more feminine flair: it is black, but here ends all the respect for the rules, because the square décolletage is so ample as to leave visible the roundness of the breasts.[114] The head is covered by a rather coquettish bonnet laced under the chin with ribbons, and the nun is holding in her left hand a very fashionable and technically strictly forbidden accessory, a fan.[115]

Further evidence on the secular style of the nuns of San Zaccaria and of the fact that they were not at all concerned about being seen by outsiders is given by the famous painting by Francesco Guardi, *The Nuns' Parlor*

Pierre Helyot, *Ordinary Habit of the Nuns of San Zaccaria in the House*, from *Histoire des Ordres Monastiques, Religieux et Militaires*, vol. VI, p. 314, fig. I, Paris, 1743. Courtesy of Biblioteca San Francesco della Vigna, Venice.

in San Zaccaria,[116] a work that effectively conveys the worldly atmosphere of this monastery.

The space is divided in two by a wall: on the public side of the parlor are the visitors, a mixed group of noblewomen, gentlemen, and children, entertained by a puppet show; at the far left is also represented a beggar, a rather common presence in conventual parlors, where they could count on the generosity of the nuns. Well visible behind the grilles are the nuns themselves. Five of them, the majority, are wearing fashionably tailored white habits, thus confirming the account by Cosimo III, three are wearing the prescribed Benedictine black, and one of them, maybe a *putta a spese*, even shows off a bright yellow dress. All of them show the hair under the coif, the *putta* even more so.

Francesco Guardi, *The Nuns' Parlor in San Zaccaria*, Venice, Ca' Rezzonico, ca. 1755. Reprinted by permission of Biblioteca del Museo Correr, Venice.

Just from the color of the dresses of the nuns one can make an informed guess about the different roles held by these women inside the conventual hierarchy. Probably those wearing white habits were choir nuns, proud to be able to wear such a precious and ennobling color. The three nuns in black were likely *converse,* servant nuns, a hypothesis supported by the fact that one of them is accepting a basket of supplies from a lay servant, a *donna delle monache*—this menial task would never have been performed by a choir nun! Furthermore, the faces of the *converse* are much less defined in their features by the artist than those of the aristocratic nuns or their likewise noble visitors, a further indication of their lesser social status inside the convent. Finally, the lady in yellow is doubtless a *putta* already engaged to be married: her dress and hair match the fashionable style of the lay gentlewomen who came to visit her, and she is amiably conversing with them as equals: her monastic confinement has almost come to an end.

The "Nymphs" of San Lorenzo

On May 20, 1664, the Grand Duke of Tuscany, Cosimo III, accompanied by his court chaplain, Filippo Pizzichi, visited the monastery of San Lorenzo, "the richest monastery in Venice." The Benedictine institution founded in 841 was very often visited by illustrious guests. According to the chaplain's account, Cosimo in fact amiably conversed in the parlor, where the curtains of the windows were left open and the grilles were so large as to be practically useless, "with the Abbess and two sisters of the noble Loredan family; and one of them, besides being extraordinarily beautiful, was also greatly admired for her grace and eloquence." The over one hundred choir nuns of San Lorenzo, "all noblewomen," are described by the visitors as "most lovely dressed, with a French-style white gown and pleated-linen bodice which the professed nuns are allowed to trim with a black lace a couple of inches wide; a small veil covers the front. Under it are visible the curled and carefully styled hair, the breast is half bare, and, overall, it is an outfit more suited to nymphs, than to nuns dedicated to a life of penance and prayer."[117]

The alluring narration of Pizzichi is echoed by the description of the outfit of a San Lorenzo nun by theologian Marco Ferro, who depicts her "dressed in fine white linen, and so vain as to resemble more a graceful and charming nymph than a chaste and modest virgin."[118] Although the traditional Benedictine color was black, the nuns of this convent had, according to Count Scipione Pannicchieschi d'Elci, since the early fourteenth century opted for the more prestigious white as the color of choice for their habits, always made of the finest linen available. Despite the efforts of some of the prioresses (among them Polissena Badoer, the one who received Cosimo III), who had repeatedly, and unsuccessfully, tried to reimpose the use of the prescribed black tunic and to forbid French-style dresses, the standard dark habit was generally worn only for solemn ceremonies or during Holy Week.[119]

Bonanni's *Catalogo* presents three different images, all numbered 19, related to San Lorenzo: two "ordinary" outfits and a choir habit, all of

Sanctimonialis Monasterÿ S. Laurentÿ
Venetiarum familiari habitu induta.

Vincenzo Maria Coronelli, *Ordinary Habit of a Benedictine Nun of San Lorenzo*, from *Ordinum religiosorum in ecclesia militanti catalogus*, Venice, 1707. Reprinted by permission of Biblioteca del Museo Correr, Venice.

them black. The first two only seem modest and demure; examining them more carefully, it is possible to notice that the dress is rather form-fitting, that the wide décolletage is scarcely, if at all, covered by the wimple, and, particularly, that the hair has been carefully curled and arranged at the sides of the front; or, in Bonanni's words, "the habit adopted by them is made of black serge, and not in the shape of a tunic, but fitted to the waist of every nun; on the head they use a white veil that does not cover the styled hair and from the head goes to cover the neck."[120] The choir habit appears to be very imposing: "When they recite their prayers in the choir or they take Communion, they wear a wide-sleeved *cocolla* with a large

Benedictina in Cænobio S. Laurentij Venetijs extructo A. DCCCXLI.

Vincenzo Maria Coronelli, *Choir Habit of a Benedictine Nun of San Lorenzo*, from *Ordinum religiosorum in ecclesia militanti catalogus*, Venice, 1707. Reprinted by permission of Biblioteca del Museo Correr, Venice.

train that lends them a majestic dignity. On the head they add a black transparent veil that reaches below the waist."[121]

Given this worldly display of décolletages, elegant dresses, and fashionable hairstyles, it does not come as a surprise that one of the most notorious Venetian sex scandals of the eighteenth century involved one of these "nymphs." Suor Maria da Riva was a beautiful inmate in San Lorenzo: born into the patrician family of Luigi da Riva e Chiara Cellini, she was, in 1719, at the age of sixteen, forced to take the veil.[122] Very intelligent, educated, and charming, she soon attracted the attention of the many visitors who flocked to the convent parlor. Among them was the French ambassador to Venice, Count de Froulay, who, having arrived in Venice in November 1733, soon discovered the refined glamour of the parlours, so similar to Parisian salons, and fell madly in love with the nun. Most evenings he arrived at the convent in his gondola, to accompany the lavishly dressed Maria to all sorts of parties and entertainments, such as a *bal masque* at the Bragadin Palace near Santa Marina on January, 20, 1735, where she arrived "dressed as a man with a *tabaro*" and from which she returned to the convent only at dusk.[123] The scandalous relationship was severely prosecuted by the government as shown by the files of the Inquisitori di Stato. Maria was transferred to a monastery in Ferrara, from which she later managed to escape again and to marry in Bologna a colonel Moroni. Given his political position, the French ambassador escaped any sort of prosecution and left Venice on December 11, 1742. His reputation was undamaged and he even received the ceremonial present of a necklace by the Serenissima.[124]

Beauty Secrets

Venice was a city renowned in Europe for the extraordinary attractiveness of its women, a charm that, despite the beliefs of Federigo Luigini, who in his *Libro della bella donna* cursed the inventors of perfumes and cosmetics because "the work of God does not have to be altered in any way,"[125] owed much to the elaborate and time-consuming beauty treatments followed by women of all social classes, and noblewomen especially, who, as Pietro Casola observed, "painted their faces a great deal, and also other parts as they show, in order to appear more beautiful."[126] In the Renaissance, outward beauty was thought to reflect inner nobility, and women used numerous recipes to achieve the ideal fair complexion and preserve the bloom of the body. Some of these beauty secrets were already known in classical times, as Roman poet Ovid documents in his *Ars Amandi*, a compendium of love and seduction tips. Since the fifteenth century, the passion for the classical world helped spread knowledge of Ovid's work and, thanks to the invention of printing, many of these formulas, previously passed down orally as women's secrets, were in Venice collected and published.

The best known among these books were the *Notandissimi secreti dell'arte profumatoria*, by Giovanventura Rossetti,[127] and the *Secreti*, by Isabella Cortese.[128] In their pages are listed dozens of beauty concoctions, the ingredients of which arrived in the city through the spice commerce between the Serenissima and the Middle and the Far East. Once in Venice, the exotic components were skillfully mixed and sold by the local *spezieri*, a cross between a pharmacist and herbalist.

Among the most common and useful recipes were lip rouges made with *verzino*, a type of wood that yielded a red dye, rose water and oil, "pezzuole di Levante," a small piece of cloth dyed with a decoction of rock alum, caustic lime, and brasil, an Asiatic plant (*Caesalpinia brasiliensis*) that produces a vivid red. It was used not only on the lips and cheeks; Venetian courtesans colored their nipples with it. There were also recipes for face creams in which rose water was combined with cinnamon, rock salt, and "urine of a virgin boy," and for a whitening paste obtained by mixing lemon juice, white wine, breadcrumbs, and nutmeg. More dangerous recipes suggested for this purpose the use of poisonous ceruse (high in lead content), while caustic lime was recommended for hair removal. Never mind that, as a consequence of this rather dramatic treatment, burns, sometimes severe, were not uncommon.

In every book of "secrets" were several formulas to bleach the hair using the *bionde*,[129] a homemade mixture composed of extravagant, if not disturbing, ingredients, such as turmeric, saffron, rock alum, lemon juice, white wine, Arabic gum, centaury, ammonia, and urine,[130] which gave the hair the trademark Venetian blond, a warm tone of gold that, as we have seen, was the mandatory color of hair for both secular and religious *novizze* on their wedding day. The color symbolized their virginity and purity, though to obtain it, it was necessary to endure an extenuating, and rather stinky, bleaching process. In fact, Venetian ladies spent endless hours on their *altane*,[131] the typical Venetian roof terraces, dressed in a light *schiavonetto*,[132] a sort of long chemise made of fine linen or light silk, usually enriched by refined laces and embroideries, the head covered with the *solana*,[133] a straw hat without the crown, and the locks spread on the brim, constantly moistened using the *sponzeta*, a small sponge, soaked in the *bionda*.

Cesare Vecellio, *Dama in altana,*
from *De gli habiti antichi et
moderni di diverse parti del
mondo . . .* , 1590, c. 112v.

These elaborate beauty practices were not unknown inside the seclusion of the monasteries. Tarabotti describes the vanity of the married
sister who bleached her flowing hair on the *altana,* while the forced nun
was deprived of the locks that Mother Nature had given to her.[134] Nuns
did not just endure the ritual tonsure during the Clothing ceremony; they
were supposed to cut their hair "at least once a month during the winter,
and every two weeks in the summer" and completely hide it under the
veil and wimple.[135]

However, from the records of the patriarchal visitations, we learn that
the custom of keeping long hair and styling and dyeing it did not stop at
the convent gates: over and over we find the patriarchs recommending
the nuns cut their hair short, "as it was customary for proper nuns,"[136]

firmly prohibiting them from showing the hair at the temples or curling it.[137]

The above comparison between the dress style of the nun of the monastery of San Secondo and the supposed courtesan confirms the use even inside monastic institutions of the forbidden *fongo*, or "mushroom," hairstyle that the nun just barely concealed underneath the thin veils that covered her head.[138] The *fongo* was a whimsical hairstyle fashionable in Venice around the end of the fifteenth century in which the hair was gathered in a sort of flat concentric chignon on top of the head. It was completely forbidden even to laywomen by sumptuary laws because, wearing this style they appeared "rather men than women,"[139] but it was nevertheless widely adopted in the city. A creative variation of the *fongo* was the *funghetti* (small mushrooms) or *monticelli*,[140] a style worn by Tarabotti, who openly disregarded the prescribed periodical tonsure and left her coif intentionally untied in order to leave the curled hair visible at the temples.

Other engravings representing monastic attires also show the hair styled according to the *a corna* fashion,[141] that is, "two horns that create a half moon shape, with the so-called horns pointed upwards, and kept this way with some sort of adhesive."[142] Patriarch Vendramin was outraged at finding the nuns of Sant'Andrea wearing "locks on the temples, and curls on the head,"[143] which he defined as "inventions of the devil."[144] Even more scandalous was the behavior of Suor Eleonora Francesca Possevino, an involuntary nun who, after having tried to escape from several convents and following the refusal of Pope Alexander VII to annul her vows in 1660, was eventually imprisoned. She used to shock her fellow inmates by refusing to wear the veil and sporting curled hair and a pair of earrings.

Unveiled heads could also sport beautiful floral decorations on the hair, or on the breast, vividly remembered by Messieur de Saint Disdier in his *Memoirs*.[145]

The disregarding of regulations caused great outrage both among government representatives and religious hierarchies. Marin Sanudo narrates a rather curious episode that happened on August 25, 1525, during the visit of Patriarch Gerolamo Querini, accompanied by the state attorney and other officials, to the monastery of Santa Maria della Celestia. The inspection was motivated by numerous reports that described "those dishonest nuns wearing long hair," and the delegation arrived so early that most nuns were not even dressed. As soon as Querini entered the convent, he immediately spotted "a nun of the Tagiapiera family with her hair in braids"; frustrated, the Patriarch himself "grabbed her and cut her hair with his own hands."[146]

However, evidently no amount of patriarchal determination could separate the nuns from these forbidden beauty indulgences, despite even the unexpected visits carried out either by the prioresses (as recommended by all the patriarchs), or, as we have seen, by the patriarch himself. In one case the set of younger nuns of the San Zaccaria monastery who had sported a rather demure hairstyle during the routine inspection went back to their usual fancy ways as soon as the patriarch was through the convent's gate![147]

Archival documentation also proves the use of the *bionde* inside the monasteries. In 1578 Giovanni Trevisan prohibited blonde and curled hair,[148] obviously to no avail, because in a letter dated September 10, 1580, the apostolic nuncio Bolognetti reported that the vast majority of Venetian nuns were accustomed to dyeing their hair with the *bionde*.[149]

If Venetian women were experienced and skilled in the use of makeup, nuns were no less proficient at it. Once again, confirmations about their beauty habits come from the files of the patriarchal visits. In 1620, for instance, Suor Chiara del Calice was accused of wearing bangs, picking her eyebrows, and hiding beauty waters and perfumes that she obstinately refused to give up, showing the same appreciation for scented waters and perfumed oils as her lay contemporaries.[150]

Venetian ladies, in fact, took care of their bodies with aromatic baths scented with rose, jasmine, and other perfumed oils; the same oils were generously sprinkled on clothing, handkerchiefs, and gloves. Unpleasant smells were disguised by fragrant paste, such as civet, Indian musk, and amber, kept in little precious jars attached to gold belts. Perfumes arrived in the West with the Crusades; it was at that time that Venice began to import sandalwood, cloves, aloe, civet, Arabian incense, Egyptian balm, and iris powder, scents generously used also by men.

Despite the recurring prohibitions, the fascination of the nuns with makeup and beauty treatments continued for centuries, following the fashions and passions of secular women. In 1635, Suor Arcangela Correr of the monastery of San Alvise, was reported to have "paint[ed] herself white and red," while a vaguely identified Suor Stella was denounced because she kept mirrors and other beauty tools in her cell, and showed herself, presumably beautifully made-up, at the window facing the canal.[151] The same passion for cosmetics was attributed to Marietta Dolfin of San Giuseppe di Castello.[152]

In the eighteenth century, when the *bionde* dyed hair was no longer chic, the nuns of the monastery of Santi Rocco e Margherita were severely reprimanded for powdering their long locks and faces and for wearing watches, another of the latest trends.[153] A year later, on September 10, 1715, two nuns from the Santa Marina monastery were similarly accused of "vanity": Elena Fortuna and Lisabetta Antonin were reported to have powdered their hair and used makeup according to the fashion of time, accessorizing their outfits with lace cuffs and high-heeled clogs.[154]

Rather extreme means were sometimes used to punish "immoral" nuns, such as social ostracism, "no nun can talk to her (the guilty nun), or give or receive anything from her with the exception of some by us authorized and under penalty of excommunication," or imprisonment. In the case of imprisonment, Patriarch Lorenzo Priuli recommended that the cell be carefully searched beforehand in order to remove all knives and any other instrument the nun could use to harm herself.[155] The bold obstinacy with which the nuns persevered for centuries in defying the unceasing prohibitions of ecclesiastical authorities reveals the value and importance that these beauty secrets had for the nuns. As for the unsuitable, if not forbidden, clothes they wore, these illicit practices offered to some of the nuns the chance to escape cloistral life, to "smell" the scent of freedom, if only through a bit of makeup and few whiffs of perfume.

Carnival: Masks, Disguises, and Theatrical Costumes for Nuns

Carnival was yet another occasion in which "forbidden" dresses played a symbolic role and became a psychological outlet for the inmates of Venetian convents. In the outside world, Carnival was the time of the year in which rules were set aside and anybody could assume the identity of anybody else: inside the convents this, too, was the time in which some latitude was allowed and it was possible for the nuns to indulge in a number of modest entertainments.

During these weeks, in many monasteries the usually already soft rules on dress became even more lax, and nuns set aside their religious habits and enjoyed themselves with masquerades. Ecclesiastical authorities, acknowledging the need for some kind of diversion, came to a compromise: they tolerated the nuns' behavior while trying at the same time to set strict rules and guidelines. While masks were, *obtorto collo* (unwillingly), allowed inside the monastery, it remained forbidden for the nuns to be seen in them in the parlors, even by their very own parents,[156] and it was especially prohibited "at any time to dress as a Man."[157]

However, apparently cross-dressing was very popular in Venetian convents. The ethical and psychological implications of this behavior were quite clear and did not escape the religious hierarchies, who tried to suppress the scandalous behavior. Numerous archival documents report, in fact, that some of the nuns used to dress up as men, with others enjoying the idea of being courted by or having imaginary relationships with these "gentlemen." They not only dressed up during Carnival, but year-round and on a regular basis. Just to mention an example, Suor Laura Querini, accused of having brought men into the convent of San Zaccaria, affirmed her innocence by stating that "nuns are accustomed to dress up, both as men and women, and to go about the convent at night."[158] Similarly, when accusing Suor Colombina of having slept with Padre Zuane, Suor Clara of San Vito di Burano could not offer a convincing description of the man; she just stated that "it could not have been another nun dressed up (as a man)."[159] Much more clear-cut was the evidence

Giacomo Franco, *Cortigiana Veneta*, from *Habiti delle donne venetiane*, 1628.

against Gasparo Busella, handyman of the convent, caught by the prioress herself while running away from the cell of the same Suor Colombina "wearing a long shirt, such as those worn by women, that reached to the heels, with a pair of red pants in his hands."[160]

The freedom experienced by the nuns in wearing these secular feminine and masculine fashions was potentially devastating for the moral order of their convents. By dressing themselves in forbidden clothes, nuns could imagine escaping their confined existence and expressing their repressed feelings. These clothes could even stir undesirable emotions among the women, attracting them to each other and letting them indulge or even act out reprehensible fantasies. Worse still, the possibility of seeing dressed-up nuns could also draw lusty visitors to the parlors.[161] In the monastery of San Mauro of Burano, Suor Angela and Vittoria Amai and Eccelsa Falier, were, in fact, accused of wearing in the parlor masculine clothes or secular feminine outfits accessorized by elegant hairstyles while entertaining too friendly relationships with local priests.[162] Similarly, on Fat Wednesday, 1660, the abbess of San Giovanni Evangelista of Torcello dressed her favourite and most beautiful nun, Eletta Querini, as a man and introduced her to a Father Domenigo from Naples who came to visit the monastery. He was so charmed that he prolonged his visit for weeks![163]

This reprehensible conduct also had the unpleasant consequence of strengthening in the outside world the already widely held notion that equated Venetian nunneries with public whorehouses. The widespread awareness that nuns dressed themselves in masculine garb placed them on a level with Venetian courtesans and prostitutes used to going about the city either dressed up as men or wearing a pair of pants under their dress.[164]

Cesare Vecellio, *Cortigiana*, from *De gli habiti antichi et moderni di diverse parti del mondo . . .* , 1590.

Augustiniana in Cænobio Venetiarum
S. Catharinæ, Cuculla induta, in Solennitatis.

Vincenzo Maria Coronelli, *Choir Habit of an Augustinian Nun of the Santa Caterina Monastery*, from *Ordinum religiosorum in ecclesia militanti catalogus*, Venice, 1707. Reprinted by permission of Biblioteca del Museo Correr, Venice.

This rather confusing behavior was played upon by the courtesans themselves, who, as Vecellio documented, often "tried to improve their reputation by appearing as honest women," wearing the demure dress of respectable widows, complete with the thick black veil used also by Venetian nuns that covered their heads and most of their bodies. However, as Vecellio notes maliciously, "since they could not remain covered all the time and needed to be seen (by the potential clients) it is impossible to not recognize them."[165]

A similar ambiguity is illustrated by an interesting eighteenth-century painting by Henry Morland that reflects the rather negative view of cloistered Catholic women in contemporary Protestant England. His *Lady in a Masquerade Habit* was first exhibited at the Free Society of Artists in 1769;[166] it was, however, soon rechristened as the *Fair Nun Un-*

Henri R. Morland, *The Fair Nun Unmasked*, 1769. © Leeds Museums and Art Galleries (Temple Newsam House) / Bridgeman Art Library.

masked and reproduced in engravings accompanied by a caption taken from Alexander Pope's *The Rape of the Lock*:

> On her white Breast a sparkling Cross she wore
>
> Which Jews may kiss and Infidels adore

The artist actually meant to portray a Venetian courtesan in a luxurious masquerade costume. But by including the meaningful detail of the black silk veil, he suggested the monastic costume of the local nuns, an allusion reinforced by the use of devotional jewellery enticingly displayed on the generous décolletage of the courtesan/nun to lure potential clients or lovers.

Another serious cause of concern for the patriarchs were the concerts and plays that were performed by the nuns during the weeks of Carnival, but also on such occasions as Clothing or Profession ceremonies. Both the nuns and the boarding girls were involved in these theatrical productions, which were allowed by the religious authorities under specific conditions: "We shall tolerate the plays as long as they are stories from the Holy Scriptures, or from the lives of the Saints; and no nun may presume to wear secular dress, whether male or female, nor it is permissible to wear masks or beards."[167]

What was subject to dispute therefore was both the plots of the plays, which often included rather irreverent topics and references or profane songs, and the costumes worn by the actresses, particularly the masculine outfits used in the plays that were borrowed from the outside world.[168] If the opposition of the Church to cross-dressing can be traced back to Deuteronomy 22:5—"the woman shall not wear that which pertaineth unto man, neither shall a man put on a woman's garment; for all that do so are abomination unto the Lord thy God"[169]—the use of masculine clothing offered the nuns the added benefit of forming interesting, if inappropriate, liaisons with people belonging to the world outside the cloister. In 1596 Patriarch Lorenzo Priuli wrote to the abbess of the monastery of San Sepolcro because he was concerned that "people talk to the nuns until late at night behind locked doors, delivering fabrics and other things for the performance of tragedies and similar shows, with great confusion inside the convent, and great scandal outside."[170] In Giovan Battista Gelli's play *La sporta* it is revealed that the nuns dress up like men for their plays: "I wish you could see them, Alamanno. They dress like men with those tights, short pants and everything; they look like soldiers."[171]

In order to neutralize the destructive consequences of these infractions, patriarchal orders threatened the nuns with severe punishment if these orders were not attended to. On January 15, 1593, Lorenzo Priuli in his "Ordini e avvertimenti" affirmed that although it was not his intention to deprive the nuns of their "honest and virtuous recreations," he was determined to forbid "everything that it is contrary to the regular life of the convent." Having, in fact, been warned that under the pretense of "devout recreations" many reprehensible acts had been committed, he sternly advised the nuns to keep their habits during the performances, warning them that wearing fancy costumes or covering their faces with masks constituted a mortal sin, punishable with being totally barred from the parlors.[172]

These representations and masquerades, however, were simply too important an outlet for the cloistral inmates: ignoring the promulgations of their superiors, they continued as much as they could to stage their shows and use the costumes as a way to escape from their monastic routine, enjoying the sense of ambiguity. At the same time, the audiences that came to see their representations increased steadily, attracted by the allure of these performances that played on the thin boundary between sacred and profane.

The list of violations against monastic rules that occurred during the bustling Carnival season would not be complete without mentioning the costumed parties and balls that took place in the monasteries. The conventual masquerades were a must-see show recommended to foreign visitors.[173] Just to recall a few, there was the memorable *bal masquée* organized in the parlor of Santa Caterina on February 1658 by a number of Venetian nobles, headed by Count Gambara; followed, in 1696, by another revelry of a group of noblemen accompanied by their lady friends, all masqueraded as Moors, who danced the night away in the parlor of the convent of San Zaccaria in the company of the nuns.[174] Violations involving visits by masqueraded friends of the nuns are also reported numerous times in the documents of the Provveditori sopra Monasteri. Ladies and noblemen visited the parlors protected by their masks, exchanged pleasantries and enjoyed meals with the nuns, and often embarked on dangerous liaisons.[175] Although precise statistical data are not available, it is well known that the most audacious among the nuns often dared to

Inscription on the wall of the former convent of Sant'Andrea, Venice, 1640.

leave the cloister at nighttime in their lovers' gondolas and then "they walked around the city going to parties, coming back only when they felt like it."[176]

Converse, Donne delle Monache, and Foreign Nuns

Converse, or servant nuns, belonged to a different social class than choir nuns. These women, who were from the middle and lower classes, were admitted into the convents with much lower dowries,[177] and did not have the possibility of rising within the internal social hierarchy of the monastery, their job being to "help with all those things that nuns could not do because of their choir duties."[178] Inside the convents the *converse* were visually distinguishable from choir nuns because of their habit, which was not as regulated as that of choir nuns, and needed to be as unassuming and humble as possible and made of the simplest wool *rascia* or *bottana*, instead of the more valuable *scotto*. It was to be worn "with modesty, not with lasciviousness,"[179] without any sort of corset underneath. It was recommended that their hair be cut short and kept hidden by veils, especially at the temples.[180]

Because *converse* did not pronounce solemn vows, they could be sent into the world to run errands for the nuns anytime it was deemed necessary. Asked if she knew anything about music being played in the parlor, a Suor Concordia answered: "I do not know anything about it, I never go into the parlors, I do my errands in the city as needed, and when I get back, I go to my cell."[181] Even while outside, they were expected to wear a modest habit and behave properly. Sanudo highlights the intrinsic danger of letting the *converse* out, expressing his concerns regarding their whereabouts in a world that he considered very treacherous because, often, they were sent by the nuns to buy forbidden items, such as laces or luxury fabrics, or to gather information about the new dress styles or the latest gossip. They could even act as messengers, carrying clandestine notes to the nuns' lay lovers. The remedy suggested by Sanudo was to allow the nuns to keep servants in the monastery, but to impose on them a monastic uniform that had to be worn at all times, making them more recognizable when outside.[182]

Definitely more free to move around were the so-called *donne delle monache*. Often confused with the *converse*, with whom they shared the mission to help the nuns with their necessities, these women lived outside the convents and performed all sort of errands for the "prisoners" inside the cloisters. Their dress was not regulated by any specific directives, and, since they belonged to the lower social classes of the city, they clearly did not have the means to follow the fashions: they usually wore a simple dark dress, covering their heads with the white *fazzuolo*. The nuns employing their services could sometimes be rather demanding or even unreasonable:

> There are about forty Female Monasteries in Venice. . . . As they are served by the converse inside the monastery, so it is necessary for them to employ some Women outside for errands and for their correspondence. Even if these tasks can be rather heavy, there are always women available for them, since it is very profitable work. For just one egg they are sent to the Pasina, and, at the same time, they need to bring another one to San Giobbe; and the work is far from over, because, back to the parlor, they find that they need to visit some of the nun's sick relatives in S. Giacomo dall'Orio, and then at Castello. Other nuns make their woman go as far as the Tolentini, and then they send her with a basket to S.S. Apostoli to the Confessor's, Doctor's or Chaplain's home. And having toured the entire city (which the nuns think is as big as their convent's cloister), being late to bring replies, they are reproached.[183]

The bubbling melting pot of the population who lived within the borders of the Serenissima was further enriched by the presence of several thriving foreign and ethnic or religious groups. The policy of openness practiced by the local government allowed, over the centuries, the creation of specific "pockets" of communities. In the Rialto area was the imposing building of the Fondaco dei Tedeschi, the warehouse and living quarters of the German merchants operating in the city, while further along the Grand Canal was the *fondaco* of the Turks.

Giovanni Grevembroch, *Donna
delle monache*, from *Gli abiti de'
Veneziani di quasi ogni età . . .* ,
vol. III, 1754.

Different religions were also tolerated, although their spaces in the
city were strictly regulated. The Jews had to live in the ghetto, while, later
on, the Armenian community settled on an island in the lagoon near
the Lido. There was also a prosperous Greek community with its own
female monastery, San Giorgio dei Greci. Although it was very close to
both San Zaccaria and San Lorenzo, it did not entertain any kind of relationship with the neighboring monasteries. According to Grevembroch,
there, guided by a wise abbess, lived only thirteen nuns (a ridiculous figure compared to the hundreds that crowded the Catholic monasteries)
following the rule of San Basilio. Grevembroch also tells us that the insti-

Giovanni Grevembroch, *Monaca greca*, from *Gli abiti de' Veneziani di quasi ogni età* . . . , vol. II, 1754.

tution, founded in 1609 with the blessing of the government, requested very reasonable dowries, only five hundred ducats. The outfits of these nuns appear from his watercolors to be far more modest than those of their Venetian counterparts, and no specific habit-related infractions were reported, but that may be due to the fact that the patriarch of Venice did not have the authority to visit or to impose his rulings on them since they obeyed the patriarch of Constantinople.

According to Grevembroch, their habit was composed of a very humble black wool cloth tunic, covered by a black cape and long black veil that reached almost to the ground; a severe wimple completely covered the neck.[184] Slightly more elaborate was the habit and veil of the abbess, which was trimmed with a stripe of *pavonazzo* fabric.[185]

Benedetto Caliari, "Istituzione del Soccorso" from the church of the Soccorso, before 1597, Venice. Courtesy of Ministero per i Beni e le Attività Culturali.

Almost Nuns: *Soccorse,* Widows, *Pizzocchere,* and Orphans

The Casa del Soccorso was just one of the numerous charitable institutions created in Venice since the beginning of the sixteenth century and was dedicated to the aid and relief of the socially forgotten.[186] Each *hospitale* targeted a specific group of the needy: the Incurabili, founded in 1521, was dedicated to medical care of the terminally ill, followed in 1528 by the Derelitti, a refuge for the destitute and hospital for the sick, while the Pia Casa delle Cittelle (also known as Zitelle) was founded in 1559 to house beautiful and poor young girls and women not safeguarded by their families. Although some institutions, such as the Incurabili and the Catecumeni, accepted boys and men too, the vast majority of the "guests" of the hospitals, considering the specific mission of some of the institutions, were female, from very young girls to more mature women. Their lives were equally and strictly organized between prayers, meals, work, and sleep, with few moments of recreation.

The main purpose of these charitable enterprises was to transform endangered girls or helpless children into women of worth that could legitimately aspire to a decent marriage or to enter a convent. The *hospitali* relied on needlework to teach to the *figlie* or *putte* (daughters) a "morally proper" craft, the profits of which were used to support the missions of the hospitals themselves, earn enough money for a dowry to allow the girl to enter a convent or, should they get married, to be able to supplement the family income.[187]

According to popular belief, the founder of the Soccorso was, in 1577, Veronica Franco, a rich and famous courtesan.[188] The purpose of the institution was to offer temporary refuge for prostitutes or, as they said, unmarried women who were living "sinfully," and for adulteresses who already lived separated from their spouses. They were accepted only if they demonstrated that they were repentant, and they could not be sick, pregnant, old, or ugly. They had to swear not to leave the house until either they were reconciled with the husband, decided to get married, or chose to enter the Convertite.[189]

The Convertite was founded in 1530 to provide cloistral asylum for repenting prostitutes and basic medical care for women affected by venereal disease. In the words of Sansovino, "the Convertite monastery was built because, as the Virgins consecrated to God have their own places, so should the repenting sinners, so that they can save themselves from their sins. Here a great number of women, all of them beautiful (because only the beautiful ones are accepted, in order not to let them fall into their sins again since their beauty is so attractive), admiringly apply themselves to create different kinds of needlework."[190]

The women of the Soccorse and the Convertite, although clearly encloistered, were not, however, considered real nuns because they did not pronounce solemn vows: they simply retired within their institution and dedicated themselves to redeeming their past sins through prayers and the constant practice of needlework.

An interesting painting by Benedetto Caliari that was once on the altar of the church of the institution, titled *The Foundation of the Soccorso* and dated circa 1570, summarizes the redemptive process of these women through the language of dress.[191] The key to redeeming their past lay in relinquishing all the worldly frills, dresses, and jewellery that were considered among the main causes that had led these women to their sins. In the painting, in fact, a group of elegantly dressed women are disrobing from their precious clothes and jewels, following the example of their leader, thought in the past to be Veronica Franco herself, but probably Laura Caravella, one of the spiritual leaders of the Casa at the time.[192] Laura appears modestly dressed in a simple black habit accessorized by a large white shawl to cover her shoulder and décolletage, a white apron, and with her hair gathered in a demure white bonnet. From the sky, a benevolent Mary Magdalene, intercessor and model of the redeemed prostitute,[193] presents the penitents to the Virgin Mary; in the lower right side of the painting some already redeemed women are busily practicing some type of needlework.

The modest outfit of Laura clearly indicated the way to be free from the temptations of the world: the luxurious gowns and jewellery the sinners used to wear could not but lead to lust and perdition, as indicated by the too generous décolletages and soft and seductive fabrics used that contrasted with the modesty and simplicity of the Soccorso "uniform." A similarly demure attire was later adopted by Elisabetta Rossi, founder of the Pio Loco delle Penitenti,[194] another important Venetian charitable institution dedicated to helping older prostitutes. The portrait of Elisabetta shows her modest black dress completed by the white *fichu* and apron; the only difference is in the color of the bonnet, no longer white, but black.[195]

A long black dress and long black veil: this was the standard outfit of Venetian widows, who, after the death of their husbands, lived a very retired life, in many ways similar to that of the cloistered nuns.[196] Vecellio

VEDOVE.

Cesare Vecellio, *Vedove*, from
*De gli habiti antichi et moderni
di diverse parti del mondo . . .* ,
1590.

writes that, in his time, widows "embrace the death of all vanities and ornaments. Because apart from dressing in black they cover their hair, firmly enclose their bosom with a heavy veil, gather their mantle up to their
forehead, and walk in the streets, with head inclined." He also highlighted
the symbolic use of dress; it was, in fact, through the use of specific and
well-known dress codes that women expressed their future intentions,
because "when they want to stay a widow, they wear a train and never
dress in colors; . . . when they want to remarry they are permitted to wear
some ornament, though not a conspicuous one, and reveal a little more
hair, which serves to signal their wishes to others."[197]

PIZZOCCHERE.

T 3

Cesare Vecellio, *Pizzochere*,
from *De gli habiti antichi et
moderni di diverse parti del
mondo . . .* , 1590.

Being dressed in black, however, did not mean that they were giving
up luxury completely; their clothes were often made with precious velvets
or other silk fabrics that were also used by most noblewomen, not neces-
sarily widows themselves.[198] Others instead retired within a convent for
the rest of their lives and abandoned worldly fashions. In the necrology
of the Corpus Domini convent is mentioned a Sister Franceschina da
Noale who "entered the convent seven days after it was enclosed, as a
widowed lady forty-nine years old. During her marriage she lived in the
world in a holy fashion and always wore a hair [therefore coarse] shirt
under her velvet. When she was left a widow she dressed humbly in a
coarse cloth."[199]

Among the figures who characterized everyday life in the Venetian *campi* and *calli* and who, in different ways, were somehow assimilated into the conventual world, were the *pizzocchere*:

> There is in Venice and elsewhere a certain type of woman, and for the most part widows, who, having retired from the world, either out of devotion, or of necessity, live in some specific places, and live off of alms and of some other honest activity, following the leadership of the heads of those orders whose habit they wear. Since they do not live in a convent, they cannot be called nuns, but *pizzocchere*, and there are as many types of them as there are orders of Mendicants, the colors of whose habits they follow. They remain chaste and unmarried, obey the rules so they can serve God, visiting the sick and preparing and accompanying the deceased at the funerals and doing other charitable things.[200]

The comprehensive definition of Grevembroch well illustrates the condition of this specific segment of the Venetian female population. These women, actually tertiary nuns who did not profess holy vows[201] and were not subject to the enclosure rule or to the close regulation of ecclesiastical authorities, after the death of their husbands or because of a precarious economic condition, abandoned secular clothes and vanities and dedicated themselves to charity work and penance; since most of them lived confined in small cells, they were also called *recluse* or *romite*.[202]

The habits they wore, made with the humblest fabric available, followed the specifications of the religious orders they chose to be affiliated with, and were blessed by a priest during a special ceremony. Although the modesty and shapelessness of their tunic was easily comparable to the unchanging garments worn by the poorest social classes, their pious life guaranteed the *pizzocchere* some social standing and made them recognizable figures. In the *Processione in Piazza San Marco*,[203] painted by Gentile Bellini in 1496, where are represented all the members of the government and the city's main public characters, appear also some easily identifiable and modestly dressed *pizzocchere*, clearly visible in the background. Identified by their dark, unfashionable dresses that vividly contrast with the one worn by the stylish lady passing nearby, and by their *ninzioleto* or *fazzuolo*,[204] the ample white cloth, occasionally trimmed by tiny muslin ruches, that was typically used to cover the head and shoulders by Venetian lower-classes women. Although the golden age of this accessory was the eighteenth century, the *fazzuolo* was already in use by the late fifteenth century, worn, for instance, by the *pizzocchera* engraved by Cesare Vecellio.[205]

However, it is in the amazing paintings by Jacopo Palma il Giovane in the Oratorio dei Crociferi that this modest accessory appears as a prominent and identifying feature of the figures in the canvas.[206] The cycle, specifically created for the purpose of highlighting the fusion between civil and religious ideologies, illustrates how the life of the doge was strictly interconnected with the lives of the benefactors of the hospice, and of its guests. The old *pizzocchere* housed in the pious institution are accurately represented by the modesty of their rather formless clothes made with a fabric of an anonymous dark colour, maybe *beretin*.[207] A touch of light is provided by the white folds of the *fazzuolo* that covers their heads and frames the wrinkled faces that are so meticulously and individually delineated.[208]

Also easily recognizable were the orphans that lived in charitable institutions. Despite having been abandoned by their families of origin, they were, Vecellio affirms, so well taken care of that they were envied by those who still lived in their parents' house,[209] thanks to an education that prepared them for a socially productive life, either in a marriage or inside a convent, because of the lace-making, weaving, or sewing skills that were taught to them.[210] All the Venetian orphanages adopted a similarly shaped uniform, with different colors identifying the respective institutions: white was, for instance, used by the Hospitale di San Giovanni e Paolo, blue for the Incurabili, red for the Pietà, black for the Mendicanti.[211] They wore an apron on the occasions when they left their "homes" and a white veil over their heads. In case of rain, a straw or black felt hat was worn on top of the veil. However, even orphans could be fashionable.

ORFANELLE.

T 4

Cesare Vecellio, *Orfanelle
degli Spedali di Venetia*,
from *De gli habiti antichi et
moderni di diverse parti del
mondo . . .* , 1590.

An interesting detail of the fresco that decorates the Sala della Musica
inside the Ospedaletto dei Derelitti represents two famous singers, *figlie
da coro*, who were educated in this charitable institution. Even behind
the thick gilt grilles that hide them from view, it is possible to make out
powdered hair and a generous neckline enriched by a beaded necklace.

Although it is entirely possible that this is just an imaginative detail, it
is not difficult to imagine that at least for the most popular singers, it was
somehow possible to keep pace with secular fashions and dress up a little.

Encloistered women usually took up some kind of work in order to
feel meaningfully engaged and useful. Most often the work of choice was
textile-related, being either lacework, embroidery, weaving, basic sewing,

or even doing laundry. They worked to gather money for the institutions they were living in, but also to earn enough so they could afford some precious little luxuries or even to lure prospective lovers to the parlor windows.

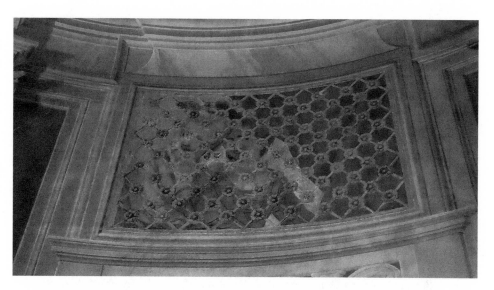

Jacopo Guarana, Agostino Mengozzi Colonna, detail with the *figlie del coro* of the fresco in the Sala della Musica, Ospedaletto dei Derelitti, Venice, 1776. Courtesy of IRE, Istituzioni di Ricovero e di Educazione Venezia, Venice.

Four

Textiles, Embroideries, and Laces
in the Convent

$\mathcal{H}$ow were the days organized inside the cloister? Monastic rules stressed the need for a routine based on regular prayer and meditation cycles, interrupted only by simple meals to be taken in the convent refectory and by work in the communal workroom because every nun needed to "escape idleness as the most dangerous thing."[1]

Nuns were asked to concentrate exclusively on their spiritual life, but, to make the forced enclosure bearable, most of them took up some type of work to while away the hours. Venetian monasteries were celebrated for their "nuns' virtues in art, music, and in the making of magnificent needle works."[2] Girolamo Priuli admiringly describes some "beautiful, noble and virtuous" nuns, so skilled that not even the most talented painter "could be compared to them."[3] It was a rather innocent, time-consuming, and quite proper activity, commonly practiced also in aristocratic households, and potentially useful within conventual economy.

Venetian patriarchs in their pastoral visits, while praising the usefulness of these activities, recommended that a communal workshop be created in every monastery, a place "where all the Nuns came to work according to the rules."[4] In fact, "It is a great disorder, and many evil thoughts are born from the fact that nuns do not work together in the workshop. We therefore order that all the nuns work in the communal workshop, and never in their own cells. . . . The Abbess has to organize turns between the nuns to have some of them reading some spiritual book during the hours of work. . . . The works executed in the workshop need to be approved by the Mother Superior, and only commissions coming from honest people of good name and reputation are to be accepted." The profits from the work of the nuns had to be managed by the abbess, while an older nun was to be put in charge of receiving the commissions at the wheel and distributing the work among the nuns.[5]

The patriarch's concerns were amply justified: the extraordinary needle skills of the nuns were often employed in frivolous works or to make presents used by the nuns to lure visitors to the parlors. Needlework presents were part of the nuns' strategy to maintain a strong connection with and to play a role within the city's social fabric: by offering extravagant handmade presents they felt appreciated and in control of their lives. It was an empowering act, a way to preserve their identities, in disregard of the basic principle of conventual life, self-humiliation. Because of this, conventual authorities tried to regulate needleworking activities, and other work practices, which, however, could not be completely stopped because of their considerable financial benefit in a competitive market.

Today, conventual-made textiles, lace, and embroideries can help us focus on the high value and consideration placed by contemporaries on these objects. For historians they represent a priceless tool in the investigation of the social and economic relationships between the convents and other similarly cloistered institutions and the people living in the outside world.

Lacework in Venice: A Brief Outline

While embroidery and sewing had never been, in Venetian society, activities reserved only to female workers,[6] laces on the contrary, have always been created exclusively by feminine hands. Lace was a matriarchal art that has for centuries tied together the fate of thousands of women belonging to the most different social classes and conditions.

According to a romantic legend, the first lace was created by a talented young Venetian woman who, to prolong the life of a magnificent sea-weed she received as a love token from her fiancée, applied herself to find a way to translate the intricate designs of the seaweed using only needle and thread.[7] Legends aside, lace, and specifically needle lace, appeared in Venice as early as the fifteenth century,[8] as a sophisticated evolution of the *reticello*[9] embroideries worked at the time by the vast majority of the women of the city. In the luxurious halls of the palaces, in middle-class homes, in convents and charitable institutions, women of different ages spent every bit of "free" time practicing all sorts of "feminine works" in order to avoid "dangerous" moments of idleness. According to contemporary philosophers and religious thinkers, in fact, these empty moments were those in which the "weak" feminine mind was more vulnerable and could indulge in morally reprehensible thoughts. To keep women constantly busy in some kind of activity was therefore deemed essential in protecting them from sin. Furthermore, aristocratic ladies needed a pastime to help them creatively spend their days, something that could not be possibly confused with actual "work," since any kind of useful manual labor was deemed absolutely dishonorable for a noblewoman.[10] The characteristic repetitiveness and relative uselessness of the needlework that filled their long hours meant that the lace was not tainted by the appearance of or social stigma of actual labor.[11]

During the sixteenth century the equivalency of feminine works and virtuous practices became rather ubiquitous in moral treatises and in common thinking. In 1547, Venetian writer Ludovico Dolce recommended careful supervision of the activities and games of young girls, suggesting that they be allowed to play with miniaturized household tools "so they will learn with delight the name and function of each."[12] Especially essential for their education was to learn to sew, because "knowing how to sew for a women is equivalent to knowing how to write for men."[13] Dolce's opinion was, years later, corroborated by Agostino Valier, who in his *Istruzione del modo di vivere delle donne maritate* (Venice, 1560) strongly recommends domestic works as the "honest" behavior for married women.[14]

Time-consuming lace making was not only socially acceptable; it was also propagandized as an ennobling occupation. This belief was clearly stated in the titles and dedications of the numerous pattern books published in Venice since the early sixteenth century.[15] Words such as "honesty," "virtue," and "nobility" regularly appear in connection with the practice of needlecraft. The captions in these books also highlight the fact that in the execution of needlework there was the possibility of expressing the "feminine talent . . . to create with the needle what was with other means expressed by Poets or Painter,"[16] thus transforming lacework into a much-needed creative outlet for upper-class ladies. In fact, Venetian dames, forbidden to pursue a more formal education, resorted to engaging in "suitable" artistic activities, such as music, painting, dancing, and singing. The curriculum was always filled out with a large number of "feminine works," ranging from spinning to weaving, from sewing to embroidering, and, of course, lace making.

How did women learn these feminine arts? Lower-class children were taught basic sewing skills by their female relatives, and orphans learned needlecrafts in the charitable institutions that housed them. While aristocratic girls became familiar with the needle during their school years, which, for most of them, took place in convents. For instance, Elena, the daughter of humanist Pietro Bembo, was placed in the monastery of San Zaccaria in 1542 to learn Greek, Latin, and embroidery.[17]

Invisible Seamstresses

Needlework was strongly encouraged by conventual authorities, but the attitude toward any sort of work inside the convent, whether was it baking, doing laundry, spinning, or weaving, related to how it benefited the common good of the monastery, not to the personal profit it generated.[18]

Almost all monasteries, in fact, needed the money they made from the sale of the laces and other needlework. Even in the rich and highly aristocratic convent of San Zaccaria, according to Filippo Pizzichi, chronicler of the visit of Cosimo III de' Medici, most of the nuns were busy making laces for "a French nobleman."[19] For less wealthy monasteries the profits deriving from the lacework business were essential for the survival of the convent. Many of them also augmented their incomes with some kind of approved work. For instance, the abbess of San Mauro of Burano stated in 1654 "that if I were not helped by some generous persons, and if we did not keep boarders in our convent, we certainly could not survive, and we . . . also contribute some money through our work, which keeps us awake day and night in addition to our daily services."[20]

In the monastery of Sant'Anna the lace-making business seemed to have had a rather well organized structure. Heading the business was Suor Arcangela Tarabotti, who, thanks to her remarkable network of important and wealthy acquaintances, was able to acquire important commissions of needle laces.

From her *Letters*, published in Venice in 1650,[21] it is possible to learn the names of some of her patrons and to read descriptions of the laces that the nuns were making for them. Arcangela corresponded with Isabetta Piccolomini Scarpi, reassuring her about her commission of a "*punt'in aria* needle lace" that is driving her "crazy,"[22] while in another letter she informed the Marquise Renata di Cleramonte that there would be some delay in the completion of the lace she ordered because "the nuns that committed themselves to the work are either sick or have left the monastery."[23] She replied to Madame de Anò, wife of the French ambassador, that the lace she had ordered would cost "no less than sixty ducats per *braccio*," assuring her that she would supervise the diligent execution of the lace and its timely delivery.[24]

Monasteries also relied on other textile-related activities, definitely less ennobling and prestigious, to satisfy their need for cash, such as spinning, weaving,[25] and doing laundry.[26]

In the documents of the Arte della Seta (Silk Corporation) are mentioned over nine hundred *incannaresse*, or weft-makers (reelers), all women, and among them are mentioned several nuns. Certainly more nuns than this were actually involved in the process, since in a declaration by some silk weavers to the Venetian Senate in 1529 it emerges that the preparation of the wefts was a common activity practiced in "local monasteries,"[27] even in the most important ones, such as Santa Maria Maggiore, San Zaccaria, San Servolo, and Corpus Domini. In the seventeenth century several prioresses mention the role played by the nuns in the silk industry, with the exception of the nuns of San'Iseppo, located in the Castello area, who being too busy "in other activities"[28] were not actively involved in the silk industry; anyhow, as they said, "every time we want to work some silk, we have as much as we can make."[29] Even the most aristocratic canonesses of Le Vergini appear to have been involved in the weaving industry. According to the account book of Marino Contarini, the owner of the Ca' d'Oro palace, they specialized in the manufacture of gold cloth, which was considered a "noble" occupation. The book details the expenses for the marriage of his daughters, Maria and Samaritana, between 1426 and 1430, and in the description of their trousseaux is included a long list of precious items such as handkerchiefs, purses, and lengths of gold cloth coming from the convents of San Salvatore and Le Vergini.[30] A far simpler type of convent-made fabric was the so-called *tela muneghina*, nun's cloth, a rather coarse linen or hemp fabric suitable for simple house linens.

However, there were not many nuns who wished to work just for the common good of the convent. In fact, deprived of most personal property and forced to live on only a modest allowance, even those nuns born to some of the richest families of Venice tried to bring in some extra income through their industriousness. The money they earned was partly used to provide for their necessities, but it also allowed them a few precious little luxuries, such as strengthening the ties with their families through extravagantly expensive gifts to relatives and friends.

However, the common practice of offering costly presents was obviously and in many ways damaging for the convents and harshly opposed by the prioresses. Suor Cipriana Morosini, for instance, prioress of the convent of Sant' Iseppo, in 1571 complained to the Provveditori sopra Monasteri that one of her nuns, Suor Deodata,[31] who worked "miraculously with pearls and jewels,"[32] instead of using her precious hands to help the convent's economy, was accustomed to lavishing precious gifts on a number of friars from the Augustinian convents of Sant' Antonio and San Salvador. The prioress appears to have been very disappointed by the fact that this nun's talent, which could really benefit the convent, was used instead to make elegant surplices—"more than twenty"—and other magnificent items for the friars. She declares: "I have seen her sewing handkerchiefs for them, as well as shirts, collars, hats stupendously embroidered. . . . She has been (here) for thirteen years, and she has never worked for the monastery, and everything she earned she spent it on what I already told you."[33] Despite Suor Deodata's defense that she sewed only few simple surplices for the friars, receiving from the friars themselves the materials she needed and just a small compensation for her work, the other nuns also accused her of routinely doing work for people outside the convent: doing laundry for the friars and sending Angelo Bressan, the convent handyman, around the city to gather the materials she needed. "She sent me to buy two or three . . . of silk, and also some gold thread from a woman called la Castellana . . . and she gave me as much money as was needed to buy things."[34]

However, once again, both the prioresses and the patriarchs found themselves unable to do much more than express disappointment with this situation. During one of his patriarchal visits to the monastery of San Daniele, Patriarch Zane remarked that, all too often, the nuns' private time in the cells was not devoted to prayer, but to laboriously sewing and embroidering clothing or handkerchiefs, making laces and even doing laundry for personal gain.[35]

The abandon with which Suor Deodata, and many other nuns, regularly donated luxurious objects was without a doubt highly therapeutic for their self-esteem. They must have greatly enjoyed the empowering sensation to be able to donate precious things to visitors and friends, and Suor Deodata especially used her skills to achieve "self-expression and individuality through gift-giving; . . . making presents for the friars and for Prete Mathio gave her life a purpose."[36]

Cloistered, but Secular, Seamstresses

The imperative of keeping women purposefully occupied in order to avoid any possible "trouble" was also a necessity for the administrators of those numerous charitable institutions that played such an essential social role in the life of the city. Women's *hospitali* were charitable refuges created in Venice at the end of the fifteenth century as safe havens where abandoned girls, young women without family protection, or other categories of destitute females were housed to safeguard them from any sort of physical or moral danger. The women housed in these institutions were the secular counterparts of the nuns, sharing a similarly secluded life, until they were either respectably married or took formal cloistral vows.

Life inside these institutions was rigidly organized by prayers, meals, work, and sleep, with very little time left for recreation and socializing. As Benedetto Palmio, founder of the Casa delle Cittelle, clearly states in the rules of the Casa, "the continuous and diligent practice of obedience and needleworks at which they attend in order to provide for themselves, makes them women of worth, and banishes from this House idleness, source of every evil."[37] The *hospitali* relied on the teaching of needlecrafts to give their *figlie*, or daughters, a "morally proper" skill. A small part of the profit deriving from the sale of laces was set aside for the dowry of the women, thus ensuring a marriage, either secular or divine, and a socially secure future, while the rest was used to support the hospitals themselves.[38]

The preservation of the *Registri Capitolari dell'Ospedaletto dei Derelitti* has given us the opportunity to understand how the work inside this Venetian hospital, and in all probability in the others, was organized. The pay system revolved around the so-called *tascha*, a term that originally indicated a slit in the dress worn by the girls and women of the hospital, inside which was kept a small fabric pouch, the *tascha*, where the tools and thread necessary for the daily work was kept.[39] The overseers assigned the work to each of the women on a daily basis, and should the task not be completed a fine or penalty was imposed.

In contrast to what happened with the laces made in the convents, which were often either donated or sold directly by the nuns, the "guests" of the hospitali were not allowed to sell, much less to donate, their laces. All the laces made by them were given to the overseers, who consigned them to trusted merchants and shopkeepers who supported the mission of the hospitals. Only the governors of the hospitals could negotiate the prices with the merchants.[40] Likewise, the "repenting sinners" of the monastery of Santa Maria Maddalena delle Convertite, on the island of Giudecca, could not negotiate the prices for the silk they spun; this was the duty of a few esteemed silk weavers.[41]

Generosity, self-affirmation, economic need: different necessities brought the women living inside the numerous Venetian cloisters to be actively involved in the making of "feminine works." The works made by the women housed in the *hospitali* had essentially a very practical purpose. Created thanks to a simple, but efficient, system that involved every "guest" of the *hospitali*, these goods were sold to contribute to the maintenance of the institution in which the women lived and through which they tried to achieve some sort of social goal (marriage or consecration) and, consequently, the hope for a relatively safe future.

Conversely, for the nuns in the convents there was no hope of self-sufficiency or agency in any form since they could not change their social status through their industriousness. As a consequence, all the lace making, sewing, washing, and spinning had for them a completely different value and meaning. Through their work they made objects, such as laces, that could be sold for a significant amount of money, liberally donated, or, not at all rare, could be scandalously worn by the same nuns who made them. The nuns felt "free" to earn money, to buy or make costly presents to be bartered for attention from people belonging to the outside world. They could use their time to make laces and other forbidden adornments that defied the rules of the convent.

The extremely varied roles of the works made in cloistered Venetian institutions makes it very difficult to simply categorize them as "feminine works." Correctly contextualized, they are actually psychological, social, and economic keys to penetrate the hidden world of these institutions, and to reveal the attempts by the nuns to achieve self-affirmation through their industriousness.

Five
Conclusions

> "This box contains two portraits of me, which are to be seen in two different ways: if you take off the bottom part of the case in its length, you will see me as a nun; and if you press on the corner, the top will open and expose me to your sight in a state of nature." . . . I followed the instructions given in the letter, and I first saw my mistress in the costume of a nun, standing and in half profile. The second secret spring brought her before my eyes, entirely naked, lying on a mattress of black satin, in the position of the Madeleine of Coreggio. She was looking at Love, who had the quiver at his feet, and was gracefully sitting on the nun's robes.
>
> Giacomo Casanova, *Memoires*, chap. 19

One person, two very different images. The hidden and audacious portraits found by Giacomo Casanova in a concealed compartment of the tobacco box given to him by his lover M. M., a nun of the convent of Santa Maria degli Angeli in Murano, well summarize the ambivalence of the dresses worn by Venetian nuns and the symbolic meaning of these clothes so deeply entwined with their lives.

While many of the nuns did follow the rules and wore the prescribed habits, an at least equal, and much more noteworthy, number of them did sport more fashionable styles. The carefree disregard for the approved habits can be explained by the fact that Venetian convents were not, for the most part, religious establishments: "It makes no sense to continue with the pretence that these institutions were composed of 'religious'

View of the church of the monastery of Santa Maria degli Angeli, Murano.

women; nuns during these years were very often secular women forced to live in an externally imposed religious context . . . many Venetian patrician nuns in this period retained highly secular interests and *mores* . . . and this secular pattern of thought and behaviors permeated the ways in which they thought about themselves and their convents."[1]

Forced therefore by economic circumstances to abandon their families, homes, and social status in order to transform themselves into poor and devoted brides of Christ, many of these "involuntary" patrician nuns felt conflicting emotions, often considerably unsuitable for consecrated women. They usually did not have the strength to oppose their families and to refuse to take the vows, apparently accepting the imposition and burying themselves in the convent enclosure. However, pride, frustration, revenge, desire of self-affirmation, and vanity simmered threateningly within their souls.

In light of these considerations, the attitude of many local nuns toward their sacred habits becomes much more understandable. The demure outfits imposed on them represented an additional prison, but one from which they could, within certain limits, run free. Although they could not physically leave the convent, they could nevertheless set aside the habit and adopt the quasi-secular lifestyles they considered rightfully their own, using their individually tailored clothes as a means of social promotion, to strengthen their self-identity and personal image.

The fashionable façades of the luxurious outfits of these Venetian nuns, then, far from denying their family origins and wealth, were used to highlight their social standing among their sisters in religion and, in their relationships with the outside world, allowed them to demand recognition of their own patrician status. Furthermore, the erotic potential of dress was of critical importance for the nuns, since seductives clothes and tantalizingly transparent veils were instrumental in seducing the numerous male visitors that flocked to the conventual parlors, satisfying the nuns' frustrated femininity.

The religious hierarchies and the government of the Serenissima were of course highly unsympathetic toward these unbecoming behaviors, leading to a *querelle* between the "involuntary" nuns determined to keep wearing and treasuring their elegant dresses and the authorities similarly determined to restrain their intemperance, which lasted for centuries.

The covered heads, cut hair, and modest habits symbolized the nuns' ritual sacrifice to God for the good of the community; therefore their curly blond hair, lacy veils, and audacious dresses constituted not only an obvious betrayal of their office, but also a treason against Venice herself, since the nuns' sins jeopardized the privileged relationship between Venice and God.

Despite the fact that nothing remains of the actual clothing of Venetian nuns, a mosaic of sources, from archival documents to engravings, from contemporary literature to paintings, supports our re-creation of them. The fading ink of the archival documents brings back to life the seductive rustling of the silks, the alluring transparency of the veils, and the rich twinkling of the jewels worn by many of the nuns, offering us an indiscreet glimpse inside the not so impenetrable, but definitely fashionable, cloistral enclosure and allowing us to understand the psychological and social meanings of the use of forbidden or even scandalous clothing inside these peculiar communities.

Appendix

*T*his appendix contains a selection of transcribed documents particularly relevant to many of the topics discussed in the book; it is in fact, especially interesting to analyze the items included in the simple baggage that accompanied Marsilia Acerbi to the convent of Ss. Rocco and Margherita as boarding girl: many of the objects are new, but many more are described as used, because, since a boarding girl was not yet charged with the social role to prove the family wealth, her wardrobe was eminently practical.

Very different was instead the role played by the trousseaux of brides Paulina Provisina Vignon and Lucietta Pasini Moretti: their families' wealth was lavishly exhibited through the gilded furniture and prestigious paintings, musical instruments, dozens of expensive lace-trimmed linens, and silver and gold brocaded dresses given to them when they entered marital life.

On the contrary, the modest provisions given to Laura Acerbi, Anna Toniuti, and Angela Minio, when they entered religious life, from one point of view respected the rules of the religious authorities, from the other prove the sour comments made on this topic by Arcangela Tarabotti. Interestingly, although the presence of lavish clothing and furnishings in the cells has been conclusively proved, they do not appear listed in the many conventual trousseau studied, with the tolerated exception of silver candlesticks and cutlery.

With the exception of document n. 2, which has been partially published, the documents contained in this appendix are unpublished.

The original Venetian has been translated into English by the author.

Documents transcribed

1. IRE, DER E 3.	Trousseau, Marsilia Acerbi, boarding girl, Ss. Rocco e Margherita, 1726
2. IRE, DER E 182, b. 9.	Dowry inventory, Paulina Provisina Vignon, 1666
3. IRE, DER E 178, b. 2.	Dowry inventory, Lucietta Pasini Moretti, 1670
4. IRE, DER E 2, b. 3.	Conventual trousseau, Laura Acerbi, Ss. Rocco e Margherita, 1715
5. IRE, DER G 1, n. 83.	Conventual trousseau, Anna Toniuti, S. Andrea di Murano, 1726
6. IRE, DER G 2, n. 83.	Conventual trousseau, Angela Minio, Convertite , 1758

Abbreviations used in the transcriptions

. . .	stands for missing or unreadable lines
n.	stands for "numero" or "number" of the items listed
p. and p.a.	stand for "para" or "pairs"
d.	stands for *ducati*

IRE, DER E 3

[On the cover of the file:]

Inventory of linens, clothes, gold and silver objects belonging to
Marsilia Acerbi, boarding girl in
the convent of S. Rocco e S.ta Margherita.

[Inside the cover:]

1726: December 22nd, in Venice
Inventory of linens, clothes, gold and silver objects belonging to
Marsilia Acerbi, currently . . . boarding girl in . . . D.a M.a. Mar-
silia . . .

the convent of S. Rocco e S.ta Margherita.

A walnut wood wardrobe with three drawers	n.° 1
New linen shirts	n.° 8
Same, shirts, used	n.° 4
Same shirts, used, made with Dutch, finer linen	n.° 2
New linen handker-chiefs	n.° 4

Used linen bed sheets	n.° 6
Same, smaller used bed sheets, made with a different cloth	n.° 4
Same, used larger embroidered bed sheets	n.° 2
New white linen handkerchiefs	n.° 4
Same, used	n.° 12
New linen napkins, without decorations	n.° 6
Same, used	n.° 6
Fine linen cuffs, with lace	p.ra 4
Fine linen shirts, new	n.° 12
Same, used	n.° 12
. . .	
Cotton cloth to be used to make linens	
Lace trimmed linen dicky	
Shirt, trimmed with used lace	n.° 1
Matching black damask bodice and skirt	n. 2
Black wool skirt, new	n.° 1
Black wool to line a bodice	
. . .	
Used bodice with matching skirt and sleeves	n.° 2

. . .	
Flannel underskirts, used	n.° 2
Same, different fabric	n.° 2
Shawls	n.° 2
Same, made with used damask	n.° 2
. . .	
New red velvet hairnet	n.° 1
Same, made with cherry red and white velvet	n.° 1
Used, blue velvet muff	n.° 1
. . .	
New cotton and wool cloth undersleeves	p. 2
blue sleeves	p. 2
Tobacco silk hand-kerchiefs	n. 2
New pewter bowl with lid	n.° 1
Small bag . . .	
Small bowl with silver handle	n.° 1
. . .	
Silver bodkin	n.° 1
Silver thimble	n.° 1
Silver bowl	n.° 1
Bottle of scented water	n.° 1
. . .	

Silver shoe buckles	p.a 2
. . .	
Black silk bracelets with two . . . and silver and gold with pearls	p.a 2
Earrings with semi-precious white stone	p.a 2
Gold ring with stone	n.° 1
Ring with two dia-monds	n.° 1
Spanish style pen-dants	p.a 1
. . .	
Silver pendant for necklace with the Virgin Mary	n.° 1
A pair of scissors in their black case	n.° 1
. . .	
A wooden rosary with small silver Cross	n.° 1
A large prayer book with its case	n. 1
A couple of small prayer books, one decorated in silver	
the other one simple	n.° 2

IRE, DER E 182, b. 9

Note: Given the quantity of elements listed in this inventory, I decided to transcribe only those that seemed more relevant to the topics discussed in the book, particularly items of clothing, linens, and precious objects, in order to highlight the importance of a marriage trousseau in comparison with a Clothing *corredo*.

August 10th, 1666

Inventory of the properties of the illustrious *signora* Paulina Provisina Mignon given as her dowry to Mr. Vettor Perozzo gentleman from Collogna

One painting with the Virgin Mary in a gilt frame, n. 1

Other smaller paintings with the Virgin Mary

One painting with S. Gierolamo

One portrait of a woman in a gilt frame

Two Roman landscapes

Nine portraits of Kings, Emperors, Dukes, Queens and Duchesses with 29 frames

Frame to be placed around the bedroom ceiling

3 Ladies' chairs

One gilded stool

One stool for the mirror

Five lace trimmed bed linens p. a (pairs)

Five trimmed bed linens, old

One pair of embroidered bed sheets, old

One pair of bed sheets decorated with large trimmings of needle lace

Six pairs of coarse bed sheets, for family use

Two pairs of trimmed bed sheets, one with lace "ponto in aiere"

Six pairs trimmed fine bed sheets, new and old

Four coarse and fine coverlets, old

One fine damask linen coverlet

Two fine, used coverlets

Two used white bed blankets

Twelve new woman's linen shirts

Twelve old linen shirts

Twelve new cotton shirts

Twenty-four old linen shirts

Twelve new cotton shirts

Twenty-four used, but still good, cotton shirts

One trimmed small linen bed sheet

Twelve towels, both coarse and fine

Two new veils trimmed with lace

Seven differently trimmed towels

One small linen bedsheet

One veil trimmed with "ponto in aiere" lace

One trimmed linen bed sheet

One linen tunic

Two new cotton tunics

Three linen half-drawsheets

Twenty-six coarse and fine coverlets

108 coarse napkins

. . .

One set of muslin to make mattress covers

One embroidered bed sheet

One white blanket

Ten new veils

Ten cotton bed sheets

Fifteen different pillowcases

Twelve embroidered napkins

Thirty-six differently trimmed used napkins

Six old silk half-drawsheets

Eighteen lace-trimmed used handkerchiefs

Two embroidered handkerchiefs trimmed with lace

Sixteen handkerchiefs trimmed with lace

Sixteen coarse hemp and cotton coverlets

One hundred new round napkins

Six handkerchiefs

Twenty-four new veils of which fifteen old and nine new, total twenty-four

Sixteen silk shawls and twelve of other kind of fabrics

Twenty-four pairs silk socks

Eight old handkerchiefs

Four *brazza* of linen sashes

Eight old handkerchiefs

One torn-up coverlet and bed sheet

One white old and torn-up blanket

Two white embroidered bedcovers

A pair of linen bed sheets trimmed with "ponto in aere" lace

Seventeen kitchen cloths

Four dishcloths

. . .

Two used bed sheets

Two new bed sheets

Four used covers

Two used silk half draw sheets

Eleven coarse and soiled napkins

One old bedcover with four handkerchiefs

. . .

Three wool mattresses

Duvet pillow

Two straw mattresses

Four gilded chests

Large money chest

One small inlaid table with four legs

Another small table with one drawer

One gilded vanity

One green pillow used to make needle lace

One lady's gilded stool

One inlaid chest for painting

One large mirror and one leather . . .

Six new girl's shirts and twenty old, total 26

One small ebony desk

One refurbished spinet

One small painting with the Virgin Mary and ebony frame

. . .

One hundred and forty-four gilded leather panels

One gilded cage

Fan, cuffs pairs 19 and three collars

Two pairs of pillowcases, one cover and one veil

Muffs made of zibeline, hermine, marten and fox furs

Five blankets of different kinds

n° 164 gilded leather panels (in the *portego*, the main room of the Venetian palaces)

Twelve leather-covered chairs

Twelve carved wooded stools

One walnut wood credenza

One walnut wood table

One small round table

Four old chairs

One length of cloth of gold (in the *portego*, the main room of the Venetian palaces)

One length of painted green cloth

Green and Yellow damask drapes, in the bedroom, n.° 36

Yellow damask . . . with base, blanket and two pillows

Red and yellow brocatelle . . .

Bed-base, blanket and two pillows

Egyptian rugs to place on the chests, n.° 8

Square Egyptian rug to place on the table

Yellow rugs to place on the chest, n. 6

Rugs to place on the chest . . .

Egyptian rug to place on the table

Yellow rug for the table

Yellow and red satin drapes, n° 46 b. a 5 wide b. z 230

. . .

Gilt iron bedframe

Two straw mattresses, on wool mattress

. . .

A pair of bedsheets on the bed

A red blanket

Eight gilded walnut chests

A stool to be used when eating

A mirror in a gilt frame

Green dress brocaded in gold

Gold and blue brocatelle dress

White taffetas *brazza* 22 trimmed in gold

Gold brocade with silver ground B. a 12 with gold trimmings to make a dress

Green dress brocaded in gold

Black wool coat

Shot silk dress

Green satin dress with gold

White patterned velvet dress

Satin dress decorated with fringes in four colours

Yellow satin dress decorated with gold dots

Black velvet patterned dress

Wool dress

Shot silk dress for child

Dress with yellow braiding

Black wool coat

Taffetas dress with yellow braiding

Floral-motif velvet dress, trimmed

Red wool cloth skirt, one for adult, one for child

Green silk skirt

Patterned velvet coat lined with soft cloth

Satin pants embroidered in gold

Doublet in green silk embroidered in gold

Red silk sash with gold tassels

Patterned-silk coat

Black velvet coat

Black satin coat with bow

Black silk coat

b[zza] a 8 of cloth in different colours

woman's jacket brocaded in silver with two pairs of sleeves of different colors

Seven hats in silk and velvet

Half of a ermine lining

Black caps, n.° 4

. . .

Handkerchiefs, some with gold stripes, n.° 4

A length of silver silk with gold flowers and

A length of white taffetas

Cotton tunic and veil and one band in a pillowcase

Round handkerchiefs and a small bed sheet

One worn out bed sheet and fragments, n.° 4

. . .

Hemp thread L 70

Raw hemp L 16

Linen thread L 63

A painting with the Virgin Mary and St. John

A painting with St. Michael and a female portarit

Vases with citrus plants n°9 with jasmine

(in the small room) a painting with Christ

Gilt iron bed, . . .

Straw mattress, wool mattress

Bed, . . . pillows, n.° 4

A pair of bedsheets over the bed

. . .

Silk veil with gold "foreign style"

Carved walnut chests, n.° 5

. . .

Black fan

One wood pyramid

Marten-lined silk coat

Squirrel-lined silk coat

Squirrel (backs) -lined coat

Dress made of floral brocade lined with squirrel (backs) fur

Squirrel fur lining for a skirt

Gilt iron bed

Walnut bed and straw mattress

Wool mattress

Bed with headboard

Stone mortar

A painting cover with a portrait

Two old paintings

Walnut credenza

A wardrobe

A walnut chest and a strongbox

A gilt lantern

One small pinewood wardrobe

. . .

Straw-bottomed chairs, n.°3

Knives to be used at the table, n.° 3

. . .

In another chamber two paintings with the Virgin Mary

Small table covered with a rug

. . .

Small bell

. . .

Gold decorated purses, n.° 5

Gold decorated shoes, n.° 2

Gold embroidered gloves, pairs, n.° 3

Cuffs

New ruff collars, n. 4 and other 4 old, total 8

Different types of fans, n.° 5

. . .

New ruff collars decorated with needle lace

Yellow silk sleeves

Voile ruff collars decorated with needle lace

IRE DER E 178, b. 1, c. 22v.-24v.

1670 Inventory of . . . goods that will be appraised by Giulio Parachini Ragman in Frezzaria, and Zuanne Magni Tailor in S. Moisè

The dress of black Spanish cloth, trimmed	d. 110
The dress of black satin "Tabin", trimmed	d. 105
The dress of black brocaded	d. 30
The dress of black "tarantella"	d. 24
The dress of silk "Bellacosa"	d. 24
The dress of pearl "tabinetto" trimmed with black	
lace and gold braiding	d. 28
The dress of black damask	d. 12
The skirt trimmed in gold and the corset . . .	
in silver with flowers trimmed with gold and silver lace	d. 80
The dress of pearl damask	

trimmed with gold lace	d. 36
The dress, or corset and skirt of striped satin	
trimmed with gold and silver lace	d. 35
The dress of cloth trimmed with gold	
and silver lace and braiding	d. 40
	d. 524
Current total	d. 524
The Polish style velvet dress trimmed with lace	d. 20
The Polish style black damask dress	d. 12
The Polish style striped satin dress,	
trimmed with silver braiding	d. 24
The Polish style rose dress, trimmed with braid	d. 12
The Polish style black and gold dress	d. 12
The Polish style pearl and flowers dress	
trimmed with lace	d. 35
The pearl dress with gold flowers and silver lace	d. 70
The striped yellow and pearl dress trimmed with	

gold and silver lace	d. 40
The skirt of green Tabin trimmed with	
silver lace	d. 27
The skirt of French moiré trimmed	
with gold and silver lace	d. 40
The skirt of yellow shot silk	
trimmed with black lace	d. 14
The pearl skirt . . .	
trimmed with gold and silver lace	d. 55
The pearl dress with trimmings	d. 55
The skirt of light silk with silver lace	d. 10
The silver . . . dress	d. 12
The dress with large floral pattern, trimmed	d. 24
	d. 1067
Current total	d. 1067
The striped . . . dress trimmed	
with gold and silver lace	d. 14
The striped pearl skirt trimmed with silver	d. 10
The striped skirt trimmed with silver	d. 12
The striped pearl skirt trimmed with silver and gold	d. 16

One light silk veil trimmed with Flemish lace	d. 120
Seven pairs of bedsheets made of convent-made	
fabric trimmed with lace	d. 70
Five pairs . . . of the same	d. 35
Ten pairs of new pillow-cases	d. 8
One gilded headboard with eagles	d. 50
n. 3 mattresses, and two pillows	d. 24
one white silk curtain	d. 16
. . .	d. 6
A wardrobe with three . . . painted	d. 16
Three identical chairs	d. 24
Gilded and painted leather panels . . .	d. 35
. . .	
One stool . . .	d. 10
One mirror and jug	d. 30
n. 160, shirts of convent-made fabric	d. 40
n. 6, same, but finer and with laces	d. 18
	d. 1486
Total . . .	d. 1486

Different shirts made with linen cloth or other fabrics, n. 28	d. 56
New napkins 50	d. 8
. . .	
. . .	
Handkerchiefs . . . n. 12	d. 18
Same, n. 10 with laces	d. 38
Linen drawsheets, n. 50	d. 168
Different handkerchiefs, n. 24	d. 128
. . .	d. 3
Pairs of shoes, n. 12	d. 2
. . . of Bulgarian (leather ?) n. 12	d. 60
	Total 1669: f

All the above-mentioned furniture has been appraised
According to our judgement and in agreement between us
And (the estimate) has been revised by Zanne Magni
Tailor in San Moisè
I, Giulio Parachini Ragman in Frezzaria
. . . d. 1673
I Zuanne Magno tailor confirm
I Giulio Parachini confirm
1670

Gold and pearl necklace	d. 501
Gold and pearl pendant	d. 361
Gold and pearl earrings	d. 301
Gold and pearl flower	d. 701
Faceted diamond rosette	d. 1220
Diamond ring	d. 408

Gold, enamel and amber earrings	d. 125
Gold, agate earrings	d. 16
Braided pendant	d. 25
Amber pendant Manini con ambra	d. 200
Gold earrings	d. 125
Gold, pear-shaped agate earrings	d. 71
Gold earrings	d. 89
Amber rosary with ruby cross	d. 120
Silver vase	d. 79
Saucers	d. 47
. . .	d. 125
Salt cellar	d. 120
Bucket	d. 79
	d. 6391

The above-mentioned jewels and silver pieces, according to the estimate made in agreement with my father in law Gio: Battista Pasini, amount to a total of d. 6391

IRE, DER E 2, 3

1715, July15th

List and accounts of the Noblewoman D.na Maria Gaetana Loredan
Nun in the monastery of San Rocco and s.ta Margarita
for the Monacation of Laura Acerbi, my (spiritual)
daughter *

List of things I have to receive of Furniture and Linens

Linens

n. 24 shirts and of these I have received enough cloth
to make 10

6 pairs of bed sheets

24 drawsheets

30 kerchiefs

2 handkerchiefs

12 *brazza* of cloth

12 cotton tights

12 linen tights

12 cotton veils of which I have received

enough to make one

. . .

2 napkins

12 pairs of pillowcases

Fabric for veils, wimples and bands brazza n . . .

Of these I have received 100 brazza for wimples and veils, or 50 of each and of bands 20 brazza; so that I still need to have 50 brazza for veils and wimples and 50 for bands; and of these you could just give me the money because you do not know much about them.

Furnishings for the cell

A walnut stool as it is customary

A walnut wardrobe with three drawers

One chest, although everybody else has two, but in order to
Save you some money I will make do with one, although
I would need the other one and would be glad to have it in order not to be
Different from everybody else.

One black walnut toilet as it is customary;
there should also be a small table, but I do not even think about it;
please, provide me with all this stuff
because I really need it
and a pinewood chest for the dirty laundry

Copper utensils

a bowl, a carafe, a bed warmer

one candlestick

Regarding the clothes I still need for the profession

Black twill brazza n° 14

boots pairs n° 2

pairs of pavonazzo linen hoses n° 2

August 4th, 1716

I, D.a Maria Gaetana Loredana, declare to having received from Ill:mo Sig.r Marin Acerbi in 3 installments as it is customary for the 3 rites for the monacation of his daughter Laura

. . .

ducati 420

In addition to the dowry paid to the Monastery for the rites, banquets and other events, according to the customs of the monastery _____ d: 420, total 1260

For the banquets of the three days of festivities for the Marriage (Clothing)

Doves, 25 pairs

. . .

Chickens, 12 pairs

. . .

Turkeys, 2 pairs

Veal, 2 quarters

Veal, liver 2 libbre

Veal, tripe, 2 libbre

Beef, libbre n. 6

. . .

Cheese, libbre 3

Small wheels of cheese 4

Sweet cheese libbre   n. 1

. . .

Salted tongue meat   n. 2

Beautiful sea-breams   n. 12

. . .

n. 12 flasks of sweet and muscat wine

——-

List of what there is to give to each of the nuns

In the monastery of SS: Rocco et Margarita

To give to the Nuns a . . . each, 40 total

To give to the same a box of cinnamon weighing half *libbra*, n. 40

Marzipan loaves   n. 40

To each of the boarding girls

Marzipan loaves weighing 10 ounces, n. 10

Rolled-up wicks weighing half *libbra*, n. 10

Sugared almonds . . . livre n. 6

To the Confessor and doctor sugar soave, n. 6

Sweet cakes n. 4 quince and pine nut cakes n. 6

To the two priests present at the ceremony half scudo each, total 1

To the sacristans, each, livre n. 2

To the maids soldi 24 each, total lire 1:4

. . .

A long list follows detailing all the ingredients needed to make *bozzoladi*, sweet biscuits enriched by cinnamon, pine nuts, rose water, almonds, and oil that were customarily baked to celebrate Clothing ceremonies and whose ingredients were provided by the families of the future nuns.

*The list, more than by D.na Maria Gaetana Loredan, prioress of the San Rocco e Santa Margherita monastery, as stated in the tile of the file, seems to have been compiled by Laura Acerbi herself, in consideration of the pleas she introduced alongside the items listed such as ". . . to save you some money I will make do with one, although I would need the other one and would be glad to have it in order not to be different from everybody else" or "please, provide me with all this stuff because I really need it."

IRE DER G 1, n. 83

Anna Toniuti was born on February, 11th 1707 and was admitted to the Derelitti hospice on September 9th, 1716. After having refused to marry an older man, she requested to be admitted into the monastery of Saints Mauro and Andrea, in the island of Murano, where she was accepted as *conversa* on September 21st, 1726. The expenses for the monachization process amounted to 600 ducats, to be delivered to the monastery in three different times.

The mother superior of that institution wrote a memo detailing what the future nun will need in her new life:

List of everything is necessary to accept a daughter as *conversa* in the monastery of Sant'Andrea

To be admitted into the monastery

2 pairs of bed sheets
2 pairs of pillow cases
6 shirts
4 drawsheets of Slovenian-made cloth
4 same, of locally-made cloth
4 same, of white cloth
12 handkerchiefs of Slovenian-made cloth
12 cotton veils
Linen cloth for the Communion
4 *Brazza* under-sleeves
4 pairs of cotton hoses
4 same, of linen
4 towels

For the admittance ceremony

Three black dresses, made of different qualities of wool fabrics
Two bodices closed in the front, with matching sleeves, made of wool cloth
Three pairs of coloured hoses, made of cotton and linen
Two pairs of slippers, one of boots
Two pairs of leather shoes
Two combs
For the winter 10 *brazza* of heavy cloth for the skirt and underdress.
After the first trial year it is necessary to give 100 ducats to the monastery; they
will be returned if the girl decides not to be clothed; 200 more ducats need to be
paid to the monastery after the Clothing

At the admittance ceremony (it is necessary to give)

One *Zechino* to the Mother Superior
Four sugar loafs weighing one and a half *libbra*
Two big candles weighing two *libbre* each
To the two Camerlenghe nuns, two
Sugar loaf weighing one and a half *libbra*
Each, total four

On the day the girl is Clothed

As presents for the Father confessor
One *Zechino*, one sweet confection weighing 24 *libbre*
Six sugar loafs weighing one and a half *libbre*
2 pairs of capons
2 pairs of doves
One quarter of a veal weighing 25 *libbre*
To his assistants
One quarter of a Ducat each, two marzipan loafs weighing half a *libbra* each
To the sacristan
For the singing during Mass 12 Ducats
For the licence to get Clothed 14 lire
For the *Bozzoladi* (typical cookies) for the day of the Clothing 20 Ducats

For her cell

One stool, two chests, a small wardrobe
Everything made of pinewood painted to resemble walnut wood
2 straw-bottomed chairs
One Crucifix consistent with the approved model
silver cutlery

bed warmer, bucket, jug and basin

. . .

Feet warmer
Two large tubs

. . .

walnut wood board to be used to starch the veils and wimples

All of the above need to be ready before the day of the Clothing

For the dinner of the Nuns
German barley for soup *libbre* 14
Chickens or pigeons . . . n. 46

. . .

Fruit according to the season
Flasks of white wine n. 20
Marzipan weighing one *libbra* n. 46
Sugared almonds *lib.re* 24

. . .

One boiled capon, with six slices of veal liver, with eight meatballs
Nove-raised small doves, braised n. 2
Roasted veal lib.re n. 3
Decorated cakes, n. 12
A large plate with fruit

For the habit of the future nun
For the Communion and Clothing dress, the habit needs to be made of
coffee-coloured cloth made with n. 7, lire 12
To the seamstress, for the dress and the fittings, l. (lire) 4

. . .

Two skirts of ordinary wool cloth
Two bodices with matching sleeves of ordinary wool cloth

. . .

A skein of black silk

One belt of the approved model
Slippers and shoes n. 2
Boots   n. 2
Linens
Bedhseets of plain cloth n. 6
Pillowcases made of convent-made cloth n. 4
Shirts made of the same fabric n. 40
drawsheets of Slovenian-made cloth n. 20
same, of locally-made cloth n. 20

same, of white cloth n. 10

. . .

Handkerchiefs n. 40

. . .

More cloth . . . braz.a n. 50
Pairs of cotton hoses n. 12
Pairs of linen hoses n. 12

. . .

(fabric for) wimple braz.a n. 100 (fabric for) veil braz.a n. 100
Napkins n. 6

For winter habits
One skirt of heavy wool cloth
Winter underdress with its sleeves made of heavy *pavonazzo* cloth
Wool *pavonazzo* hoses

. . .

For her bed
One mattress, with two pillows,
bedcover, two blankets,
One white cotton blanket

IRE DER G 2, n. 82

Receipt of Anzola Minio once boarding girl of the Hospital
before her Profession in the monastery of the Convertite at the Giudecca
on June, 14th, 1758.

Document written by D. Franc. O Todeschini N.V. (Nobile Veneto)

In the eternal name of God
amen
in the year 1758 from the Incarnation of our God Jesus Christ
June 14th

Having been inspired by Our Lord to retire
In the Monastery of the Convertite at the Giudecca
Among the Nuns, *Signora* Angiola Minio
Daughter of Antonio, boarding girl at the
Pio Ospitale de' poveri Derelitti has brought into effect
Her Holy vocation thanks to the support
Of the above mentioned Ospitale, as decided on December 5th and 19th
1757,
    March 10th and May 22nd (1758)

List of expenses for the Clothing, and Profession of Anzola Minio

May, 20th Venice

Needs to give

2 lenghts of cotton cloth for veils	à 11	22
18 b.za (brazza) of convent-made cotton cloth, ¼	1.15 width	136.10
18 b.za same . . .	1.10	108
18 (b.za) same . . .	1.5	22.10
36 (b. za) fine linen cloth	2.14	97.4
. . .	2.2	50.8
12 ¼ (b.za) fine cotton cloth	1	49
6 ½ . . . fine . . .	1.8	9.2
30 Fine cotton cloth flesh-coloured	1	30
18 (b.za) cloth. . . .	1.4	21.12
8 (b.za) Indian cotton cloth from Holland	2.16	22.8
12 (b.za) light cloth ¼ wide	1.2	13.4
12 hemp napkins, tablecloth	1.8	17.10
7 17 (b.za) same, finer	1.14	12.15
49 (b. za) striped cotton and linen cloth	1.6	63.14

7 (b. za) fine wool cloth from Scotland	6.20	45.10
5 (b. za) same . . .	5.5	26.5
12 (b. za) fine wool cloth made with camel hair	2.12	31.4
3 ½ (b. za) extra-fine wool cloth	2.5	7.17
13 (b. za) yellow fine cotton veil	18	11.14
2 (b.za) same, black	18	1.16
2 (b. za) same, cinnamon-coloured	18	1.16
7 ribbons . . . from bologna	6	2.2
3 ½ (b. za) black veil 6/4 wide	2.10	8.15
6 ½ (b.za) same width . . .	1.12	10.8
8 black doublets	1.15	10
10 pairs of linen hoses	3	30
4 cotton sleeves	1.14	6.16
. . . 890		

. . .

8 coloured linen handkerchiefs
2 cotton shirts
P . . . 2 Linen ribbons
2 same . . .
1 black silk . . .
2 coloured ribbons
White silk ribbons
One large quilted blanket and
6 b.za Cloth
8 (b. za) Flannel
1050
Lorenzo Ambrosioli, alla Madonna del Rosario da B . . . June 12, 1758

Notes

Introduction

1. "Le monache che sono in Venetia in numero grande et per ordinario tutte nobili, per che tutti quei Clariss.mi che hano figlie femine, da pute le mettono nel Monasterio, e come per forza le fano far monache, per non spendere tanto nelle doti. . . . Da che nasce che . . . (le monache) dicono pubblicamente che già che se sono fatte monache per forza, vogliono fare il peggio che possono . . . vivono senza spirito o devotione. Vestono alcune monache più lascivamente con ricci, con petti scoperti, quasi dell'istesse secular."

   "There is in Venice a large number of nuns, usually from noble families since all the noblemen who have daughters send them to monasteries to be educated when they are still very young, later forcing them to become nuns in order to save their dowries. . . . From this custom derives that (the nuns) publicly declare that, since they have been forced to take their vows, they are allowed to behave as badly as they want . . . living without any sort of religious spirit or devotion. Some of the nuns dress in a very seductive fashion, curling their hair, wearing large décolletages, much more than the laywomen." From "Relazione del Stato, Costumi, Disordini et Remediis de Venetia," a seventeenth-century manuscript cited in Pompeo Molmenti, *Storia di Venezia nella vita privata* (Trieste: Lind, 1973), 2:467–68.

2. See Jutta G. Sperling, *Convents and the Body Politic in Late Renaissance Venice* (Chicago: University of Chicago Press, 1999), 244–45. According to Giovanni Spinelli, "I religiosi e le religiose," in *La Chiesa di Venezia nel Seicento*, ed. Bruno Bertoli (Venice: Studium, 1992), nn. 74 and 190, in 1656 there were in Venice 2,508 nuns distributed among thirty convents. See also Stanley Chojnacki, "Gender and the Early Renaissance State," in *Women and Men in Re-*

naissance Venice: Twelve Essays on Patrician Society (Baltimore: John Hopkins University Press, 2000), 39; Marin Sanudo, *De origine, situ et magistratibus urbis Venetae overo la città di Venetia*, ed. Angela Caracciolo Aricò (Milan: Cisalpino-La goliardica, 1980), 45. "Wholesale monacation caused awkward results for the government: in 1553 the magistracy that supervised nuns went unfulfilled because of the impossibility of finding a patrician who could meet the requirements of not having daughters, sisters, or cousins in convents." Chojnacki, "Gender," n. 64.

3. Compare with the tables in Sperling, *Convents*, 246–48, in which for each patrician family is specified the number of nuns and number of brides in the years between 1590 and 1670.

4. "Nel vivere et nelle obbedienze et nel vestire . . . tutte quelle agevolezze . . . dentro i termini dell'onestà . . . se non più consolate, almeno assai meno di scontente, riflettendo in me stesso come esse siano nobili, allevate e nodride con somma delicatezza et rispetto, che se fossero d'altro sesso ad esse toccarebbe il comandare e governare il Mondo . . . che si sono confinate fra quelle mura, non per spirito di devozione ma per impulso dei loro, facendo della propria libertà . . . un dono non solo a Dio, ma anco alla Patria, al Mondo, et alli loro più stretti parenti." Among the honest comforts allowed by Tiepolo were, for instance, wool shirts and bed linens (*camiscie et lenziol di lana*). BMC, Codice Cicogna 2570, ff. 299–304.

5. Venice was usually represented as a blonde noblewoman, as can be seen in such paintings as Paolo Veronese's *The Triumph of Venice*, 1579, or Jacopo Tintoretto's *Apotheosis of Venice*, 1584, both in Palazzo Ducale, Sala del Maggior Consiglio, Venice.

6. On the holy day of the Ascension the doge renewed the dominion of Venice over the Adriatic Sea by "marrying it" and throwing a gold ring in the waves, "thereby underscoring the authority of the patriarchal father in the blending of public and private life which was the essence of patrician culture." Stanley Chojnacki, "Subaltern Patriarchs: Patrician Bachelors," in Stanley Chojnacki, *Women and Men in Renaissance Venice: Twelve Essays on Patrician Society* (Baltimore: John Hopkins University Press, 2000), 247.

7. ASV (Archivio di Stato, Venezia), Provveditori sopra Monasteri. For more on this, see Innocenzo Giuliani, "Genesi e primo secolo di vita del Magistrato sopra monasteri, Venezia 1519-1620," *Le Venezie Francescane* 28 (1961): 42–68, 106–69.

8. The dress of an individual has been defined as "an assemblage of modifications to the body and/or supplements to the body. Dress, so defined, includes a long

list of possible direct modifications of the body, such as coiffed hair, colored skin, pierced ears, and scented breath, as well as an equally long list of garments, jewelry, accessories, and other categories of items added to the body as supplements." Mary E. Roach-Higgins and Joanne B. Eicher, "Dress and Identity," *Clothing and Textile Research Journal* 10, no. 4 (1992): 1–8.

9. Rosita Levi Pisetzky, *Il costume e la moda nella società italiana* (Turin: Einaudi, 1978), 9.

10. Stripes were also a characteristic pattern worn by children, indicating in this case their extraneity to social dynamics. Michel Pastoreau, *La stoffa del diavolo: Una storia delle righe e dei tessuti rigati* (Genoa: Il melangolo, 1993), 15–40.

11. "In all societies dress is first and foremost a means of communication, conscious and unconscious, but inescapable. Metaphorically a language, dress, like all languages, is constantly subject to change, both in detail and in meaning." Stella M. Newton, *The Dress of the Venetians, 1495–1525* (Aldershot: Scolar Press, 1988), 5. Dress can to be interpreted, using the concepts of Saussure, as *langue*, that is, an "institution . . . , an abstract body of constrictions" in contraposition with the *parole*, "the momentary part of the institution itself that the individual uses in order to communicate": inside this research the *parole* is represented by the different dress styles. For more on this, see Roland Barthes, *Sistema della moda* (Turin: Einaudi 1970), 20–21; Ferdinand de Saussure, *Corso di linguistica generale* (Bari: Laterza, 1966); Giovanna Perini, "Meyer Schapiro: Incunaboli di una lettura semiotica dell'arte figurativa," in Meyer Schapiro, *Per una semiotica del linguaggio visivo* (Rome: Meltemi, 2002), 12.

12. See Daniel Roche, *Il linguaggio della moda* (Turin: Einaudi, 1991), 46; Roland Barthes, "Histoire et sociologie du vêtement," *Annales, ESC* (1957): 430–31.

13. Maria Calabrese, *Psicologia della moda: Abbigliamento come linguaggio* (Milan: Igos, 1990), 17. "Dress . . . as an aspect of social history . . . is unparalleled. In forecasting revolutionary movements it is as sensitive as it is in the foretelling of a return to conservatism." Newton, *Dress of the Venetians*, 6.

14. Francesco Sansovino, *Venetia Città Nobilissima et Singolare Descritta in XIII Libri da M. Francesco Sansovino* (in Venetia appresso Iacomo Sansovino, 1581).

15. Schapiro highlights the fact that "the greatness, the social or spiritual importance were expressed through . . . the dress or the attitude." Schapiro, *Per una semiotica*, 112. Rosita Levi Pisetzky also stresses the "special relationship between the dress and the wearer," especially significant when "the dress has the symbolic value of dignity," and mentions "the key importance" of clothing in the portraits of magistrates, portraits that seem to be "an allegory of the power and magnificence of Venice." Levi Pisetzky, *Il costume*, 13–14.

16. "Questo Habito rappresenta veramente la felice & bene principiata grandez-za di questa Repubblica Cristianissima, fondata sopra lo scoglio fermo della Santa Fede per conservatione, & ornamento di tutta l'Italia, come chiaramente si vede, che ella fino à questi nostri tempi si è conservata Vergine intatta. Lo Habito dunque sopraposto è di gran decoro, & grandezza di questa Serenis-sima Repubblica." Cesare Vecellio, *De gli habiti antichi, et moderni di diverse parti del mond libri due, fatti da Cesare Vecellio, & con discorsi da lui dichiarati* (in Venetia: presso Damian Zenaro, 1590), 27.

17. See Giulio Bistort, *Il Magistrato alle Pompe nella Repubblica Veneta* (Bologna: Forni, 1969). Further reading: Doretta Davanzo Poli, *I mestieri della moda a Venezia, Documenti* (Venice: Edizioni del Gazzettino, 1984–86).

18. Doretta Davanzo Poli, "La moda nella Venezia del Palladio," in *Architettura e Utopia*, ed. Lionello Puppi (Milan: Electa, 1981), 219–34. "In sixteenth centu-ry Venice the meaning of dress was precise . . . [and] to ignore its rules could be dangerous and, in extreme cases, amount almost to blasphemy." Newton, *Dress of the Venetians*, 5. In the same period "the only members of the popula-tion free to dress as they pleased were the working classes. . . . Every effort was made to regulate the dress of middle and upper-class women." Newton, *Dress of the Venetians*, 7.

19. Monsignor della Casa highlights how it was necessary that the dress fit not only the person, but also the status of the wearer: "Stia bene non solo al dosso, ma ancora al grado di chi la porta. E oltre a ciò che ella si convenga eziandio alla contrada ove noi dimoriamo." See Stefano Zuffi, *Dettagli di stile: Moda, costume e società nella pittura italiana* (Milan: Mondadori, 2004), 98.

20. Rona Goffen, *Titian's Women* (New Haven, CT: Yale University Press, 1997), 83.

21. Donald E. Queller and Thomas F. Madden, "Father of the Bride: Fathers, Daughters, and Dowries in Late Medieval and Early Renaissance Venice," *Re-naissance Quarterly* 46, no. 4 (Winter 1993): 698. See also Diane Owen Hughes, "Sumptuary Law and Social Relations in Renaissance Italy," in *Disputes and Settlements: Law and Human Relations in the West*, ed. John Bossy (Cambridge: Cambridge University Press, 1983), 97.

22. Roche, *Il linguaggio*, 12; the quote is from Ludovico Ariosto.

23. Ibid. Regarding the symbolic value of the colors, see Sicillo Araldo, *Trattato dei colori nelle arme, nelle livree, et nelle divise* (Venice: D. Nicolino, 1565); Levi Pisetzky, *Il costume*, 64–85. About the dying techniques, see Franco Brunello, *L'arte della tintura nella storia dell'umanità* (Vicenza: Neri Pozza, 1968).

24. For the meaning of colors in Catholic liturgy, see Johann Braun, *I paramenti*

sacri: Loro uso, storia e simbolismo (Turin: Marietti, 1914).

25. The importance of colors in the dresses worn by the aristocrats while in public office is highlighted by the fact that, among the duties of the most feared Council of Ten, the council elected by the Senate to preserve homeland security, was the supervision of the clothing worn by Venetian public officials. See Newton, *Dress of the Venetians*, 21. See also Roche, *Il linguaggio*, 11.

26. Goffen, *Titian's Women*, 83.

27. A fifteenth-century account of dress as the sole means open to a woman for expressing herself and her status is that of Niccolosa Sanuti in Bologna. See Catherine Kovesi Killbery, "Heralds of a Well-Instructed Mind: Niccolosa Sanuti's Defence of Women and Their Clothes," *Renaissance Studies* 13, no. 3 (1999): 99–120. (I thank Jane Bridgeman for the suggestion.)

Chapter 1

1. Fanciullette semplicelle
Pure, o sciocche ne' primi anni
Furono fatte Monacelle
Con lusinghe e con inganni
Ci vestiron questi panni

. . .

Padri e madri ci han scacciate
Come lor mortal nimiche

. . .

Questa dea che al mondo regna
Cieca, sorda, aspra e fallace
A chi è madre, a chi matrigna
Tolle et da come a lei piace
Se son più sorelle l'una
Siede in grembo alla fortuna
L'altre son da lei scacciate
Monacelle incarcerate
L'una è sempre in doglia e pianto
L'altra sempre in gioco e feste
L'una ha il vezzo e ricco manto
L'altra ha il negro velo in testa.

Benedetto Cingulano, "Barzelletta delle Monacelle," BNM, Cl. It., IX, 369 (7203), Poesie varie, sec. XVI, cc. 48v–51r.

2. ASV, Notarile Testamenti, b. 166, n. 124, December 17, 1680.

3. "Voglio che Bianca, e Cecilia mie figlie siano messe monache à suo tempo, se ci andavano volentieri, e le prego andarvi, che starano molto meglio che se si maritassero (che non hò modo di farlo) . . . e esorto e prego andar Monache a servir à Dio che non possono servir sig. Maggiore." If the two girls decided not to become nuns they were to live in the paternal home until their mother's death, living off the usufruct of seventy ducats each. Archivio IRE, DER E 150, b. 5, will of Zuane Falier, April 10, 1601, cc. 19r and v.

4. ASV, Notarile Testamenti, b. 167, n. 177, April 1, 1670. Sometimes young women were cloistered because they remained orphans. For instance: BNM, *Componimenti poetici in occasione che professa la regola di San Benedetto nel nobilissimo monastero di S. Giovanni Evangelista di Torcello la nobil donna Augusta Zorzi al secolo, ora D. Maria Elena* (Venice: presso Gio. Antonio Curti q. Vito, 1793) affirms that the girl has been placed in monastery in order to save her from the "dangers of the life" after the sudden death of both her parents; not incidentally, the abbess of the monastery was her aunt.

5. ASV, Notarile Testamenti, b. 65, n. 119, August 2, 1647

6. Queller and Madden, "Father of the Bride," 704.

7. Chojnacki, "Subaltern Patriarchs," 249.

8. James C. Davis, *A Venetian Family and its Fortune, 1500–1900: The Donà and the Conservation of Wealth* (Philadelphia: American Philosophical Society, 1975), 77–154.

9. Stanley Chojnacki, "Introduction: Family and State, Women and Men," in *Women and Men in Renaissance Venice*, 1–24.

10. Chojnacki, "Subaltern Patriarchs," 253.

11. F.N. Donà, Biblioteca, Lettere varie, "Instruttione paterna d'Antonio Ottoboni N.V. a Pietro suo Figliolo," 22, 23, cited in Davis, *Venetian Family*, 153.

12. Sir Henry Wotton, English ambassador in Venice, wrote in a letter dated 1608 that young women were forced into convents by their parents "who to spare so much marriage money (dowries), impose commonly that life upon three daughters at least if they have five, and so in proportion." Henry Wotton, *Life and Letters*, ed. Linda Pearsall Smith (Oxford: Clarendon Press, 1907), 1:438–39 (letter to Sir Thomas Edmondes, November 14, 1608). Alexander Cowan, "Rich and Poor among the Patriciate in Early Modern Venice," *Studi Veneziani*, n.s., 6 (1982): 147–160. Spinelli, *I religiosi*, 189–198.

13. "mia mare vol che la vada munissela
    Per sparagnar la dote a mia sorela,
    E mi par obedir la mama mia,
    Tagio i capelli e munissela sia."

Venetian folk song

14. IRE, DER E 3, b. 1

15. Chojnacki, "Introduction: Family and State," 11. Following the defeat of the Venetians at Agnadello, many customs perceived as unnecessarily luxurious were abandoned in the belief that sobriety would be appreciated by God, who would, in turn, lend a more favorable ear to the prayers of the Venetians.

16. Just as there was forced monacation, there were forced marriages. Vittoria Cesana in her petition to invalidate her marriage declared that her father extorted her consent to the wedding with Giovanni Battista Barbaro at knife point, "and, fearing he would kill me with that knife, I told him I would obey, with my voice, but not with my heart . . . the marriage never derived from my will or consent." Cited in Joanne M. Ferraro, *Marriage Wars in Late Renaissance Venice* (New York: Oxford University Press, 2001), 41.

17. Sansovino, *Venetia*, 402. After 1501 this custom gave way to registration with the *avogador* (state attorney) of any dowry over one thousand ducats. See Patricia Labalme, Laura Sanguineti White, and Linda Carroll, "How to (and How Not to) Get Married in Sixteenth Century Venice (Selections from the Diaries of Marin Sanudo)," *Renaissance Quarterly* 52, no. 1 (Spring 1999): 45n5.

18. Labalme, White, and Carroll, "How to (and How Not to)," 60.

19. Chojnacki, "Introduction: Family and State," 10.

20. "Nei matrimoni è prima da considerare la quantità della dote e poi la donna, perchè non arricchiscono le case la virtù delle donne, ma le facoltà ch'elle in casa del marito portano." See Manlio Bellomo, *La condizione giuridica della donna in Italia* (Turin: Eri classe unica, 1970), 68.

21. Queller and Madden, "Father of the Bride," 690.

22. Further reading: Sperling, *Convents*, 5–17. Nuns too gave up any pretension to their families' patrimony: N.D. (Nobil Donna) Caterina Barbaro issued to the father and brother a formal receipt confirming that she had received her dowry and nothing else was due to her: "Hauer hauuto, & effettivamente riceuuto per conto della Dote Spirituale del suo Monacto, e professione, come pure per le fontioni occorre, tutti li dinari, argenti, suppellettili, vestimenti, biancherie per suo uso per la summa de Lire dodecimille settecento quarantanove soldi nove, over a qual sopradetta summa tanto specialmente quieta, & rinuncia al medesimo Nobil Homo s. Zorzi Barbaro suo Padre qui presente; & accettate ogni sua raggione, attiene presente, e futura che quouismodo le potesse spettare, & appartenere ne' beni paterni, Materni, Fraternali Sororali, Auiti, & di qualunque altra sorte." ASV, S. Maria delle Vergini, b. 32, "Contratto tra la Nob. Do. Barbaro e Zorzi @ quattro Marzo 1708."

23. Queller and Madden, "Father of the Bride," 686.

24. ASV, Senato, Misti, R. 53, fol. 70. The law, proposed by consigliere Giovanni Garzoni, reads as follows: "Cum inter cives nostros pessima consuetudo orta sit et quotidie augeatur in matrimoniis fiendis propter importabiles sumptus dotium, corredum, donorum atque rerum inutilium, que omnia ascendunt ad tantum numerum quod non est possibile quod multi nobiles nostri possint eorum filias maritare, ac etiam divitum substantia attenuatur in maximum damnum et preiuditium suiorum heredum et quanquam maximam quantitatem pecuniae expendant, tamen minima pars est que in utilitate virginum ponatur in dotem, propter quod aliqui eorum filias coguntur in monasteriis carcerare, cum dignis lacrimi set plantibus ipsarum, aliqui tenent ipsas innuptas, cum rubore et periculo. . . ."

25. ASV, Senato, Misti, R. 53, fol. 70r.

26. "Parte veneziana dura una settimana." Girolamo Priuli, *I Diarii*, ed. Arturo Segre, (Città di Castello: 1912), 4:115.

27. ASV, Senato, Terra, R. 15, c. 78

28. ASV, Senato, Terra, R. 37, c. 107

29. See Labalme, White, and Carroll, "How to (and How Not to)," 43–72.

30. Ibid., 48.

31. Ibid. Cites Sanudo, *Diarii*, February 26, 1498, 1:885–86.

32. IRE, DER E 178, b. 2, marriage contract and dowry inventory of Lucietta Pasini Moretti, 1670, cc. 21v, 22r. In the inventory are mentioned a mirror with a ewer, mattresses, chairs, and numerous jewels made with gold, pearls, amber. A silver salt cellar is listed with the jewels. See the transcription in Documents, no. 3, in the appendix. Unpublished.

33. Gilded foods were frequently served during important events. Molmenti, *Storia di Venezia*, 2:390, reports that they were considered beneficial to the heart.

34. "Sono così ben guardate e custodite nelle case paterne, che ben spesso né anche i più stretti parenti le veggono se non quando elle si maritano. . . ." Vecellio, *De gli habiti antichi*, c. 124v. Even when they were allowed to leave the house, Venetian maidens were kept hidden from the eyes of the people on the streets by thick veils over their heads.

35. Labalme, White, and Carroll, "How to (and How Not to)," 48, cites Marin Sanudo, October 4, 1506, *Diarii*, 6:437.

36. Sanudo, May 2, 1513 (*Diarii*, 16:206–7). It is worth mentioning that Venice was still in the middle of the war of the League of Cambrai. Sanudo also meticulously described the lavish wedding of the granddaughter of Doge Andrea Gritti and ser Polo Contarini in 1525; see *Diarii*, 37:440, 445, 447, 470–75.

37. Gastone Geron, *Carlo Goldoni, cronista mondano* (Venezia: Filippi, 1972), 85.

. . . per far tropo no le va in sconquasso . . .
Le pol laorar, se laorar ghe piase,
Le pol lezer, studier, divertirse,
Meggio che no le fa in te le so case.
No le gh'ha quela pena de vestirse
Tre o quatro volte al dì, de star tre ore
Soto del peruchier a infastidirse. . . .

38. Sperling, *Convents*, 25.

39. "Venetians faced the problems of rising dowry levels by restricting the number of daughters who married. Those whose marriages would have eroded their sister's dowries were forced to take the veil, a practice that led to moral disorders in convents." Chojnacki, "Introduction: Family and State," 10–11.

40. "Figlia mia fate monica
E non ti maridar
Ti faro far la tonica
Hor la voglia portar,
Fuor d'ogni affanno
Starai a officij e a messa
e appresso alla badessa
tu potrai sempre star.

. . .

Madre non mi far monica
Che non mi volgio far
Non mi tagliar la tonica
Che non la voi portar
Star tutto el zorno
A vespero e a messa
poi la madre badessa
non fa se non gridar."

Antonio Pilot, "Figlia mia fate monica," in *Niccolò Tommaseo*, a. II, no. 9–10 (Arezzo: Stab. tip. E. Linatti, 1905).

41. Arcangela Tarabotti, *Paternal Tyranny*, ed. and trans. Letizia Panizza (Chicago: University of Chicago Press, 2004), 54. Although unable to leave the monastery, Tarabotti was allowed visitors: her friends brought news of the outside world and, more importantly, books that allowed her to make up for her limited education. From the 1630s her visitors included members of the Accademia degli Incogniti, a group of freethinkers rather influential in Venetian cultural life; its founder, Giovan Francesco Loredan, arranged for the publication of at least two of her works. By 1643 Tarabotti had written and circulated among her

friends *La tirannia paterna* (Paternal tyranny), and *L'inferno monacale* (Monastic hell). In the same year came her first publication, *Il paradiso monacale* (Monastic paradise), the praise of monastic life for those who had freely chosen it. Together with *L'inferno monacale* and another planned (but apparently unwritten, or lost) work, *Il purgatorio delle mal maritate* (The purgatory of unhappily married women), the three would have made a Dantean trilogy on women's lives. In the following year, Tarabotti published *Antisatira in risposta al lusso donnesco*, a reply to a humorous satire mocking women's vanity, published years earlier, in which she defended a woman's right to adorn herself. *Antisatira* resulted in several written attacks on the author, in part because Venice was always concerned with enforcement of its sumptuary laws, and in part because the text had identified the author as a nun, who, the critics said, should oppose vanity in all its forms. In 1650 appeared a collection of letters *(Lettere familiari e di complimento)*, the only work to be published under her own name, not anonymously or under a pseudonym. In the next year she published another polemic, *Che le donne siano della spezie degli uomani* (That women are of the human species), in response to a recent Italian translation of a 1595 Latin treatise. A year later Tarabotti died, but in 1654 *La semplicita ingannata* (Simplicity deceived) was published; it is a revision of her very first attempt at writing, *La tirannia paterna*, but since little of the earlier work survives, we can't know how much the later work resembles the earlier. *Semplicita* harshly criticizes civic and ecclesiastical leaders for allowing the coercion of women, but it also presents an argument that those leaders could understand: the need to acknowledge God's gift of free will to women as well as men.

42. "Luogo antico & abitato parimenti da monache, & per la sua molta vecchiezza, quasi del tutto nudo di bellezze: ma venerando, si per le donne dalle quali è officiato, & per lo sito nobile dove è posto." Sansovino, *Venetia*, 5. The convent was also known for having been the home of two of the daughters of painter Jacopo Tintoretto, Ottavia and Perina, called "le Tentorette." See Isabella Campagnol, "Invisible Seamstresses: Needlework in Venetian Convents from the Fifteenth to the Eighteenth Century," in *Women and Things: The Material Culture of Needlework and Textiles, 1650–1950*, 2 vols., ed. Maureen Daly Goggin and Beth Fowkes Tobin (London: Ashgate, Arizona State University, 2009), 2:167–78.

43. "[Y]ou have buried some of us within a convent's four walls, knowing that had we been free and assisted by an education, we would have made known to the world all your tyranny's treacheries with truthful tongue and faithful pen!" Tarabotti, *Paternal Tyranny*, 133. "Whenever I see one of these hapless young girls, betrayed by their very own parents, I am reminded of what happens to

a pretty little bird: from within the tree's foliage or along riverbanks, it delights the ear with sweet chirping and charming song, soothing the hearts of its audience—when suddenly it's trapped in a treacherous net, robbed of precious liberty." Ibid., 59.

44. "Sino inganandole con far vedere loro albori sui quali, avendo inestati confetti e frutti di zuccaro . . . non mancano le provvisioni di balli, canti, suoni, mascherate e colazioni." Francesca Medioli, *L'Inferno monacale di Arcangela Tarabotti* (Turin: Rosemberg & Sellier, 1990), 32.

45. ASPV, Archivio Segreto, Visite pastorali, Badoer, S. Mauro, n. 23, 1693: "Non dovendosi poi colla facilità praticata admetter all'Habito Monacale le Figliole senz'il previo esperimento della loro stabilità, è sufficienza nel tempo già in questa materia prescritto, affine che le medesime quando hanno ricevuto l'Habito, e doppo fatta la Santa Professione non habbino à lamentarsi d'essere state ingannate."

46. Alessandro Visconti, *L'Italia nell'epoca della controriforma* (Milan: Mondadori, 1958), 71.

47. Sister Lucia Tiepolo, prioress of the convent of Corpus Domini, during the war between Venice and Padua, addressed her nuns, saying: "My dear daughters, our Lord God is greatly offended. All the war's tribulations are due to the great sins of the world. I pray that He may give victory to this state, and he replies to me that not in armis, sed in precibus, so that dear daughters, you should be fervent in your prayers if you want this city to be victorius." Sister Bartolomea Riccoboni, *Life and Death in a Venetian Convent: The Chronicle and Necrology of Corpus Domini, 1395–1436*, ed. and trans. Daniel Bornstein (Chicago: University of Chicago Press, 2000), 76.

48. "Se voria remediar a le cause che induce la peste, chè li pecati orendi che si fa: . . . quando vien qual che signor in questa terra, li mostrate li monasteri di monache, non monasterii ma prostibuli e bordelli publici. Serenissimo principe! Io so che non siete ignorante, e che tutto sapeti meglio cha mi. Provedete, provedete, e provedereti a la peste." Sanudo, *Diarii*, December 24, 1497. However, it must be remembered that in some monasteries the behavior of the nuns was strictly pious and sober. Eugenio Musatti, *La donna in Venezia* (Bologna: Forni, 1975), 101.

49. Gerolamo Priuli, *I Diarii* (a. 1499–1512), ed. Renato Cessi, in *Rerum Italicarum Scriptores*, t. XXIV, pt. III, vol. IV (Bologna: 1938–1941), 33–37, 115. Sperling, *Convents*, 11–13.

50. May 14, 1509. Venice was defeated by the combined military forces of the League of Cambrai, which included Spain, France, the Holy Roman Empire,

and the papacy. Writes Priuli: "Li monasteri dele monache conventuale . . . se putevano reputare pubblici bordelli et pubblici lupanari con grandissima offensione divina . . . et vergogna della republica veneta che le nobile fiole deli primi nobili . . . dela citade, poste in li monasteri et dedicate et disposte al culto divino, fussero diventate pubbliche meretrice. . . . Et erano simili monasterij publicamente noti a tuti li forastieri che venivano a Venezia . . . et molti di questi forestieri si innamorano di simili monache, belle et giovane." Cited in Pio Paschini, "I monasteri femminili in Italia nel '500," in *Problemi di vita religiosa in. Italia nel Cinquecento* (Padua: Antenore, 1960), 45.

51. An example of the mischief committed by involuntary nuns is offered by the figure of Monaca di Monza, the nun described in Alessandro Manzoni's *Promessi Sposi.* This literary character was based on the historical figure of involuntary nun Marianna Maria de Leyva-Suor Virginia. Further reading: *Vita e processo di Suor Virginia Maria de Leyva monaca di Monza*, ed. Giancarlo Vigorelli (Milano: Garzanti, 1985). An interesting statistic about immoral behavior in Venetian convents from the archives of the Provveditori sopra Monasteri is given by Bartolomeo Cecchetti, "Saggio di statistica di alcuni processi per malcostume, nei conventi di Venezia e dello Stato Veneto, sec. XVII e XVIII," in Bartolomeo Cecchetti, *La Repubblica di Venezia e la corte di Roma nei rapporti della religione* (Venice: Prem. Stabilim. Tipog. di P. Naratovich, 1874), 2:98–103.

52. "La è una buona zovene, ma Dio perdona à chi mette le fie in Monestier per forza," ASV, Provveditori sopra Monasteri, b. 347, fasc. 5, June 10, 1604; "Vorrei piuttosto esser nata da un fachin," ASV, Provveditori sopra Monasteri, b. 347, fasc.7, June 19, 1604.

53. "L'ho sentita à maledir padre, et madre, et chi l'ha messa munega, et l'ho sentita dir mal de Zorzi . . . suo cugnado che mai l'ha fatto ben, che l'ha ruinà casa sua." Provveditori sopra Monasteri, S. Iseppo, 1571, b. 263, fasc. 4, fol. 4v.

Chapter 2

1. The Immaculate Conception is a Catholic dogma proclaimed by Pope Pious IX on December 8, 1854, with the bull *Ineffabilis Deus*; it decrees that the Virgin Mary was immune from original sin since the moment of her conception.

2. "Un abito candido, e bianco di tutto punto snello, et attillato, secondo apparteneva alla candidezza et innocenza di ben educata fanciulla." Vecellio, *De gli habiti antichi*, 1590, cc. 126v–127r. See also Giovanni Grevembroch, *Gli abiti de' Veneziani di quasi ogni età con diligenza raccolti e dipinti nel secolo XVIII*, ed. Giovanni Mariacher (Venice: Filippi, 1981), IV, no. 118.

3. Araldo, *Trattato dei colori*, c. 19r., cited in Davanzo Poli, *Abiti antichi*, 72.

4. Sara Piccolo Paci, *Le vesti del peccato: Eva, Salomè e Maria Maddalena nell'arte* (Milano: Ancora, 2003), 21–22.

5. See also Newton, *Dress of the Venetians*, 18. On the doge wearing white and gold, see Giovanni Bellini, *Portrait of Doge Leonardo Loredan*, 1501–4, London, National Gallery; Grevembroch, *Gli abiti*, II:7, 113. Further reading: Daniele Ferrara, "Il ritratto del Doge Leonardo Loredan: Strategie dell'abito tra politica e religione," *Venezia Cinquecento* 2 (1991): 89–108.

6. A black with rusty red overtones.

7. Cloth originally made of camel hair, but later also with silk. It was also known under the names of *camelotto, zambellotto, cambellotto*. See Achille Vitali, *La moda a Venezia attraverso i secoli: Lessico ragionato* (Venice: Filippi, 1992): 109–11.

8. "Le giovani destinate o per Marito, o per Monastero, sì Nobili, che Cittadine . . . portano in testa un velo di seta Bianca, ch'esse chiamano fazzuolo, d'assai ampia larghezza et con esso si coprono il viso e' l petto. Portano in questo tempo pochi ornamenti di perle, et qualche picciola collana d'oro di poca valuta. Le sopravesti di queste sono la maggior parte di color rovano o nere, di lana leggiera, over ciambellotto o altra materia di poca valuta, benché sotto vadano vestite di colore, et vanno cinte d'uno di quei retini di seta ch'esse chiamano poste." Vecellio, *De gli habiti antichi*, 101–2; Grevembroch, *Gli abiti*, 1:42.

9. In the *Capitolare de sartoribus* it is in fact specified that "che nessuna tunica femminile possa avere uno strascico lungo oltre un braccio . . . eccezion fatta per la sposa che per l'abito nuziale potrà avere la coda che vorrà" ("no feminine tunic can have a train longer than a *braccio*, . . . with the exception of the bridal dress that can have a train as long as they want it"). Cited in Doretta Davanzo Poli, *I mestieri della moda: Documenti* (Venice: Edizioni del Gazzettino, 1984–1986), 1:139. Other exceptions were made for the visits of foreign kings and dignitaries. Participating in the festivities organized for the arrival of King Henry III of France were two hundred noblewomen all magnificently dressed in white with priceless pearls around their necks. See Grevembroch, *Gli abiti*, 1:137.

10. "Mezo di restagno d'oro e mezo bianco, ch'è contra la leze." Sanudo, *Diarii*, XXIIII, col. 341.

11. "Vestura di raso bianco e restagno d'oro." Ibid., col. 71.

12. Bistort, *Il magistrato*, 38.

13. "Vestura scachada di restagno d'oro e raso biancho, qual per le parti non si pol portar e al collo in forma di cadena, et molte grosse perle." Sanudo, *Diarii*, XXIIII, col. 14.

14. Sanudo, *Diarii*, January 1555, XXXVII: col. 474. Vitali mentions a Senate decree dated May 5, 1541, in which the pearl necklace is described; Vitali, *La moda*, 146.

15. Harula Economopoulos, "Considerazioni sui ruoli dimenticati: Gli 'Amanti' di Paris Bordon e la figura del compare dell'anello," *Venezia Cinquecento* 2, no. 3 (1992): 101.

16. "Sei Spose con capelli distesi filati d'oro." Grevembroch, *Gli abiti*, 1:131.

17. IRE, DER E 182, b. 9, August 10, 1666, Inventario di dote di Paulina Provisina Vignon. See Documents, no. 2, in the appendix.

18. For a detailed description of the shape, materials, and evolution of this garment, see Vitali, *La moda*, 414–22.

19. "Dopo aver salutato lo sposo e ringraziato i presenti faceva 'un passo e mezzo' poi un salterello modesto e inchinandosi con un bell'inchino prendeva licenza." Giacomo Franco, *Habiti delle donne veneziane*, ed. Lina Urban (1610; Venice: Centro Internazionale della Grafica, 1990), 7.

20. The cabin that covered part of the gondola.

21. "Fuori del felze, & si pone a sedere sopra un seggio alquanto rilevato, coperto per tutto di tappeti (& questo modo si chiama andare in trasto) seguendola un gran numero di altre gondole, & se ne va a visitar i monisteri delle monache, dove hanno, o sorelle, o parenti & congiunte." Sansovino, *Venetia*, 149. The *trasto* was a bench placed outside the felze.

22. For more on this, see "Ordini a quelli che hanno a parlar con Monache." BMC, Codice Cicogna, 2583, c. 128v, July 7, 1594.

23. Medioli, *Inferno*, 70.

24. Gabriel Bella, *Sposalizio di una nobil donna venetta*, before 1782, Venice, Fondazione Querini Stampalia.

25. About her mystical marriage, see Gabriella Zarri, "La vita religiosa tra rinascimento e controriforma: Sponsa Christi: Nozze mistiche e professione monastica," in *Monaca, moglie, serva, cortigiana: Vita e immagine delle donne tra rinascimento e controriforma*, ed. Sara Matthews Grieco and Sabina Berveglieri (Florence: Morgana edizioni, 2001), 118–21.

26. "Io sono la sposa di Cristo. Egli è la mia gloria, Egli è il mio amante, la mia dolcezza, il mio amore" See Jacopo Da Varagine, *Legenda Aurea* (Florence: Libreria Editrice Fiorentina, 1976), anastatic reprint, 788–98.

27. "The hair was held back on the top of the head by a jewelled hair band decorated by pendants and amazingly beautiful pearls." Grevembroch, *Gli abiti*, II, no. 131.

28. Hendrick Golzius, from Dirck Barendszen, *Matrimonio veneziano*, 1584,

Princeton University Art Museum, Princeton, New Jersey.

29. Circa 1575, Paolo Veronese, Venice, Gallerie dell'Accademia. The painting, widely appreciated by its contemporaries and known all over Italy thanks to a 1582 engraving by Agostino Carracci, was removed from its site for safekeeping during World War I and moved to its present location. See Anton Maria Zanetti, *Della Pittura Veneziana e delle opere pubbliche de' Veneziani Maestri Libri V* (Venice: nella stamperia di Giambatista Albrizzi a S. Benedetto, 1771), 183.

30. "Il cielo, e ne' quattro elementi l'aere." Sicilo Araldo, cited in Davanzo Poli, *Abiti antichi*, 23.

31. Work of Jacopo Tintoretto and his *bottega*, dated between 1582 and 1585, Venice, Palazzo Patriarcale.

32. See also cols. 520–21 and 538–39, XLIX, col. 429.

33. For a very extensive analysis of the peculiar history and traditions of the Vergini monastery, see Kate J. P. Lowe, *Nun's Chronicles and Convent Culture in Renaissance and Counter-Reformation Italy* (Cambridge: Cambridge University Press, 2003).

34. Cronica del Monistero delle Vergini di Venetia, BMC, Ms. Correr 317, fol. 18v.

35. The colored dresses worn by the top tiers of the Venetian government were called *veste segnade*, and they differentiated the public officials from the rest of the aristocracy, usually dressed in black.

36. Newton, *Dress of the Venetians*, 12. Vitali, *La moda*, 425n34.

37. The color "occupied a curious position in the chromatic hierarchy of Venetian official clothing." It could be used for half-mourning, but was also a proper mourning colour and could have different meanings depending on the circumstances in which it was used. Lodovico Dolce in his *Tratto dei colori* affirms that warm purple was "in those times known as *Paonazzo*." See Newton, *Dress of the Venetians*, 18–19.

38. Vitali, *La moda*, 421.

39. Davanzo Poli, *Abiti antichi*, 55; Newton, *Dress of the Venetians*, 12–15.

40. Giustina Renier Michiel, *Origine delle feste veneziane* (Milano, 1829), 2:66.

41. See Kate J. P. Lowe, "Secular Brides and Convent Brides: Wedding Ceremonies in Italy during the Renaissance and Counter-Reformation," in *Marriage in Italy, 1300–1650*, ed. Trevor Dean and Kate J. P. Lowe (Cambridge: Cambridge University Press, 1998), 41. In the poetic compositions traditionally dedicated to novices on the day of their Clothing, they are constantly referred to as *sposa sacra* or "holy bride." See BMC, *Componimenti poetici in occasione che la nobil*

donna Teresa Priuli veste il sagro abito di Santo Agostino nel nobilissimo monastero di Santa Giustina prendendo il nome di Maria Cecilia (Venice, 1746); BNM, *Componimenti poetici in occasione che professò l'abito di S. Benedetto nel nobilissimo monastero di S. Zaccaria di Venezia la nobile donna Cecilia Gritti che prese il nome di Cecilia Maria* (Venice: Stamp. Casali, 1784).

42. Lowe, "Secular Brides," 44.

43. Goffen, *Titian's Women*, 83.

44. "Come se andassero a nozze." Molmenti, *La storia di Venezia*, 2:467.

45. Lowe, "Secular Brides," 51.

46. IRE, DER E 182, b. 9. See Documents, no. 2, in the appendix.

47. "Ordiniamo che [i monasteri] non ricevino . . . in una sol volta una somma di danari . . . ma [una] annua entrata sufficiente al modesto, et regolato vitto e vestito d'una persona." BMC, Codice Cicogna 2583, c. 127r, November 24, 1593.

48. "Spese veramente immoderate e vane che sin hora si sono fatte in banchetti, doni, o altro che a monache particolare si è dato nella solennità del vestire." Ibid., c. 128.

49. "Sono accresciute a tanto eccesso le spese che si fanno nel monacar figliole, così nella quantità della dote, come nelle casse et in alter dispendiose instruttioni poco necessarie e del tutto superflue, che per ogni rispetto devesi provvedere a questi abusi et pessime corrutele, s' che possano egualmente le famiglie di questa Città accomodar le figliole al servizio del Signor Dio, senza essere astrette a spese maggiori di quello che ricerca il dovere ed il commodo universale." Further reading: Bistort, *Il Magistrato*, 253.

50. The dowry for the *converse*, who served the choir nuns as maids, was considerably smaller, around three hundred ducats. See Mary Laven, *Virgins of Venice: Enclosed Lives and Broken Vows in the Renaissance Convent* (London: Viking, 2002), 39–48.

51. ASV, Pregadi, April 15, 1610, CL, b. 288, cc. 411r–v.

52. Quote from Victoria Primhak, "Women in Religious Communities: The Benedictine Convents of Venice, 1400–1500," PhD diss., University of London, 1991, 151.

53. ASV, Manimorte, Sant'Anna, pacco 6472, n. 2.

54. "Stimo più 'ste sante lane
Che de ganzo le sotane.
Tanti bezzi, no, no voggio,
Che per mi se buta via
In t'un stuchio, in t'un reloggio,
In recami e biancaria:

Malignase sia pur tute,
Coi tabari le baute.
Sento dir che a una novizza
i ghe manda un arsenal; xe le cosse che fa stizza
tanta roba a trar de mal.
Prima gnanca che lo goda,
Quel vestir va zo de moda."
"Canzone in lengua veneziana dedicata alle N.D. Contarina, Alba, ed Elena Lip-
pomano per la vestizione della sorella Maria Teresa Serafina Lippomano." See
Geron, *Carlo Goldoni*, 82.

55. Doretta Davanzo Poli, "Merletto ad ago e a fuselli," in *Storia di Venezia: Temi:
L'arte* (Roma: Istituto della Enciclopedia Italiana, 1995), 2:985–1003; ASV, Arte
Marzeri, b. 312.1.

56. Arcangela Tarabotti's Clothing ceremony took place on September 8, 1620.

57. "Le più grosse e ruvide tele per le camise delle sventurate che sovente non
riescono di bastevole lunghezza e le maniche sono a tal'una diverse dal rima-
nente." Medioli, *L'Inferno monacale*, 43.

58. *Rassa*: coarse wool cloth, generally black, but also available in other colors.
See Vitali, *La moda*, 321.

59. "La condannata alla tomba di un chiostro è necessitata a coprirsi la gamba
di rozza rassa et adatarsi al piede un zoccolo di legno malvestito di cuoio . . .
usano due casse delle più tarlate." Ibid., 47.

60. "Anche questa e la misera dote viene fatta lor pesare, quasi dovessero vestirsi
di capelli, come la discepola amante." Ibid., 40–41.

61. IRE, DER E 2, b. 3. See Documents, no. 4, in the appendix. Unpublished.

62. *Boccassini*: veils made with fine cotton and linen fabric. See Vitali, *La moda*,
61.

63. IRE, DER E 2, b. 3, c. 7: "Avvicinandosi il tempo della mia professione in
chiesa e non vedendomi niente di fornimenti di cella, né meno di biancheria,
tenendoli in grande necessità, è anche in stesso tempo devo avere quello li ò
mandato scritto nella polizza tutto per la professione. Caro sig. Padre . . . (pre-
ga) di farmi il mio bisogno che mi arosischo vedendomi tra queste religiose è
mie compagne novizie che hanno tutto il suo è di cella è di robba in somma
tutto quello che si ha bisogno; adesso che è il tempo della sensa che si trova più
a buon marcato el vadi a comprare, come le noghere et anco li rami è telle che
se ne trovano di belle è bene; per farmi delli boccassini, poi io mi ritrovo avere
due pezzi di mussolo giusto à proposito per mè, è sono bona robba che alle
botteghe si trova più cara è poi è debole, onde se il Comanda che si mandi à

casa per vederla è comprarla mi farò delli boccassini; bisogna meterci alla forza Caro Sig. Padre mi mancha solo due mesi è giorni alla professione, già quando mi averà fatto tutta là robba à dato il mio bisogno lei non averà pi da me niun disturbo, è anche sarà di decoro alla Casa che pare siamo tanti pitocchi per vedere che ò una cella pezo dell'Ultima Conversa con tutto che è mendica. Si po l'immaginare che mi rende non poter comparire come le altre; onde replico Caro Sig. Padre il suplico fare un bon animo, se lei non à tempo da perdere el faci che Piero mio fratello con il Sig. Zio fazzi loro che li farà di avantaggio; non mi posso persuadere perche non mi venghi più a visitare, forse perché li predico il bisogno mio fa parlare, il . . . à comprarmi il bisogno è venghi pure a ritrovarmi che sono tanto desiderosa, che vederà se li dirò nula; li raccomando anche li 9 ducati è mezo che ho avuto in presuto è il suplico perdonarmi è abbaciandola sono sua D.V.SSma."

64. Ibid.

65. IRE, DER G 1, n. 83. See transcription in Documents, no. 5, in the appendix. Unpublished. See also the document about the monacation of Angela Minio at Le Convertite (IRE, DER G 2, no. 83) in Documents, no. 6, in the appendix. Unpublished.

66. "Dopo tre giornate di esperim.ti finalm.te jeri anno elletto la loro Badessa le Dame delle vergini e l'ellezione cadette sopra la Mora Sig.ra povera e perciò senza volerlo minoreranno le spese; anno già cominciato jeri sera a dar saggi di ciò, mentre il popolo che non aveva avuto da bere non gridava eh viva." Letter of Elena Mocenigo Querini to her husband Andrea Querini on June 18, 1774, in *Ci vuole pazienza: Lettere di Elena Mocenigo Querini 1733–1788*, ed. Antonio Fancello and Madile Gambier (Venice : Fondazione Querini Stampalia, 2008), 126.

67. See *Ordo rituum et caeremoniarum suscipiendi habitum monialem, & emittendi professionem. Ad Venetae diocesis usum. Olim jussu . . . Francisci Vendrameni Patriarchae Venetiarum, & c. Editus nunc vero curantibus sororibus Theupolis degentibus in Monasterio S. Luciae recenter typis commissus* (Venice: Apud Andream Poleti, 1694).

68. Two angels playing instruments are depicted in Veronese's *Mystical Marriage of Saint Catherine*, yet another connection with secular marriages.

69. "Non debbano . . . entrare pomposamente, né con vestimenti di seta, né ornamenti di ori, gioie, perle." Antonio Grimani, *Constitutioni, et decreti approvati nella sinodo diocesana sopra la retta disciplina monacale sotto L'illustrissimo, Reverendissimo Monsignor Antonio Grimani Vescovo di Torcello. L'anno della Natività del Nostro Signore, 1592. Il giorno 7. 8. & 9 d'Aprile* (Venice, 1592), c. 15r.

70. Grimani, *Constitution*, c. 17r.

71. *The Clothing in San Lorenzo*, by Gabriel Bella (1789), Venice, Querini Stampalia Museum. The painting represents a ceremony inside one of the two most important Venetian convents, where almost all the nuns came from an aristocratic lineage.

72. BNM, Provveditori sopra Monasteri, *Proclama pubblicato d'ordine degl'illustrissimi, & eccellentissimi signori Provveditori sopra monasterj. In materia di spese, rinfreschi, ed apparati in occasione di vestir figlie monache* (Venice: per li figlioli del qu. Z. Antonio Pinelli stampatori ducali, 1749). Dated August 24.

73. Milan, Biblioteca Ambrosiana, A 125 sup. fol. 90r. See Renata Cipriani, *Codici minati dell'Ambrosiana* (Vicenza: Neri Pozza, 1968), 5.

74. "Accipe signum Christi in capite tuo ut uxor eius efficiaris." *Pontificale sacrorum rituum sacrosantae romanae ecclesie* (Venice: Lucantonio de Giunti, 1520), 86v.

75. Venice, BNM, Cod. Lat. III, 3401, fol. 2r.

76. *Dizionario degli Istituti di perfezione,* ed. Guerrino Pelliccia and Giancarlo Rocca (Milan: Paoline, 1975), I, cols. 1235–36.

77. "Me totam in hostiam viventem offero, & sacrifico." *Ordo rituum*, 26–27.

78. Zanette, *Suor Arcangela*, 85.

79. Medioli, *Inferno monacale*, 67.

80. So wrote Saint Clare of Assisi in her *Lettere ad Agnese: La visione dello specchio,* ed. Giovanni Pozzi and Beatrice Rima (Milan: Adelphi, 1999), 138.

81. "Surge Filia, & orna lampadem tuam, ecce sponsus venit, exi obviam ei." *Ordo rituum*, 24.

82. Zanette, *Suor Arcangela*, 26.

83. *Brazzo*: Venetian unit of length. It corresponds to 63.8 cm for silk fabrics and 68.2 cm for wool fabrics. See Giuseppe Boerio, *Dizionario del dialetto veneziano* (Torino: Bottega d'Erasmo, 1867), 99.

84. L'ha scambià nome, e l'ha scambià cussì

L'oro, la seda, e fin la tela in lana.

Vestia l'ano passà l'ho vista mi

Con quatordeze brazzi de sotana.

Adesso de na tonega avalìa

Tuta da capo a pié la va vestia.

Geron, *Carlo Goldoni*, 81

85. *Andrienne:* feminine dress typical of the first half of the eighteenth century and characterized by two pleats in the back that opened in an imposing train. See Vitali, *La moda*, 36–40.

86. Le zoggie, i merli, i abiti
   Ricchi, no la i vol più;
   la li ha portai pochissimo,
   la ne li lassa a nu . . .
   Quanto xe meggio el bavaro
   Invece del toppè!
   Quanto val più la tonega
   Dei cerchi e de l'andriè!
   . . .
   Per le vestir le muneghe
   Le gh'ha un pensier de manco.
   . . .
   Dove xè andà le scarpe recamae,
   . . .
   La le ha da brava in zoccoli scambiae,
   larghi, comodi, e boni ogni stagion.
   Scuffie e cascade dove xele andae?
   La le ha trate con sprezzo in t'un canton.
   Tute l'ha renonzià . . .
   ricca, nobile nata in aurea veste,
   potrebbe abch'essa, come tante fanno,
   con nastri, trine e gemme ornar la cresta.
   . . .
   Sprezza Angiola le pompe, e sotto à piedi
   Tiensi l'oro e l'argento, e in umil lana
   Le molli membra imprigionar la vedi.
   Geron, *Carlo Goldoni*, 85–86

87. Francesca Cortesi Bosco, *Gli affreschi dell'Oratorio Suardi: Lorenzo Lotto nella crisi della riforma* (Bergamo: Bolis, 1980), 106, 108–10, 112.

88. "La povertà le sia sempre compagna, guardandosi di non tener, dare, ne ricever giamai cosa senza licentia della R.da Abbadessa, et tenendola con licentia non stimarla però come sua propria, né affezionandosi ad essa, servendosene solamente nelle sue necessità come cosa commune del Monasterio , e con animo sempre di privarsene quando gli fosse fatto un minimo cenno dalla R.da Abbadessa, altrimenti sarebbe in stato di peccato mortale, et come proprietaria saria indegna di sepoltura sacra in tempo di morte." ASPV, Archivio Segreto, Visite pastorali , b. 1, S. Biagio e Cataldo, October, 21, 1521.

89. "Apostolus muliebrem sexum in signum subjectionis, humilitatis, & honestatis vlamn super caput suum . . . habe praecepit." *Ordo rituum*, 6.

90. "Rozza cintura di cuoio." Medioli, *L'Inferno monacale*, 43.

91. "Accipe Cingulum super lumbos tuos . . . in signum temperantiae et castita-tis." *Ordo rituum*, 12. See "Abito religioso," in *Dizionario degli Istituti di Perfezi-one*, I, cols. 50–79; *La sostanza dell'effimero: Gli abiti religiosi in Occidente*, exhi-bition catalogue, ed. Giancarlo Rocca (Roma: Edizioni Paoline, 2000), 70–71.

92. Arcangela compares the nun "deprived of the locks given to her by nature" to the bride busy in taking care of her flowing hair. Medioli, *L'Inferno monacale*, 43.

93. Anonymous Venetian painter, *Saint Clare's Clothing*, sixteenth century, Rome, Quadreria della Cassa Depositi e Prestiti.

94. "Succingat crinem tuum modestia, sobrietas, continentia." *Ordo rituum*, 13.

95. "Demum turpissimae mortis tuae dulcis sposni sui memoriam hoc viduitatis inditium sepè mentis eius oculis repraesentet." *Ordo rituum*, 10. The covered head was in Venice symbolic of widowhood: "scufia in testa - che all'uso di questa patria nell'altre donne è un lugubre contrassegno della morte di cari mariti." Medioli, *L'Inferno monacale*, 43.

96. "La superiora le da poscia tre ponti ad un velo . . . che chiamasi sorazzetto e serve per coprirle il capo." Zanette, *Suor Arcangela*, 70.

97. "Tanto in chiesa, quanto fuori ne' parlatory, o altri luoghi, acque, sorbetti, caffè, cioccolata ed altri rinfreschi e così pure mazzetti di fiori." Ibid.

98. Primhak, "Women in Religious Communities," 154.

99. Victoria Primhak, "Benedictine Communities in Venetian Society," in *Women in Italian Renaissance Culture and Society*, ed. Letizia Panizza (Oxford: Euro-pean Humanities Research Centre, 2000), 92.

100. "Purchè si velino, il tutto va bene." Zanette, *Suor Arcangela*, 153.

Chapter 3

1. The church was built between 1481 and 1489 by architect Pietro Lombardo and his sons, Tullio and Antonio. For more on this, see *Santa Maria dei Miracoli a Venezia: La storia, la fabbrica, i restauri,* ed. Mario Piana and Wolfgang Wolters (Venice: Istituto Veneto di Scienze, Lettere ed Arti, 2003).

2. Some elements of the habit were to be worn even at night.

3. Further reading: Roland Barthes, "Storia e sociologia del vestiario: Osservazi-oni metodologiche," in *La storia e le scienze sociali*, ed. Ferdìnand Braudel (Bari: Laterza, 1974), 136–52.

4. ASPV, Archivio Segreto, Visite pastorali, *Visite pastorali,* b. 1, fasc. 14, S. Maria dei Miracoli, April 8, 1647: "Il nostro Vestimento d'Inverno è di Pano, e l'estate di Rassa" ("Our habit is made of wool cloth in the winter and of Rassa in the

summer"). In the instrucitons posted in the refectory of the monastery of San Biagio e Cataldo dated September 26, 1565 is established that "the petticoats are to made with rassa, as it has always been made," "le gonelle . . . Siano fatte de rassa come è sempre stato." ASPV, Archivio Segreto, Visite pastorali, Trevisan, S. Biagio e Cataldo.

5. ASPV, Archivio Segreto, Visite pastorali, b. 1, fasc. 13, S. Maria della Redenzione, 1647: "Circa del vestire, il quale è di Griso, tanto l'inverno, q.to l'estate, et ci è concesso un abito convenienti, e poi uno in . . . , e una Tonica l'inverno, e un mantello per una e del resto tutto in Comunità, cioè, Bavere, velli, e facioleti."

6. ASPV, Archivio Segreto, Visite pastorali, Cornaro, S. Sepolcro, February 13, 1635: "Che riduciato l'habito alla forma et colori che ordina la regola di s.ta Chiara, prohibendo le rascie bianche" ("The dress needs to correspond to the prescriptions of the rule of St. Claire, and white wool cloths are forbidden").

7. See Cordelia Warr, "The Striped Mantle of the Poor Clares: Image and Text in Italy in the Later Middle Ages," *Arte Cristiana* 86 (1998): 415–30; Giovanni M. Del Basso, "Il sigillo delle monache: Autorità e modello," in *Donna, disciplina creanza cristiana dal XV al XVII secolo: Studi e testi a stampa*, ed. Gabriella Zarri (Rome: Edizioni di storia e letteratura, 1996), 347–66, fig. 1.

8. ASV, Santa Croce di Venezia, February 19, 1601; Laven, *Virgins of Venice*, 216. For the symbolic meaning of burial clothes, see Lia Luzzatto and Renata Pompas. *I colori del Vestire: Variazione: Ritorni, persistenze* (Milan: Hoepli, 1997), 35.

9. Coronelli's work was resumed and improved by Pierre Hélyot, in his *Storia degli ordini monastici, religiosi, e militari, e delle congregazioni secolari dell'uno, e l'altro sesso, fino al presente istituite, con le vite de' loro fondatori, e riformatori,* eight volumes published in Lucca: per Giuseppe Salani e Vincenzo Giuntini, 1737–39.

10. "E' necessario che in ogni Monasterio ci sia un vestiario commune dover si conservino le cose communi, et necessarie per vestir le Monache; et sirene nel nostro Monasterio le Monache hanno licenza dall'Abbadessa di tenirsi li suoi panni separati così del vestire come del dormire, servirà almeno detto vestiario per conservare le robbe delle Monache che morirono, le quali poi si dovevano da dispensare col tempo in beneficio del commune ò per necessità delle Monache bisognose come parerà all'Abbadessa et quivi anco s'havevano da tagliare, et cucire li abiti delle Monache nuovi tutti d'una forma. . . . Non ardisca la detta Maestra (addetta al vestiario) tagliar vestimenti, che non siano di materia, colore, et forma communi, et conformi all'uso e buon stato della Religione, et particolarm.te aborrisca di tagliar il capilli. et vascapi ristretti in maniera che le monache non mostrino le carni, come si è riduto con scanda-

lo." ASPV, Archivio Segreto, Visite pastorali, Priuli, b. 1, S. Biagio e Cataldo, October 21, 1521.

11. Riccoboni, *Life and Death in a Venetian Convent*, 37.

12. ASV, S. Zaccaria, b. 94, "Libro di Vestiario."

13. Francesco Morosini left to his nun daughter Fiusina an annuity of twenty-five ducats; Ermolao Pisani in 1469 bequeathed one hundred ducats to the convent of Santa Giustina to fund an annuity of ten ducats for his daughter Gabriella, and finally, Zanetta Contarini left forty ducats to her three professed sisters that were free to invest them as they saw fit. Chojnacki, "Gender and the Early Renaissance State," 41.

14. For more on this, see chap. 4.

15. "Do not take pleasure in dresses or veils, and even less in your appearance; think instead about your behavior and none of them keep special seals, or a ring to be used as a seal . . . do not paint your hands or décolletage, do not accept gifts of jewels . . . abandon wordly and vain veils and fabrics." Levi Pisetzky, *Il costume*, 183.

16. ASPV, Archivio Segreto, Visite pastorali, Priuli, S. Rocco e Margherita, 1591, b. 1, fasc. 23.

17. ASPV, Archivio Segreto, Visite pastorali, Priuli, Santa Marta, May 16, 1594, c. 184v: "Le putte a spese sono di gran disturbo nel monastero . . . vano per il dormitorio e dove più le piace vagando senza alcuna regola et giocano alle carte la notte con grande scandolo."

18. To have an idea of the richness of the trousseau that the *putte* brought with them, see IRE, DER E 3, "Inventario biancheria per figlia a spese," Documents, no. 1, in the appendix. Unpublished.

19. ASPV, Archivio Segreto, Visite pastorali, Cornaro, Spirito Santo, undated, b. 6: "Che le figliole secolari in educazione non debbino andar vestite vanamente, e massime di seda, né di color proibito, con vane et artificiose conzature di testa con ornamenti d'oro o di gioie, né al collo, né alle braccia, et altre vanità da mondane . . . che portino i loro bavari serrati dinnanzi, in modo che non si vedino spettorute."

20. "Mandamus . . . aliquo modo puellas, et mulieres, ut vulgo dicitur Novitias ante earum desposationem, et transductionem vestimentis, et indumentis nuptialibus indutas in Parlatories, et locis Monasteriorum vestrorum admittere." Patriarch Francesco Contarini, November 25, 1554, BMC, Codice Cicogna 2570, cc. 164–65.

21. "Non si possino far Sposalitij in alcuna chiesa di essi Monasterij, né trattar de contrazzer Matrimonij nelli parlatori, over alle Finestre di Chiesa, né mostrar

le Novizie per contrazer essi Matrimoni." Patriarch Giovanni Trevisan, "Ordini Generali," November, 24, 1578, BMC, Codice Cicogna 2570, c. 243.

22. ASPV, Archivio Segreto, Visite pastorali, Vendramin, S. Servolo, September 10, 1610: "Le figliuole che saranno per tempo a spese fatte che sono novezze siano mandate a casa loro, et non si permetta, che stiano . . . vestite da maridate, né li mariti le venghino à visitare con scandalo alle finestre."

23. ASV, Provveditori sopra Monasteri, b. 270, fasc. 5, March 17, 1656: "è tanto scandalosa . . . andando vestita pomposamente."

24. Listeners. They were older and trusted nuns charged with the responsibility of checking the appropriateness of the conversations in the parlors. ASPV, Archivio Segreto, Visite pastorali, Priuli, S. Biagio e Cataldo, b. 1, October, 21, 1521. The only possible exceptions were for the visits of close relatives such as fathers, brothers, or female relations.

25. Patriarch Priuli stressed the need for the grilles of the parlor windows to be "double and thick" and closed by curtains. ASPV, Archivio Segreto, Visite pastorali, Priuli, S. Biagio e Cataldo, October, 21 1521, b. 1. On the contrary, exemplary of the relaxed atmosphere of the parlors is the famous painting by Giovanantonio Guardi representing the parlor of San Zaccaria (1740–50, Venice, Ca' Rezzonico) and the engraving by Petrus van der Aa depicting the parlor of San Lorenzo (from J. G. Graevious, *Thesaurus antiquitatum et historiarum Italiae*, Leiden, 1722, vol. 5, pt. 2, following p. 69, Venice, Biblioteca Nazionale Marciana).

26. ASPV, Archivio Segreto, Visite pastorali, Priuli, S. Biagio e Cataldo, October 21, 1521, b. 1: "In alcun tempo né da alcuna persona si mangi o bevi, si suoni, canti, balli, né si giouchi, né faccia alcun atto profano." For more on this, see Bartolomeo Cecchetti, *La Repubblica di Venezia e la corte di Roma nei rapporti della religione* (Venice, Prem. Stabilim. Tipog. Di P. Naratovich, 1874), 2:99–113.

27. Andrea Moschetti, "Il Gobbo di Rialto e le sue relazioni con Pasquino," *Archivio Veneto*, 1893, t.V, 39.

28. Poellnitz, *Memoires* (Liége, 1737), 675, cited in Molmenti, *La vita privata*, 2:375.

29. Cecchetti, *La Repubblica di Venezia*, doc. 11, 2:108.

30. ASPV, Archivio Segreto, Visite pastorali, Zane, S. Daniele, 1604: "Non è dubbio che dalli abiti modesti, et dalli ornamenti di vista troppo affettati, et a vere religiose indecenti nascono li pensieri vani che allontanano le sue Spose dall'Amore del Iddio, et dal suo Santi Servitio, oltre che questo esteriore è di gran scandalo a i secolari, at apporta molto negativo pregiudizio."

31. Tarabotti, *Paradiso monacale*, 9–10.

32. Medioli, *L'Inferno*, 61: "coprirsi d'habbiti lascivi."

33. Ibid.,75: "abbellite d'habbiti vani, onde si imprimon nell'animo desio poc'honesto d'imitarle et anche superarle nell'inventioni del vestire."

34. Ibid., 10: "monaca solo d'habiti e non di costume, questo pazzamente vano, quello vanamente pazzo."

35. Ibid., 85: "religiose nel nome, ma nel cor et opere mondane."

36. Cited in Molmenti, *La vita privata*, 2:450.

37. Sansovino, *Venetia città nobilissima*, 269.

38. See Documents, no. 1, in the appendix. IRE, DER E 3, Marsilia Acerbi.

39. ASPV, Archivio Segreto, Visite pastorali, S. Biagio e Cataldo, October 21, 1521: "Adoprino camise, et lenzuoli di lana conformi alla Regola, et Constitutioni, et in quilli non si permetta né sottigliezza, né cordelle, né camizzi, né lavori di sorte alcuna, né cassi duri, né manco teneri, cose tutte lontane dalla vita Monastica."

40. ASV, Senato, Terra, r. 35, c. 24, in Bistort, *Il Magistrato*, 141: "Oltre il danno della molta spesa che vi va nel farli" e pericolosa perché "succede che per il patir che fano le done nel portarli, spese fiate molte gravede hanno disperso et molte ancho sono morte et li figliuoli sono nasciuti debilitati, infermi et guasti et sturpiati, oltra quelli che per ciò sono stati partoriti morti."

41. Ibid.: "Cassi longhi con ponte, ma siano senza ponte, tutti tondi et uguali di lunghezza da ogni canto."

42. ASPV, Archivio Segreto, Visite pastorali, Trevisan, c. 54v, November 24, 1578: "Che (le monache) . . . non possano portar Vardacuori, scarpe, over scarpette alla Romana, Cassi duri, camise increspate, et lavorate alla condizione, et al modo delle mondane, fazzoletti lavorati, che si portano in mano, et altre vanità, come capelli biondi, rizzi, e bende stoccate."

43. ASPV, Archivio Segreto, Visite pastorali, Barbarigo, S. Gerolamo, 1714, b. 6: "Busti longhi, ponte, Relogio ma coperto et i Fazzoletti sopra le Spalle come usano le dame. . . . Il suplico, letta sta carta, subito sia lacerata."

44. Pietro Casola, *Viaggio a Gerusalemme*, ed. Anna Paoletti (Alessandria: Edizioni dell'Orso, 2001), 101: "Esse done veneziane se forzano quanto pono in publico, precipue le belle, de monstrar el pecto, dicto le mamelle e le spalle, in tanto che, più volte vedendole, me sono maravigliato che li panni non ghe siano cascati dal dosso." Vecellio too mentions necklines so wide "that the breasts are almost all visible" ("quasi si vedono tutte le mammelle"). Vecellio, *De gli habiti antichi*, 1598, cc. 94, 98.

45. New York, Metropolitan Museum of Art, Robert Lehman Collection, (1975.1.85).

46. Art connoisseur Michele Contarini described it along with its pendant representing Alvise Contarini as "un ritratto a l'incontro d'una monacha da San Segondo . . . di mano di Iacometto, opera perfettissima" ("a portrait of a nun of San Secondo. . . . It is by the hand of Jacometto, a most perfect work"). The two paintings then became part of the collection of Gabriele Vendramin, with the attribuition to Giovanni Bellini: "Un altro quadreto con una munega de man de Zuan Belin." See the manuscript by Marcantonio Michiel, BNM, Ms. It., XI, 67. For more on the painting, see *Art and Love in Renaissance Italy*, ed. Andrea Bayer, exhibition catalogue, New York, Metropolitan Museum of Art (New Haven, CT: Yale University Press, 2008), 265–67.

47. BMC, Codice Cicogna 2583, c. 134: "Il portar veli et bende di seta stoccate, con lasciarsi vedere li capelli, et ancor arricciati, et le carne scoperte con grande scandalo" ordina quindi che "si conservino le monache nella loro purità degli abiti antichi, con li capelli tagliati che non is vedano, con li veli non di seta, nè stoccati, et con le carni coperte dai vascapi et dai veli" ammonisce anche che "noi medesimi entreremo all' improvviso nei monasterii, et contra le inobedienti eseguiremo severa giustizia."

48. ASPV, Archivio Segreto, Visite pastorali, S. Giuseppe di Castello, 1692, fasc. no. 21, 9: "abuso reprensibile . . . d'alcune monache di portare Li Velli sopra le spalle assai ristretti, et in varie forme molto differenti che sembri agli occhi de le seculari, che le monache siano di nuovo diverso Habito, et Istituto; ordiniamo che tutte si riformino, et riportino li Velli in forma modesta, et religiosa, che coprono totalmente le spalle, et il Seno."

49. "La maschera scoperta di Filofilo Misoponero all'Ill.mo Signor Conte Andrea Barbozza, principe dell'Ill.ma Accademia degli Indomiti di Bologna." Biblioteca Universitaria di Genova, MS E .II.39, fols. 1–115, 232.

50. ASPV, Archivio Segreto, Visite pastorali, Cornaro, Spirito Santo, undated, b. 6: "ne manighe larghe, né abiti di sotto di seda, ò di color proibito." ASPV, Archivio Segreto, Visite pastorali, Vendramin, S. Andrea della Zirada, November 12, 1609.

51. ASPV, Archivio Segreto, Visite pastorali, S. Giuseppe di Castello, 1692, fasc. no. 21, 10: "Usandosi pure nel tempo dell'Estate da molte monache andar senza Maniche e con Habiti trasparenti con scandalo de' seculari, et vilipendio del Santo Habito, che hanno vestito; ordiniamo che le medeme debbano depore tanta vanità, et riformarsi."

52. See Patricia Fortini Brown, *Private Lives in Renaissance Venice: Art, Architecture, and the Family* (New Haven, CT: Yale University Press, 2004), 174–79.

53. ASPV, Archivio Segreto, Visite pastorali, Priuli, S. Biagio e Cataldo, 1593.

54. BNM, *Ordini generali per le monache*, Badoer, 1692, art. 25: "deformar l'abito di sopra, convertendolo con puntature vanissime in veste attillata."

55. Pietro Vendramin, pastoral letter, January, 4, 1619.

56. Arcangela Tarabotti, *Lettere familiari e di complimento*, ed. Meredith Ray and Lynn Westwater (Turin: Rosemberg & Sellier, 1995), lettera 200, 253: "all'Illustrissima signora Andriana Malipiero": "L'uso del nostro monasterio è questo, che subito quando le monache hanno reso l'anima la Creatore, si chiudono le celle e non s'aprono si che non è terminato il mese; si che Vostra Signoria Illustrissima non può rimaner servita delle maniche sin al primo maggio."

57. "Me pareva de veder tante monache de l'ordine de Santo Benedetto." Casola, *Viaggio a Gerusalemme*, 101.

58. Sperling, *Convents and the Body Politic*, 141.

59. ASPV, Archivio Segreto, Visite pastorali, Cornaro, S. Sepolcro, February 13, 1635: "non lasciate portar alle Monache in modo alcun . . . anco velli gialli, ò tinti di zafferano . . . d'oro o d'argento."

60. ASPV, Archivio Segreto, Visite pastorali, Cornaro, Convertite, November 20, 1635: "Sono del detto Proibiti i bavari, et veli di seta, overo stoccati, . . . gli anelli all'orecchie, et alle ditta, gli aghi d'oro, et d'argento." ASPV, Archivio Segreto, Visite pastorali, Cornaro, Spirito Santo, undated, b. 6: "Ordiniamo che le Monache non portino capelli lunghi, né fuori delle Tempie, né calzette di seta, ne veli di seda o bende con la colla né aghi d'oro o d'argento."

61. ASPV, Archivio Segreto, Visite pastorali, Trevisan , September, 23, 1579 c. 54v.

62. Cited in Molmenti, *Storia di Venezia*, 1:288. Further reading: Davanzo Poli, *I mestieri della moda*, 1:16; Vitali, *La moda*, 87–91. An appalled English visitor describes the *calcagnetti* as "dangerous instruments," often "curiously painted: some also I have seen fairly gilt: so unseemly a thing (in my opinion) that it is a pitty this foolish custom is not cleane banished and exterminated out of the citie." Thomas Coryat, *Coryat Crudities: Hastily Gobled up in Five Months of Travels* (London, 1611), cited in Fortini Brown, *Private Lives in Renaissance Venice*, 119.

63. Actually, on March 2, 1430, the Maggior Consiglio decided that the calcagnetti could not be higher than 10 cm. See Vitali, *La moda*, 91.

64. Grevembroch, *Gli Abiti*, 1:136: "An old man proposed to order the women to wear the *calcagnetti* and rich and heavy dresses because, if it had been easy for them to walk, they would have never grown tired of going about the city."

65. "La donna deve per ogni rispetto andare innalzata dalle ordinarie bassezze." Arcangela Tarabotti, *Antisatira in risposta al "Lusso donnesco" satira menippea del Sig. Francesco Buoninsegni* (Siena: 1660), 143.

66. ASPV, Archivio Segreto, Visite pastorali, Cornaro, Spirito Santo, undated, b. 6.

67. Zanette, *Suor Arcangela*, 180.

68. ASPV, Archivio Segreto, Visite pastorali, Priuli, S. Iseppo, 1595, cc. 514–16.

69. Toldo Costantini, *Del giudicio estremo: Poema sacro* (Padua: Sardi, 1651), canto 14, str. 65.

70. Bartolomeo Cecchetti, *La vita dei Veneziani nel 1300, Le vesti* (Venezia: Tipografia Emiliana, 1885–86), 79–80.

71. ASPV, Archivio Segreto, Visite pastorali, Convertite, November 20, 1635: "Sono del detto Proibiti i bavari, et veli di seta, overo stoccati, . . . gli anelli all'orecchie, et alle ditta, gli aghi d'oro, et d'argento. Le calzette di seda di tutte le sorte et altre calzette di colore aperto e chiaro. Se ben fossero di lana ogni sorte di vestito di sotto, poste di seta, strenghe di seta, scarpe si deve essere seta e oro . . . seda, oro, ò colore che sia contrario alle Regole, et allo stato di Monaca."

72. See BNM, Badoer, *Ordini generali per le monache*, 9, 10, 11, 12.

73. ASPV, Archivio Segreto, Visite pastorali, Trevisan, 1578, c. 50v: "Che . . . non possino portar . . . fazzoletti lavorati che si portano in mano, et altre vanità."

74. See BNM, Badoer, *Ordini generali per le monache*, 9, 10, 11, 12.

75. ASPV, Archivio Segreto, Visite pastorali, Trevisan, 1578, c. 50v: "Che nelle vostre Celle non possiate tenir Tapedi, spaliere, panni rossi, o d'altri colori attorno li muri, letti sontuosi et superbi con sponzali, coltri di seda, o copertori lavorati et ricamati, et massimamente li lenzuoli o cussini, et cussinelli, ne . . . da letto."

76. ASPV, Archivio Segreto, Visite pastorali, Priuli, S. Biagio e Cataldo, 1521, cap. XII: "Si avertisca nel far le casse alle Monache che siano tutte robbe utili, et per usi necessarij di esse Monache, lasciando in tutto la vanità degli ornamenti delle celle."

77. Giuseppe Tassini, *Feste, spettacoli, divertimenti e piaceri degli antichi Veneziani* (Venezia : Filippi, 1971), 19–20.

78. Ibid.: "Sotto pena à che portasse una ò più delle cose sudette, ò altra simile . . . stasse rinchiusa per mese, et dopo essere priva per due ani di voce attiva, et passiva, et dei Parlatori."

79. BMC, Codice Cicogna 2583, parte II, c. 23; BMC, Codice Cicogna 2570, c. 288.

80. BNM, Badoer, *Ordini generali per le monache*, 40: "obligando li confessori tutti . . . a non ammettere le ostinate a' Santissimi Sagramenti."

81. Sanudo, *Diarii*, 39:345, August 25, 1525: When Patriarch Querini decide to incarcerate two unlawfully dressed nuns of La Celestia, he was stopped by the violent protest of all of the other nuns: "tutte le altre comenzono a cridar et metersi a la porta sichè non sono lassate meter."

82. Laven, *Virgins of Venice*, 57–63.

83. Isabella Campagnol, "Costume in the Italian Renaissance," in *Greenwood Encyclopedia of Clothing through World History*, 3 vols. (Westport, CT: Greenwood Publishers, 2007), 2:21.

84. Further reading: "Canonichesse secolari," in *Dizionario degli Istituti di Perfezione* (Milan: Paoline, 1975), II, cols. 41–45; Maria Pia Pedani, "Monasteri di agostiniane a Venezia," *Archivio Veneto* 125 (1985): 35–78.

85. Lowe, *Nuns' Chronicles*, 148.

86. Vincenzo Maria Coronelli, *Ordinum religiosorum in ecclesia militanti catalogus, eorumque indumenta, iconibus expressa, auctus, nec non moderatus posteriori hac editione, anni 1707 . . . a p. generali Coronelli consecratus . . .* (Venice: 1707), XXXII. See also Flaminio Corner, *Notizie storiche delle chiese e monasteri di Venezia e Torcello*, anastatic reprint (Bologna: Forni, 1997), 97: "Smodata libertà delle monache, che tali solo di nome e di vestito vivevano, senza legame de' voti, e senz'obbligo di clausura: onde uscir a loro agio potevano e contrar anche sponsali"; *La sostanza dell'effimero: Gli abiti degli Ordini religiosi in Occidente*, exhibition catalogue, ed. Giancarlo Rocca (Rome: Edizioni Paoline, 2000), 108, 255–58.

87. Sanudo, *De origine*, 62.

88. Compare with the dress of the canonesses of Mons in Coronelli, *Ordinum religiosorum*, XXX. Further reading in *La sostanza dell'effimero*, 256–57.

89. Casola, *Viaggio a Gerusalemme*, 93.

90. ASV, S. Daniele, b. 12, fol. 6: "per le muneghe venero in S. Daniel."

91. From which were born at least five illegitimate children. For more on this, see Guido Ruggeri, *The Boundaries of Eros: Sex Crimes and Sexuality in Renaissance Venice* (New York: Oxford University Press, 1985), 78.

92. Corner, *Notizie storiche*, 98.

93. "Se si imitasse, anco in altri Monasteri, ove l'uguaglianza all'abito delle Nobili Coriste somministra alle Sorelle occasione di fasto e ne segnano poscia dissensioni e inquietezza."

94. Francesca Zorzi died in 1428. After the destruction of the monastery, between 1844 and 1869, the tomb slab, made of Istrian stone, was moved to its present location in the courtyard of the Seminario Patriarcale, Venice.

95. For more on this, see Emanuele Antonio Cicogna, *Delle inscrizioni veneziane* (Bologna: Forni, 1969), 5:91.

96. Now in Berlin, Gemaldegalerie Berlino. See Alvise Zorzi, *Venezia scomparsa* (Milan: Electa), 1984, 245–47.

97. Now in the Seminario Patriarcale, Venice. See Lowe, *Nuns' Chronicles*, 380.

98. Filippo Bonanni, *Catalogo degli ordini religiosi della chiesa militante espressi con imagini, e spiegati con una breue narrazione, offerto alla santita di n.s. Clemente 11. dal p. Filippo Bonanni della compagnia di Gesù*, 3 vols. (Rome: nella stamperia di Antonio de' Rossi nella strada del Sem. Romano).

99. Coronelli, *Ordinum religiosorum*.

100. Pierre Hélyot, *Storia degli ordini monastici, religiosi, e militari, e delle congregazioni secolari dell'uno, e l'altro sesso, fino al presente istituite, con le vite de' loro fondatori, e riformatori*, 8 vols. (Lucca: per Giuseppe Salani e Vincenzo Giuntini, 1737–39), t. III, p. 50, fig. II.

101. "E perchè io intendeva una grande fama de alcuni monastery de done, io andai pure acompagnato a visitarne qualche uno, precipue el monastero de santo Zacharia. Sono asai done de zovene e de vegie, se lassana volentera vedere. . . . Se dice sono molto riche e non si fano molto cura de esser vedute." Casola, *Viaggio a Gerusalemme*, 93.

102. Primhak, "Benedictine Communities," 92.

103. "Fra tutti i monisteri di donne monache, quello di San Zaccaria è nobilis. per diverse sue qualità. Tra queste le reliquie, come il panno di Santa Maria , ò vero de vestimenti del Salvatore." Sansovino, *Venetia città nobilissima*, 26.

104. Further reading: Giustina Renier Michiel, *Origine delle feste veneziane* (Milano: Editori Annali Universali delle Scienze e dell'Industria, 1859), 91; Piero Pazzi, *Il corno ducale o sia contributi alla conoscenza della Corona Ducale di Venezia volgarmente chiamata Corno* (Treviso: Trivellari, 1996), 10.

105. ASPV, Archivio Segreto, Visite pastorali, Priuli, b. 1, S. Biagio e Cataldo, October 21, 1521: "Nuns cannot be seen by anyone" ("le Monache non possono essere vedute da alcuno").

106. They taught embroidery, Latin, and Greek to Elena, daughter of the famous humanist Pietro Bembo. Pedani Maria Pia, "L'osservanza imposta: I monasteri conventuali femminili a Venenzia nei primi anni del Cinquecento," *Archivio Venento*, ser. 5, vol. 144 (1995), p. 123 (113–26).

107. ASR, Congregazioni religiose femminili 4226/4 (miscellanea), Memoria del monasterio di san Zaccaria, fol. 1v.

108. Pizzichi, *Viaggio per l'alta Italia*, 3:453.

109. "Però debbano le Monache . . . col capo velato in maniera che niente si veda dei capelli. . . . Li velli delle spalle siano tanto copiosi et ampli che coprano tutta la carne, siano sottili ma non trasparenti." ASPV, Archivio Segreto, Visite pastorali, Vendramin, S. Zaccaria, October 19, 1609.

110. Pierre Hélyot, *Storia degli ordini monastici*, t. V, p. 314, fig. II.

111. Very large sleeves. See Vitali, *La moda*, 180.

112. Antonio Zonca, *Doge's Easter Visit to San Zaccaria*, 1690 ca, Venice, Church of San Zaccaria.

113. See Documents, nos. 4 and 5, in the appendix.

114. Hélyot, *Storia degli ordini monastici*, t. V, p. 314, fig. I.

115. BNM, Badoer, *Ordini generali per le monache*, 11, 12, 13.

116. 1740–50, Venice, Ca' Rezzonico, Museo del Settecento Veneziano.

117. "Vestono leggiadrissimamente, con abito bianco, come alla franzese, il busto di bisso a piegoline, e le professe trina nera larga tre dita sulla costura di esso; velo piccolo cinge loro la fronte, sotto il quale escono i capelli arricciati e lindamente accomodati, seno mezzo scoperto, e tutto insieme abito più da ninfe che da monache." Federico Pizzichi, "Viaggio per l'alta Italia del Serenissimo principe di Toscana, poi granduca Cosimo" (Florence, 1828), in Fabio Mutinelli, *Storia arcana ed aneddotica d'Italia raccontata dai Veneti ambasciatori* (Venice: Pietro Naratovich, 1858), 3:454.

118. Enilio Zanette, *Suor Arcangela: Monaca del seicento veneziano* (Venice-Rome: Istituto per la collaborazione culturale, 1960), 141.

119. ASV, "Nunziatura a Venezia del Conte Scipione Pannocchieschi d'Elci," b. 7, vol. 19, March 3, 1652.

120. "L'abito da esse adottato è di Saja nera, non in forma di tonaca, ma adattata alla vita di ciascuna; in capo usano un velo bianco, il quale non cuopre affatto le culture de' capelli, e steso dal capo si ravvolge intorno al collo." Bonanni, *Catalogo degli ordini religiosi*, no. 19.

121. "Quando però in choro recitano l'Offizio Divino, ò si accostano all'altare per comunicarsi, portano una cocolla con maniche larghe, e con strascino steso per terra, che lor concilia un maestoso decoro , e devozione. Al capo aggiungono un velo nero trasparente, che pende libero oltre la cintura, conforme si vedere espresso nella immagine." Bonanni, *Catalogo degli ordini religiosi*, no. 19.

122. The document detailing her dowry is preserved in ASV, S. Lorenzo, b. 13.

123. Musatti, *La donna in Venezia*, 38. See also Fulin, *Studi nell'Archivio degli Inquisitori di Stato* (Venice: Visentini, 1868), 431 sseg.

124. Fulin, *Studi*, 175.

125. Federigo Luigini, *Il libro della bella donna*, cited in Isabella Campagnol, "Costume in the Italian Renaissance," 2:34.

126. Casola, *Viaggio a Gerusalemme*, 101.

127. Giovanventura Rossetti, *Notandissimi secreti de l'Arte profumatoria* (Venice: F. Rampazzetto, 1560).

128. Isabella Cortese, *I Secreti* (Venice: G. Fornetti, 1584).

129. In the *Ornamenti delle donne*, published by Marinello in 1569, are given

no less than twenty-six recipes to dye hair different shades, from red to ash-blonde. See Isabella Campagnol, "Costume in the Italian Renaissance," 2:35.

130. "In altana convien far solana a sbiancarse la testa con una sponzetta ligata a la cima di un fuso e colorir de liscia forte, con mille armati dentro, lume di feccia, scorze di arancia, cenere, scorze de ovo e mile altre vanità" ("in the altana they bleach their hair with a sponge secured to a small stick and mixing thousands of ingredients such as wine dregs, orange peels, ashes, egg shells and many other vain things"). Giuseppe Passi, *I donneschi difetti* (Venezia: Somasco, 1605), 280.

131. Vecellio, *De gli habiti antichi*, 107v.

132. See Vitali, *La moda*, 346. See also Documents, no. 2, in the appendix.

133. A topless hat that protected their fair skin from the sun. See Vitali, *La moda*, 357.

134. Medioli, *Inferno monacale*, 43.

135. ASPV, Archivio Segreto, Visite pastorali, Miscellaneous, b. 1, S. Biagio e Cataldo, October 21, 1521: "Si tosino almeno una volta il mese l'inverno , et ogni quindici giorni l'estate, guardandosi di non far comparire neanco sotto le bende capilli alti né rizzi, perché saranno da noi securamente castigate."

136. ASPV, Archivio Segreto, Visite pastorali, Miscellaneous, fasc. 23, S. Rocco e Margherita, 1591: "et li capilli tagliati bassi conforme all'uso delle buone religiose."

137. ASPV, Archivio Segreto, Visite pastorali, b. 1. Patriarch Matteo Zane ordered them to cover their temples: "coprino li capelli delle tempie," S. Daniele, 1604. Years later, Patriarch Federico Cornaro needed to repeat the recommendation not to allow the nuns to wear their hair long: "non lasciate portar alle Monache in modo alcun i capilli longhi et scoperti," S. Sepolcro, February 13, 1635, and Convertite, November 20: "Che niuna Monaca porti i capelli lunghi, ne scoperti troppo fuori delle tempie."

138. G. Nicoletti, *Intorno alla acconciatura del capo o calzature delle donne veneziane, sec. XV e XVI, per nozze Allegri* (Venezia: G. Cecchini, 1884), 21: "1513, Adi XIII April in Pregadi si decide che le donne de questa città, che se conzano i capelli in fongo, et i capelli suso le spalle . . . non possano conzarse la testa come al presente se fano, ma ben possano conzarse con le scuffie de velo de seda"; cited in Davanzo Poli, *Abiti antichi*, 61. Vitali remembers that the origin of this forbidden hairstyle was to be found in the fight of Venetian women, and courtesans particularly, against sodomy. Further reading: Vitali, *La moda*, 193. "Dishonest women, in order to solicit men, adopted a masculine look and dress and partially hid their face with the hair knotted in a *fongo*, as this hairstyle was called"; Molmenti, *Storia di Venezia*, 2:457.

139. Casola, *Viaggio a Gerusalemme*, 101.

140. BMC, Codice Cicogna 2570, 205, January 4, 1619.

141. See images 2.005, 3.2.3–003, 3.2.3–004.

142. "Due ricci che fanno la forma d' una meza luna, con le punte o corna (che questo nome anchora hanno sortito)" rivolte all'insù, mantenuti in forma "con draganti." Passi, *I donneschi difetti*, 257. Vecellio describes them as "ricchi che fanno la forma d' una mezza luna con le punte ò corna," *De gli habiti antichi*, c. 113v. The bizarre haistyle, disapproved because visually evocative of the horns of the devil, was nevertheless defined by Modesta Pozzo de' Zorzi (Moderata Fonte) as "nulla più di un costume, una moda e un passatempo, e, quando è fatta con saggezza . . . apporta grazia al volto" ("nothing more than a fashion, a passing fancy, and, when well done . . . it donates grace to the face"). *Il merito delle donne ove chiaramente si scopre quanto siano elle degne e più perfette de gli uomini*, ed. Adriana Chemello (Venice: Eidos, 1988), 167.

143. ASPV, Archivio Segreto, Visite pastorali, Vendramin, S. Daniele, 1609.

144. ASPV, Archivio Segreto, Visite pastorali, Vendramin, S. Girolamo, 1610.

145. Alexandre-Toussaint Limojon de Saint-Didier, *De la ville et la République de Venise* (Paris: Claude Barbin, 1680), cited in Zanette, *Suor Arcangela*, 49.

146. "Andarono a la Celestia perché quelle monache Conventuali molto disoneste portano ì caveli longi etc. E . . . loro visto una fia . . . Tagiapiera con drezuole in testa di cavelli, il Patriarca l'aferò e di soa man li taiò i cavelli." Sanudo, *Diarii*, 39:345.

147. ASPV, Archivio Segreto, Visite pastorali, b. 1, S. Zaccaria, 1596, fol. 578r.

148. ASPV, Archivio Segreto, Visite pastorali, Trevisan, c. 54v.

149. See Paschini, *I monasteri femminili*, 57.

150. ASPV, Archivio Segreto, Visite pastorali, Tiepolo, fasc. 9, September, 23, 1620: "Porta zuffo, si pella le ceglie, tien acqua da viso, . . . et non vuol obbedire . . . Porta odori, e muschi."

151. ASPV, Archivio Segreto, Visite pastorali, Cornaro, S. Alvise, August 24, 1635.

152. Zanette, *Suor Arcangela*, 50.

153. ASPV, Archivio Segreto, Visite pastorali, Barbarigo, Ss. Rocco e Margherita, b. 6.

154. ASPV, Archivio Segreto, Visite pastorali, Barbarigo, b. 6: "Portano delle vanità, cascade, e Zoccoli, portano della polvere di Cipro sopra li Capelli."

155. ASPV, Archivio Segreto, Visite pastorali, Priuli, January 12, 1590: "Niuna adisca di ragionar, ne trattar con lei, ne darli, ne ricever da lei cosa alcuna, eccetto quelle che saranno deputate da noi sotto pena di scomunica . . . far la cerca nella sua cella, et vi leviate coltelli, et ogni altro in strumento con quale lei si potesse offender."

156. BMC, Codice Cicogna 2570, c. 368.

157. ASPV, Archivio Segreto, Visite pastorali, Barbarigo, Convertite della Giudecca, April 7, 1717, c. 130v.

158. ASV, Provveditori sopra Monasteri, b. 265, 1614, S. Zaccaria, f. 5v.

159. "Non poteva esser altra monaca travestita." ASPV, *Torcellania Criminalia Monialum*, b. 23, fasc. S. Vito di Burano, March 4, 1608, c. 16r.

160. ASPV, Torcellania Criminalia Monialum, b. 23, fasc. S. Vito di Burano.

161. De Saint-Didier, *De la ville et la Republique de Venise*, 317, affirms having seen nuns dressed as men going around the parlors wearing feathered hats and bowing with good grace.

162. ASPV, *Torcellania Criminialia Monialium*, b. 23, fasc. S. Mauro di Burano, cc. 39r–49v, January 24, 1652.

163. Ibid.

164. See Pietro Bertelli, *Courtesan and Blind Cupid* (flap print with liftable skirt), ca. 1588, New York, Metropolitan Museum of Art, 55.503.30, in Andrea Bayer, ed., *Art and Love in Renaissance Venice* (New Haven, CT: Yale University Press, 2008), 210–11.

165. "Cercano di acquistar credito col mezzo della finta onesta . . . non potendo stare serrate et coperte con la cappa che portano, et non potendo d'altra parte essere vedute, sono finalmente sforzate a scoprirsi alquanto, et è perciò impossibile ch'elle non sieno conosciute qualche gesto." Vecellio, *De gli habiti antichi*, 106v–107r.

166. Henry Robert Morland, London, 1730?–1797. The painting is preserved in the collections of the Temple Newsam House, Leeds, UK. Morland is first mentioned as a painter in 1754. Starting in 1760 he began exhibiting works in crayon and oil and, occasionally, engravings, specializing particularly in domestic scenes influenced by both Dutch genre paintings and French works of art, such as *A Laundry Maid Ironing* (exhibited 1768, London, Tate Gallery).

167. BMC, Codice Cicogna 2570, 182–83, January 15, 1593: "We shall tolerate the plays as long as they are stories from the Holy Scriptures, or from the lives of the Saints; and no nun may presume to wear secular dress, whether male or female, nor it is permissible to wear masks or beards." See also Grimani, *Constitutioni*, 45v.

168. "Vestono da huomeni, per far dimostrazioni." ASPV, Archivio Segreto, Visite pastorali, Priuli, 1592–96, Miracoli, fol. 369r.

169. "Non induetur mulier veste virili, nec vir utetur veste feminea: abominabilis enim apud Deum est qui facit haec."

170. "Si serrano dentro [il parlatorio piccolo] persone à parlar con le monache à hore proibite, facendo portare avanti, e indietro tutto il giorno drappi, et altre

robbe per recitar tragedie, overo dimostrazioni con gran confusione nel monasterio e gran scandalo fuori." ASPV, Archivio Segreto, Visite pastorali, Priuli, S. Sepolcro, 1595, fol. 398v.

171. "Io vorrei che le vedessi Alamanno. Elle si veston da uomo con quelle calze tirate, con la brachetta, e con ogni cosa, ch'elle paion proprio soldati." Giovan Battista Gelli, *La sporta*, act. III, sc. 4, in *Opere*, ed. Amelia Corona Alesina (Naples: Fulvio Rossi, 1970–72).

172. "Non deponete i suoi abiti ordinarij, . . . né mettersi maschera sopra il volto, perché alle monache questo è proibito sotto pena di peccato mortale." BMC, Codice Cicogna 2583, c. 127v.

173. For more on this, see Andrea Moschetti, "Il Gobbo di Rialto e le sue relazioni con Pasquino," *Archivio Veneto*, 1893, t. V, 5–93.

174. Giuseppe Tassini, *Curiosità veneziane* (Venice: Filippi, 1970), 351.

175. Some violations to the rules regarding the visits to the parlors are cited in Cecchetti, *La Repubblica di Venezia*, vol. 2, doc. 11, "Saggio di statistica di alcuni processi per malcostume, nei conventi di Venezia e dello Stato Veneto, sec. XVII e XVIII," 108:

> February 8, 1682: Some masqueraders are seen in the parlor of the monastery of San Sepolcro.
>
> February 26, 1682: Few masqueraders had lunch in the parlor of the monastery of S. Antonio di Torcello with the nuns participating from the other side of the grille.
>
> February 9, 1684: Two men dressed as women were seen in a chapel of the church of the convent of the monastery of Ss. Sepolcro.
>
> February 1658: In the monastery of S. Caterina and Corpus Domini in Venezia masqueraders were seen at night-time in the parlor.

176. "In tempo di carnevale molte Suore si mettono la maschera e i loro innamorati con la gondola vengono a pigliarle e poi a piedi vanno per tutta la città a festini e tornano quando li pare." Luciano Menetto and Giuseppe Zennaro, *Storia del malcostume a Venezia nei secoli XV e XVI* (Abano Terme: Piovan, 1987), 57.

177. Because of this, *converse* often needed to supplement their income, for instance doing laundry for lay men and women, an activity forbidden by patriarchal dispositions. See ASPV, Archivio Segreto, Visite pastorali, Barbarigo, S. Sepolcro, December 28, 1716.

178. ASPV, Archivio Segreto, Visite pastorali, Lorenzo Priuli, S. Biagio e Cataldo, October 21, 1521: "Cap.XIJJ Delle Converse: Sono introdotte le Converse nei Monasterij per aggiutar il commune à far quelle cose, alle quali non si possono

applicare le Monache in officio per l'obligo grande che hanno di attender al choro."

179. ASPV, Archivio Segreto, Visite pastorali, Morosini, January 17 1651, b. 6: "con modesta, non con lascivia."

180. ASPV, Archivio Segreto, Visite pastorali, Zane, S. Daniele, 1604: "Li vestimenti dovranno essere per le monache semplicemente di scotto, et per le converse di rascia o di bottana. Li capelli si porteranno sempre bassi, particolarmente sopra la fronte, et le tempie." Both nuns and converse were also forbidden to wear "cassi duri, tanto fatti per mano di monache, quanto da altri, ma solamente . . . di tella semplice."

181. ASV, Provveditori sopra Monasteri, b. 347, fasc. 17, fol. 3v: "E mi no savezo dir cosa altra perchè non vado mai nelli parlatorij, vado per la città come occorre, et quando vengo à casa, vado nella mia cela."

182. Sanudo, *Diarii*, VIII, cols. 454–56, June 29, 1509: "In dicti monasterij di monache conventual tengono fantesche de suo servitio in abito seculare, le qual escono et intrano nei monasteri a loro beneplacito, operando molti mali effeci con le sue pratiche e mezzanità . . . debino le predecte monache, vogliando aver persone a li loro servitii, tegnir converse in abito monasticho, justa la costituttion delle loro regule, le qual uscir debano dei moansterij con lo abito religioso."

183. "Contiene il circuito di Venezia circa quaranta Monasterj di Donnne. . . . Come che nell'interno della Clausura vengono esse pefettamente servire dalle loro Converse, così rendesi indispensabile al di fuori, per le quotidiane provvigioni, e corrispondenza, valersi di certe Donne approvate. Quantunque sia pesante questo impiego, si rinvenne sempre chi lo esercitò pazientemente, perche non senza congruo interesse. Sono mandate per un sol'uovo alla Pasina, e nello stesso tempo hanno debito di portarne un'altro a San Giobbe; ne qui sta il temine dell'incombenza, poiche ritornate al Parlatorio, ritrovano l'incarico di visitare Parenti infermi a S. Giacomo dall'Orio, indi a Castello. Ad altre Religiose non le basta far caminare la loro Donna sino ai Tolentini, mà la obligano, con una Cesta, pervenire anche a S.S. Apostoli alla Casa, o del Confessore, o del Medico, o del Cappellano. Girata in simile guisa tutta la Città (che da esse stimasi grande, quanto il recinto del loro Convento) e forse troppo tardi restituendosi coloro a recare le risposte, ne conseguiscono rimproveri." Grevembroch, *Gli abiti*, 3: 67, 103.

184. Grevembroch, *Gli abiti*, 2:57, 58; 3:71: "L'Abito delle Religiose greche fu una veste di sotto in luogo di Tonica di panno nero, o rovano, e di sopra un Manto nero, posto sopra il Capo che quasi scendeva in terra. Aveano un Bavaro, o

Soggolo, come le Monache Latine, e portavano in mano divotamente le Corone. Altre simili Donne, ch'erano state Mogli di Preti, o Papassi, e che non si potevano in stato vedovile più maritare, stante il divieto nazionale, e regolare, coprivano la Testa con un Mantello fino a mezza Gamba."

185. Grevembroch, *Gli abiti*, 2:56.

186. Further reading on this and on other Venetian charitable institutions: Bernard Aikema and Dulcia Meijers, "Il Soccorso: Chiesa e ospedale di Santa Maria Assunta," in *Nel regno dei poveri: Arte e storia dei grandi ospedali veneziani in età moderna, 1474-1797*, ed. Aikema and Meijers (Venice: IRE, 1989), 241-48.

187. Brian Pullan, "La nuova filantropia nella Venezia cinquecentesca," in *Nel regno dei poveri: Arte e storia dei grandi ospedali veneziani in età moderna, 1474-1797*, ed. Bernard Aikema and Dulcia Meijers (Venice: IRE, 1989), 19-33.

188. Regarding the involvement of Veronica Franco in the Soccorso, see IRE, SOC G 1, t. primo, c. 2. In the archive of the Soccorso is a petition to the Venetian Senate written by Franco on behalf of the Soccorso; however, on the edge of the letter is the annotation "it was not presented."

189. Bernard Aikema and Dulcia Meijers, "Il Soccorso: Chiesa e ospedale di Santa Maria Assunta," in *Nel regno dei poveri*, 241.

190. Sansovino, *Venetia*, 92: "Si fabbricò il monistero delle Convertite, accioche come le Vergini consecrate al servitio di Dio hanno ricetto per conservarsi, così le peccatrici pentite, habiano parimenti dove salvarsi tutto da i pecati. Quivi dimorando assai gran numero di donne & tutte belissime (perciohe non vi si accetano se non quelle cha hanno soma beltà, accioche pentendosi non ricaggino ne peccati per la forma loro attrattiva de gli altrui deisderj si essercitano con ordine mirabile in diversi artifici."

191. The painting was certainly completed before 1597, the year in which are registered some payments to the artist. See Aikema and Meijers, "Il Soccorso," in *Nel regno dei poveri*, 245.

192. See Silvia Lunardon, "Il gioco dell'amore. Le cortigiane di Venezia dal trecento al Settecento," Catalogo della mostra. Venezia, Casinò Municipale Ca' Vendramin Calergi, 2 febbraio–16 aprile 1990 (Berenice, Milano, 1990), 180.

193. "The diffusion of the theme of the Magdalene in Renaissance and Baroque paintings can be read as a reminder of immorality, a meaning highlighted by the jewels that are by her abandoned to follow a life of penance, mortification, and sanctity." Zuffi, *Dettagli di stile*, 170.

194. See Aikema and Meijers, "Le Penitenti. Chiesa e ospedale di Santa Maria," in *Nel regno dei poveri*, 273-80.

195. Anonymous Venetian painter, eighteenth century, Venice, IRE.

196. Compare with Jacopo Tintoretto's painting *Portrait of a Lady in Mourning*, 1550–1594, Dresden, Gemaldegalerie Alte Meister, published in Andrea Bayer, ed., *Art and Love in Renaissance Italy*, 284–85.

197. Vecellio, *De gli habiti antichi*, c. 134v. Also compare with Grevembroch, *Gli abiti*, 1:144–45.

198. See Grevembroch, *Gli abiti*, 1:129, 138, 140, 141.

199. Riccoboni, *Life and Death*, 72.

200. "In Venezia, ed altrove evvi una certe specie di Donne la maggior parte Vedove, le quali ritirate dal Mondo, o per devozione, o per necessità si riducono in certi luoghi a ciò deputati, e così vivono di limosine, e di qualche onesto esercizio, stando soggette a capi di quelle Religioni, delle quali vestono l'Abito. Queste perché non osservano la strettezza de Chiostri non possono chiamarsi Monache, ma Pizzocchere, le quali sono di tante differenze, di quante sono le Religioni de Frati Mendicanti, a cui esse si conformano almeno ne colori. Si mantengono caste, e libere da Mariti sotto ubbidienza, osservando alcune regole, ed ordini de suoi maggiori, onde possono servire a Dio, visitando comodamente Infermi, vestendo, ed accompagnando Morti alle Sepolture, e frequentando altre opere pie." Grevembroch, *Gli abiti*, II, no. 44, "Pizzocchere." "Involto il Mondo in grandi travagli non possono, che deplorarsi da buone Persone le calamità. Alcune Donne, che per distinta pietà vi tengono tanto d'interesse, risentendo vivamente le afflizioni proprie, o altrui, s'impegnano con ogni premura, e con continue orazioni ad implorare dal Cielo providenza, o guarigione. Come però prevale il buon'esempio, fù istituito anche in remoti tempi un Abito quasi religioso, composto e divoto, del quale vestitesi queste tali, osservano con esattezza, e li dogmi, e li Riti Cristiani, non che la ufficiatura, e le regolari Costituzioni, impetrando incessantemente le ineffabili beneficenze, e l'estensioni delle grazie, che solo possono procedere dalla Misericordia Divina." Grevembroch, *Gli abiti*, 2:43.

201. "Bizzoche," in *Dizionario degli Istituti di Perfezione*, vol. 1, cols. 1476–77.

202. Secluded or hermits. Some cells used by the *pizzocchere* or *romite* are still visible in the churches of San Giovanni Evangelista, S. Maurizio, S. Agnese, S. Samuele, S. Margherita, Ss. Apostoli, S. Angelo. Mutinelli, *Del costume veneziano*, 38. The *pizzocchere* too occasionally received visits from the patriarch: on July 22, 1593, Lorenzo Priuli visited the twenty-seven *pizzocchere* belonging to the tertiary order of the Franciscans in the Angelo Raffael neighborhood (ASPV, Archivio Segreto, Visite pastorali, Priuli).

203. Venice, Gallerie dell'Accademia. The *pizzocchera* is portrayed in the upper left side.

204. For more on this, see Boerio, *Dizionario*, ad vocem; Vitali, *La moda*, 263–67.

205. Vecellio, *De gli habiti antichi*, 115r: "Sono in Venetia tante differenze di pizzocchere quante sono le religioni de' frati mendicanti."

206. The Ospizio dei Crociferi was founded in 1177, but the paintings were not executed until the end of the sixteenth century, between 1582 and 1592. Stefania Mason Rinaldi, "Jacopo Palma il Giovane e la decorazione dell'Oratorio dei Crociferi," in *Hospitale S. Marieae Cruciferorum*, ed. Silvia Lunardon (Venice: IRE, 1984), 87–148. Further reading: Stefania Mason Rinaldi, *Jacopo Palma il Giovane: Opera completa* (Milan: Electa, 1984).

207. Dark brown, although Boerio describes it as "grayish, a colour similar to ashgray." *Dizionario*, ad vocem. See also Vitali, *La moda*, 455.

208. Jacopo Palma il Giovane, *Pasquale Cicogna assiste alla messa*, 1586–87, Venice, Ospedale dei Crociferi. As described by Carlo Ridolfi, the "poor women . . . are so well depicted that they seem alive." *Delle Maraviglie dell'arte: Ovvero le vite degli illustri pittori veneti e dello stato* (Venice: G. B. Sgava, 1648), 532–33.

209. Vecellio, *Orfanelle delli spedali*, 115v–116r; Grevembroch, *Gli abiti*, 2:46.

210. Further info on the textile-related economic activities in the convents and charitable institutions is in chap. 4: "Textiles, Embroideries, and Laces in the Convent."

211. Grevembroch, *Gli abiti*, 2:45: "Alcune Orfane Fanciullette, che per lo più non hanno Persone congiunte vengono condotte a gli Ospedali della Carità de fedeli, al fine di essere ben custodite, e civilmente allevate . . . Quanto all'Abito, quelle dello Spedale dell'Incurabili lo hanno di color turchino, quelle di S.S. Gio. e Paolo di bianco, quelle della Pietà di rosso, e quelle de Mendicanti di nero." 46: "S.S. Gio. e Paolo Vestono di bianco, e portavano il grembiale fuori di casa . . . hanno un Velo bianco in Capo, che cade dalle Spalle, e sopra di esso sostengono un cappello di paglia o di panno nero in sporgenza della pioggia. . . . Abito nero , ed il Velo pendente sul volto in occasione di feste di santi o per accompagnare i morti al sepolcro."

Chapter 4

1. "Sfugga ogni una l'otio come cosa pestilentissima." ASPV, Archivio Segreto, Visite pastorali, Priuli, S. Biagio e Cataldo, October 21, 1521, cap. XI "Degl'habiti, vita, et costumi dele Monache."

2. "Erano simili monasterij de Venetia conventuali pubblicamente noti a tutti li forasteri che venivano a Venetia per sentire et aldire le virtude loro in l'arte musica ed etiam in vedere cose bellissime cum lo ago e la mano facte." Giuliani, *Genesi e primo secolo*, 12.

3. "Monache formosissime, delichatissime et piene de ogni virtude . . . quello che facevanno cum le manno sue et cum lo ago et azze, chosse veramente che pictori cum loro penello non lo sapevanno fare." Cited in Molmenti, *Storia di Venezia*, 2:459.

4. ASPV, Archivio Segreto, Visite pastorali, Priuli, S. Servolo, July 4, 1597, c. 164: "Si accomodi un lavoratorio commune, o nel lavoratorio della Priora, ò in quello che chiamano della Seda, dove tutte le Monache convengano à lavorare conforme alla regola."

5. ASPV, Archivio Segreto, Visite pastorali, Priuli, S. Biagio e Cataldo, October 21, 1521: "Grande disordine, et origine di molti mali nasce dal non ridursi le moanche à lavorare nel lavoratorio commune; Però ordiniamo che tutte debbano ridursi à lavorare in un commune lavoratorio, e non mai nelle celle particolari. . . . Si deputi dalla M.re Abbadessa qualche Monaca scambievolmente che legga in lavoratotio qualche libro spirituale, et usino le Monache cantare insieme qualche salmo come si fa nei Monasterij ben regolati. . . . Si lavorino solamente cose approvate dalle Superiori, utili per il Monasterio, per persone oneste, di buon nome et che non diano scandalo." "At the wheel": every monastery had a wheel that was used to pass objects, messages, sometimes even abandoned newborns from the inside of the convent to the outside without physical contact and without been seen. It was a window that had a partition rotating on a central axis: you would place the object on your side, ring a bell, and somebody from the inside would rotate the wheel to retrieve the object.

6. Tailors and embroiderers were usually men, regularly enrolled in a corporation, something that lacemakers were never allowed to do. Further reading: Grazietta Butazzi, "Le scandalose licenze de'sartori e sartore: Considerazioni sul mestiere del sarto nella Repubblica di Venezia," in *I mestieri della moda a Venezia*, exhibition catalogue (Venice: Il Cavallino, 1988), 63–69; Doretta Davanzo Poli, "Dalle origini alla caduta della Repubblica," in Doretta Davanzo Poli and Stefania Moronato, *Le stoffe dei veneziani* (Venice: Albrizzi, 1994), 45, 58–59.

7. The algae supposedly was *Halymedia opuntia*, also known as the "lace of the mermaids."

8. Archival documents attest to the presence of laces in Venice since the second half of fourteenth century. Especially significant is a law dated 1476 that intended to limit the excessive amount spent by aristocratic families to buy "ponto in aire sì facto ad ago, come facto d'oro over d'arzento," thus confirming the presence of elaborate needle-made laces created with gold or silver thread. See Bistort, *Il Magistrato*, 354.

9. The *reticello* was worked by pulling away some warps and wefts from a linen

fabric that was subsequently embroidered using buttonhole stitches made with extra-fine linen thread.

10. No less than three *dogaresse* have been associated with the sponsorship of lace. In 1458 Giovanna Malipiero Dandolo supported a protective law in favor of laces, much as did, a century later, Lidia Priuli Dandolo. According to tradition, Morosina Morosini Grimani even created a lace workshop in her own palace in the Santa Fosca area. See Doretta Davanzo Poli, "Il merletto: Un'arte tutta veneziana," in Doretta Davanzo Poli and Silvia Lunardon, *Merletti: Esposizione di una selezione di antichi merletti veneziani dalle collezioni IRE* (Venice: IRE, 2001), 23.

11. Margaret L. King, *Le donne nel Rinascimento* (Roma: Laterza, 1991), 93.

12. Lodovico Dolce, *Dialogo della institution delle donne* (Venice: Gabriel Goito de' Ferrari, 1547), 8v–9r: "Consiglierei, che . . . le si ponessero tra le mani gli strumenti di tutte le bisogne della casa, in certa picciola forma, . . . che esse impareranno con diletto & il nome, & l'ufficio di ciascheduno."

13. Dolce, *Dialogo*, 12–12v: "Che il saper cucire a noi Donne tanto appartien, quanto a voi uomini el saper scrivere."

14. In sixteenth-century Italy there are innumerable representations of industrious women; for instance, Anton Francesco Doni (1552) depicts a Venetian woman laboriously sewing, with a number of busy ants in the background and masculine objects neglected at her feet.

15. Among the most famous pattern books are Alessandro Paganino, *Il Burato, libro de recami* (Venice, 1527); Nicolò Zoppino, *Gli universali de i belli Recami antichi e moderni: ne i quali un pellegrino ingegno, si di uomo come di donna, potrà in questa nostra età vertuosamente eserictarsi* (Venice, 1537); Mathio Pagan, *L'honesto essempio del vertuoso desiderio che hanno le donne di nobile ingegno, circa lo imparare i punti tagliati a fogliami*, (Venezia 1550); Francesco Calepino, *Splendore delle vertuose giovani: Dove si contengono molte e varie mostre a fogliami* (Venice, 1563); Cesare Vecellio, *Corona delle nobili et virtuose donne* (Venice, 1591); Isabella Catanea Parasole, *Teatro delle vertuose donne* (Venice, 1593); Lucrezia Romana, *Ornamento nobile per ogni gentil matrona* (Venezia, 1620). The equation needlework = honor is stated also by Federigo Luigini: "The needle belongs to all women, both high and low, but where the poor find utility in these arts, the rich, noble, and beautiful lady wins honor" ("l'ago appartiene a tutte le donne, ma dove la povera ricava solo utilità da questa arte (il lavoro d'ago) la nobile e bellissima signora vi conquista anche l'onore"). *Il libro della bella donna* (Venice: A. Pietrasanta, 1554), 32.

16. "L'ingegno donnesco . . . per far con l'ago quanto da Poeta ò Pittor mai fusse

espresso," in Alessandra Mottola Molfino and Maria Teresa Binaghi Olivari, *I pizzi: Moda e simbolo* (Milan: Electa, 1977), 28. The artistic possibilities offered by needlework were mentioned by Venetian humanist Augurello, who, in his Latin verses, describes a certain Perulla so gifted with the needle as to be able to exactly replicate the brushwork with her stitches. See Giuseppe Pavanello, *Un maestro del Quattrocento G. A. Augurello* (Venice, 1905), 142.

17. Maria Pia Pedani, "L'osservanza imposta: I monasteri femminili a Venezia nei primi anni del Cinquecento," *Archivio Veneto*, ser. 5, vol. 144 (1995): 123.

18. Regarding the work in monasteries outside the Venice region, see Marina Carmignani, *Ricami e merletti nelle chiese e nei monasteri di Prato dal 16. al 19. secolo: "La Tediosissima fatica": Prato, Palazzo Pretorio, 9 marzo–8 aprile 1985.* 1985 [S.l.] : Nova zincografica fiorentina, 1985.

19. Giovanni Mariacher, *Il merletto veneziano* (Venice, 1974), 5–6.

20. ASPV, Archivio Segreto, Visite pastorali, S. Mauro, c. 39.

21. Arcangela Tarabotti, *Lettere* (Venice: Guerigli, 1650).

22. "Quel merlo di punt'in aria che mi fa dar al diavolo." Ibid., 23.

23. "Quelle Suore che si presero l'incarico di fare i lavori parte s'ammalarono e parte uscirono di monasterio." Ibid., 219. See also Davanzo Poli, "Il merletto," 29–30. The mention of nuns leaving the monastery probably refers to the custom of allowing nuns to briefly return home before pronouncing the solemn vows, especially to recover from an illness. Arcangela herself returned home twice before pronouncing her solemn vows in 1629. See Zanette, *Suor Arcangela*, 72.

24. "Ch'ella rimanga servita a pieno per quanto s'estenderà il potere del mio debol impiego e diligenza." Ibid., 71, 145.

25. A type of rather coarse linen or hemp cloth was known in Venice as *tela muneghina*, or "nuns' cloth," because it was originally woven in convents. See Davanzo Poli, *Abiti antichi*, 200.

26. ASPV, Archivio Segreto, Visite pastorali, Miscellanea, 1592–96, S. Zaccaria, 1596, fol. 576v. At San Zaccaria the convent's laundry room became the center of social life; often, parties and banquets were held there.

27. "In molti monasterii di monache cittadine." ASV, Senato, Terra, R. 25, c. 204v, October 26, 1529, in Luca Molà, "Le donne nell'industria serica veneziana del Rinascimento," in *La seta in Italia dal Medioevo al Seicento: Dal baco al drappo*, ed. Luca Molà, Reinhold C. Mueller, and Claudio Zanier (Venice: Marsilio, 2000), 424.

28. "In altri lavorieri." ASV, Arte della Seta, b. 32, fasc. 651, polizza n. 6, October 27, 1587.

29. "Ma ogni volta che volgiamo seda per lavorar ne abiamo quanto ne possiamo far." Ibid.

30. ASV, Procuratori di S. Marco de Citra, b. 269 bis, libretto IV, 30v–31r.

31. Daughter of Pietro da Lesina, captain of a ship belonging to Hieronimo Mocenigo. She entered S. Iseppo in 1553. Laven, *Virgins of Venice*, 187

32. ASV, Provveditori sopra Monasteri, b. 263, 1571, S. Iseppo, fol. 2r–v.

33. "(La ghe ha cupido) . . . (dei) capelli stupendissimi con recami d'oro, arzento soprarizzo, perche lei lavora miracolosamente con perle et con zogie. . . . Lè stata 13 anni , che la non ha mai lavoratoper el monastero, et tutto quel che ha vadagnato l'ha messo in suo uso, et speso ogni cosa in le cose che ho ditto." ASV, Provveditori sopra Monasteri, b. 263, fasc. "copia processu Sancti Josephi Venetiarum contra il Confessor et gasparo suo fratello, 13 agosto, 1571."

34. ASV, Provveditori sopra Monasteri, b. 263, 1571, S. Iseppo, ff. 12v–13r: "La me ha dato da comprar doi o tre . . . de seda, et anco dell'oro filato da una dona che se chiama la Castellana . . . me dava tanti danari quato importava la robba," fol. 19v. Whenever she washed her own clothes, she also washed the surplices of the friars. Ibid., fol. 23v.

35. ASPV, Archivio Segreto, Visite Pastorali, Miscellanea, 1452–1570, S. Daniel. Even the converse, or servant nuns, were forbidden to do laundry for people outside the monastery. ASPV, Archivio Segreto, Visite Pastorali, Barbarigo, S. Sepolcro, December 28, 1716.

36. Laven, *Virgins of Venice*, 193.

37. "L'occupazioni continue che hanno nei lavorieri, che fanno li uffizij dell'obedienza, alli quali solecitamente e con molta carità attendono per sovvenire a i bisogni e alle necessità della presente vita, fanno che diventino donne di valore, e da questa Casa bandiscano l'ozio fomento di tutti i mali." IRE, Notatorio, ZIT B 1, 73. The daily work also helped make the days seem shorter: "Siccome l'ozio fa parere i giorni troppo lunghi, così l'occupazioni scuoprono la gran brevità loro" ("since idleness make the days unbearably long, needleworks make them shorter"). IRE, ZIT A 1, 109.

38. Documents from the second half of the sixteenth century show that married women of the middle/lower classes sold their needlework in order to help support their families. See Isabella Campagnol, "Laces and Documents: The Istituzioni di Ricovero e Educazione (IRE) Collections in Venice," in *Textiles and Text: Re-establishing the Links between Archival and Objects-based Research*, ed. Maria Hayward and Elizabeth Kramer, post-prints from the AHRC Centre for Textile Conservation and Textile Studies Third Annual Conference,Winchester, 2006 (London: Archetype Publications, 2007), 79n6.

39. For an analysis on the regulations regarding the *tascha*, see Campagnol, "Laces," 77.

40. See Campagnol, "Laces," 78–79.

41. In 1553 the Convertite obtained permission to build a spinning mill inside the monastery, since there were more than 220 women involved in the weaving activity. ASV, Senato, Terra, filza 17, fasc. March 18, 1553, Supplica procuratori monastero, Convertite, March 2, 1553; ibid., reply of the Provveditori di Comun, March 6, 1553, ibid., filza 18, fasc. November 20, 1553. During the 1587 inquiry, the nuns of the convertite affirmed that they had never been without silk to spin: "Non ne sono mai mancato de lavorar de sede de ogni sorte perfin al giorno presente." ASV, Arte della Seta, b. 651, fasc. 32, polizza n. 2, October 22, 1587.

Chapter 5

1. Kate J. P. Lowe, "Power and Institutional Identity in Renaissance Venice: The Female Convents of S. M. delle Vergini and S. Zaccaria," in *The Trouble with Ribs: Women, Men, and Gender in Early Modern Europe*, ed. Anu Korhonen and Kate J. P. Lowe (Helsinki: Helsinki Collegium for Advanced Studies, 2007), 130.

Glossary

Accia, azza: Linen, cotton, or silk thread.

Aere, ponto in: Needle lace.

Altana: Roof terrace.

Amuerro: Heavy silk moiré fabric.

Andrienne: also, *andriè*: Eighteenth-century feminine dress characterized by two large pleats in the back that opened up in a small train.

Armaro: also *armer*: Wardrobe.

Bareta: Hat.

Bavaro: Collar that covers shoulders and décolletage.

Becchetto: Final part of a man's headwear.

Bellacosa: Silk fabric often decorated by a watering effect.

Beretino: Color between ash-gray and brown.

Bionda: Blonde hair dye.

Boccassin: Linen and cotton fabric used to make the homonymous veil.

Bombaso: Cotton.

Bottana: Hard-wearing cotton fabric.

Brazzo: Unit of measure. It equals 63.8 cm for silk fabrics, 68.2 cm for wool fabrics.

Bucole: Pendant earrings.

Burato: Thin, transparent fabric often used as base fabric for embroidery.

Cagiarin: From Cairo; usually referred to rugs.

Calcagneti: also, *calcagnini*: Clogs characterized by a very high wedge, sometimes as high as 50 cm.

Calcetti: also, *calzetti*: Socks.

Cambeloto: also, *cammellotto* or *zambellotto*: Wool fabric, originally made with camel hair, hence the name, and later with silk.

Camisa: Shirt.

Camiseta: Shirtfront, usually decorated by laces or ruffles.

Cambrada: Very fine linen fabric, from the French city of Cambrai.

Carega: Chair.

Carnizza: Thin linen fabric.

Carpetta: Skirt.

Cascade: Lace cuffs.

Casso: Bodice without sleeves.

Cendal: Very light silk fabric similar to taffetas.

Ciriesa: Cherry red color.

Cocolla: Religious dress.

Cordela: Ribbon.

Costanza: White linen fabric made in the German city of that name.

Cufia: Bonnet; often decorated with pearls and jewels.

Curame: Leather.

Damasco: Damask.

Dimito: Fabric made either with cotton or a combination of cotton and linen.

Dizial: Thimble.

Ducali (maniche): Very large sleeves that in secular clothes were often lined either in contrasting fabric, or with furs. Characteristically used in the ceremonial dress of the doge and of government officials.

Ducato: Venetian gold coin; it was the only currency accepted by Muslim countries.

Facioli: Large square of light fabric, often silk, to be used to cover the head.

Fillo: Linen.

Fiuba: Buckle.

Fongo: Mushroom. It indicated a forbidden hairstyle in fashion at the end of the fifteenth century.

Fustagno: Fustian or a white cotton fabric usually characterized by a geometric decorative pattern.

Galozze: also, *galoscie*: Wooden clogs.

Ganzante: Shot silk, made with differently colored warp and weft; made since the fifteenth century.

Garza: Gauze; originally from the city of Gaza.

Gonnella: *Gonna*, *gonnella*, or *sottana*: Petticoat.

Gottonado: Lined with a cotton fabric.

Griso: Gray.

Habito: Dress.

Indiana: Indian-made cloth.

Intimella: Pillow case.

Libra: Unit of weight; it corresponds to 0.4760 kg.

Lira: Monetary unit divided into 20 *soldi* or 240 *denari*.

Maneghetti: also, *manili*: Cuffs made of laces or ruffled fabric.

Maniza: Muff, often made with heavy fabrics, such as velvet, and lined with furs.

Merlo: Lace.

Momperiglia: Small silk decorations.

Morello: Purple-brown.

Muneghina: Linen or hemp cloth woven inside the convents by nuns (*muneghe* in Venetian dialect).

Mussola: Originally from Mosul, a transparent silk, cotton, or wool fabric.

Ninzioli: Bed sheets.

Ninzioleto: Cotton cloth used by women of the lower classes to cover their heads.

Noghera: Walnut wood.

Ormesin: Silk fabric, originally from the island of Ormuz.

Pavonazzo: Purplish blue, peacock blue.

Pera: Pair.

Polacca: Short feminine dress worn with a matching underskirt.

Ponsò: Bright red.

Pontizado: Dotted.

Posta: Silk sash.

Rassa: also, *rascia*: Coarse wool fabric, originally from Serbia.

Roan: Dark brown-red.

Rocheto: Shirt.

Renso: Very fine linen fabric manufactured in Reims, France.

Sargia: also, *sarza*: Ordinary wool twill.

Schiavonetto: Long, usually embroidered tunic worn by women during their beauty treatments on the altane.

Scoto: Wool twill; so-called because the best came from Scotland.

Solana: Crown-less straw hat used to protect the face while bleaching the hair.

Soldo: monetary unit. See above: *lira*.

Sotana: See *gonna*.

Stricada: also, *striccà*: Striped.

Tabaro: Traditional Venetian cape, usually black.

Tabin: also, *tabinetto, tabì*: Sort of heavy moiré taffetas. The name derives from *al-attabija*, the area of Baghdad where it was initially manufactured.

Taffeta: Taffetas; from the Persian *tafteh*.

Traversa: Sort of apron worn inside the house by women of the lower classes and by nuns.

Vari: Fur of a species of squirrel.

Veludo: Velvet.

Ventolo: Fan.

Vestura: Generic word for dress.

Zalo: Yellow.

Zendado: also, *zendado, zendal*: Light silk fabric.

Zecchino: Monetary unit instituted in 1284, divided into 18 *grossi*, each of 3.56 grams.

Zupon: Jacket.

Bibliography

Archival Documents

State Archive, Rome (ASR)

Congregazioni religiose femminili 4226/4 (Miscellanea), *Memoria del monasterio di san Zaccaria*, fol. 1v.

State Archive, Genoa

Carteggio diplomatico, Roma, b. 32

State Archive, Venice (ASV)

Arte Marzeri, b. 312.1
Arte della Seta, b. 651, fasc. 32, polizza no. 2
Notarile Testamenti, b. 166, no. 124, December 17, 1680
Notarile Testamenti, b. 167, no. 177, April 1, 1670
Notarile Testamenti, b. 65, no. 119, August 2, 1647
Pregadi, April 15, 1610, CL, b. 288
Provveditori sopra Monasteri, b. 263, fasc.6, b. 265, b. 347, fasc. 7
Procuratori di S. Marco de Citra, b. 269 bis, libretto IV
San Daniele, b. 12
S. Lorenzo, b. 13
Santa Maria delle Vergini, b. 32
San Zaccaria, b. 94
Senato, Misti, R. 53
Senato, Terra, R. 15, 37

Archivio Storico del Patriarcato di Venezia (ASPV)

Archivio Segreto, Visite pastorali, Badoer, S. Mauro, no. 23, 1693

Archivio Segreto, Visite pastorali a monasteri femminili

Miscellaneous, October 15, 1452–November 15, 1730

Patriarch Trevisan, *Monialium visitationum sub R.mo D.no Ioanne Trivisano patriarcha Venetiarum, 1560–1589,* October 26, 1560–May 25, 1589

Patriarch Priuli, *Visite de monache, 1592–1596: Priuli,* April 9, 1592–August 21, 1596

Patriarch Vendramin, *Visitationes ecclesiarum et monasteriorum monialium Venetiarum facta ab Ill.mo et R.mo D.no card: Vendramino patriarcha Venetiarum incipientes ab anno 1609 usque ad annum 1718,* October 6, 1609–August 29, 1718

Patriarch Tiepolo, *Visite di monache, 1620–1627: Tiepolo,* March 27, 1620–August 29, 1627

Patriarch Barbarigo, *Visite de chiese di monache e monasteri, 1711–1725: Barbarigo,* February 29, 1710–June 28, 1724

Torcellania Criminalia monialium, b. 23

Archive of the Istituzioni di Ricovero ed Educazione (IRE)

DER E 3, b. 1

DER E 2, b. 3

DER E 87, b. 2

DER E 105, b. 2, 4

DER E 150, b. 5, will of Zuane Falier, April 10, 1601, c. 19r and v.

DER E 178, 1670

DER E 182, b. 9

DER G 1, no. 83

DER G 2, no. 83

SOC G 1, t. primo, c. 2

ZIT B 1, 73

ZIT A 1, 109

Biblioteca del Museo Correr (BMC)

Codice Cicogna 2583, *Ordini et avvertimenti che si devono osservare nei monasteri i monache.*

Codice Cicogna 2570, *Raccolta di documenti relativi alla riforma dei monasteri di monache.*

Ms. Correr 317, Cronica del Monistero delle Vergini di Venetia

Alcuni avvertimenti nella vita monacale, utili et necessari à ciascheduna Vergine di Cristo, Venetia, 1575.

Componimenti poetici in occasione che la nobil donna Teresa Priuli veste il sagro abito di Santo Agostino nel nobilissimo monastero di Santa Giustina prendendo il nome di Maria Cecilia. Venice, 1746.

Biblioteca Nazionale Marciana (BNM)

Cingulano, Benedetto. "Barzelletta delle Monacelle," BNM, Cl. It., IX, 369 (7203), Poesie varie, c. 48v–51r.

Componimenti poetici in occasione che professa la regola di San Benedetto nel nobilissimo monastero di S. Giovanni Evangelista di Torcello la nobil donna Augusta Zorzi al secolo, ora D. Maria Elena. Venice: presso Gio. Antonio Curti q. Vito, 1793.

*Componimenti poetici in occasione che professò l'abito di S. Benedetto nel nobilissimo monastero di S. Zaccaria di Venezia la nobile donna Cecilia Gritti che prese il nome di Cecilia Maria.*Venice: Stamp. Casali, 1784.

Deliberazioni, dell'eccelso Conseglio di 10. e terminationi, et ordeni delli eccellentissimi sig. Proueditori sopra li monasterij di monache di Venetia, e Dogado: Che si republicano al presente, a notitia di cadauno, non derogando pero alle altre deliberationi, e terminationi fatte in altre materie. Venice: stampate per Antonio Pinelli, stampator ducale. A S. Maria Formosa, in Calle del Mondo Nouo.

Parte presa nell'eccellentiss: Conseglio di Pregadi: A' 27 di agosto 1620: In materia della dote delle figliuole, che vogliono monacare. Venice: stampata per Antonio Pinelli, stampator ducale. A S. Maria Formosa, in cale del Mondo Nouo.

Proclama publicato d'ordine degl'illustrissimi, & eccellentissimi signori Proveditori sopra monasterj: In materia di spese, rinfreschi, ed apparati in occasione di vestir figlie monache. Venice: per li figliuoli del qu. Z. Antonio Pinelli stampatori ducali, 1749.

Terminatione delli eccellentiss.mi signori Proueditori sopra li monasterij: In materia di quelli, che vanno a mangiare nelli parlatorij de' monasterij di monache. Venice: stampata in Calle dalle Rasse, per il Rampazetto.

Terminatione delli illustriss.mi signori Proueditori sopra li monasterij: In materia delle meretrice. Venice: stampata in calle dalle Rasse per il Rampazetto.

Essential Bibliography

Aikema, Bernard, and Dulcia Meijers. *Nel regno dei poveri: Arte e storia degli ospedali veneziani nell' età moderna, 1474–1797.* Venice: IRE, 1989.

Alcuni avvertimenti nella vita monacale, utili et necessari à ciascheduna Vergine di Cristo. Venice, 1575.

Araldo, Sicillo. *Trattato dei colori nelle arme, nelle livree et nelle divise.* Venice: D. Nicolino, 1565.

Barthes, Roland. "Histoire et sociologie du vêtement." *Annales: Économies, Sociétés, Civilisations* 12, no. 3 (1957): 430–441.

———. *Sistema della moda.* Turin: Einaudi, 1970.

———. "Storia e sociologia del vestiario: Osservazioni metodologiche." In *La storia e le scienze sociali*, edited by Ferdìnand Braudel, 136–52. Bari: Laterza, 1974.

Battiston, Odilla. *Un piccolo regno teocratico nel cuore di Venezia: Il monastero di San Lorenzo*. Venice: Filippi, 1993.

Bayer, Andrea, ed. *Art and Love in Renaissance Italy*. Exhibition catalogue. New York: Metropolitan Museum of Art, 2008; New Haven, CT: Yale University Press, 2008.

Bell, Quentin. *Of Human Finery*. London: Hogarth Press, 1947.

Bellomo, Manlio. *La condizione giuridica della donna in Italia*. Turin: Eri classe unica, 1970.

Buonmattei, Benedetto. *Del modo di consegnar le vergini secondo l'uso del Pontifical Romano con la dichiarazion de'misteri delle Cerimonie, che in quell'azion si fanno del dottore Benedetto Buonmattei aggiuntavi in fine l'ordine che in alcuni monasteri si tene nel dar l'abito a esse Vergini*. Venice: Appresso Antonio Pinelli, 1622.

Bistort, Giulio. *Il Magistrato alle Pompe della Repubblica di Venezia*. Bologna: Forni, 1969.

Boerio, Giuseppe. *Dizionario del dialetto veneziano*. Torino: Bottega d'Erasmo, 1867.

Bonanni, Filippo. *Catalogo degli ordini religiosi della chiesa militante espressi con imagini, e spiegati con una breue narrazione, offerto alla santita di n.s. Clemente 11. dal p. Filippo Bonanni della compagnia di Gesù*. 3 vols. Roma: nella stamperia di Antonio de' Rossi nella strada del Sem. Romano, 1706–10.

Braun, Johann. *I paramenti sacri: Loro uso, storia e simbolismo*. Turin: Marietti, 1914.

Brunello, Franco. *L'arte della tintura nella storia dell'umanità*. Vicenza: Neri Pozza, 1968.

Buoninsegni, Francesco. *Contro 'l lusso donnesco, satira menippea del sig. Fran. Buoninsegni, con l'antisatira D. Arcangela Tarabotti in risposta*. Venice: per Francesco Valvasensis, 1644.

Butazzi, Grazietta. "Le scandalose licenze de'sartori e sartore: Considerazioni sul mestiere del sarto nella Repubblica di Venezia." In *I mestieri della moda a Venezia*, exhibition catalogue, 63–69. Venice: Il Cavallino, 1988.

Calabrese, Maria. *Psicologia della moda: Abbigliamento come linguaggio*. Milan: Igos, 1990.

Campagnol, Isabella. "Costume in the Italian Renaissance." In *Greenwood Encyclopedia of Clothing through World History*, 3–61. 3 vols. Westport, CT: Greenwood Publishers, 2007.

———. "Invisible Seamstresses: Needlework in Venetian Convents from the Fifteenth to the Eighteenth Century." In *Women and Things: The Material Culture of Needlework and Textiles, 1650–1950*, edited by Maureen Daly Goggin and Beth Fowkes Tobin, 2:167–178. London: Ashgate, Arizona State University, 2009.

———. "Laces and Documents: The Istituzioni di Ricovero e Educazione (IRE)

Collections in Venice." In *Textiles and Text: Re-establishing the Links between Archival and Objects-based research*, edited by Maria Hayward and Elizabeth Kramer, post-prints from the AHRC Centre for Textile Conservation and Textile Studies Third Annual Conference, Winchester, 2006, 76–81. London: Archetype Publications, 2007.

———. "Mode e tessuti veneziani negli Habiti Antichi di Cesare Vecellio." In *Il vestito e la sua immagine: Atti del convegno internazionale in omaggio a Cesare Vecellio nel quarto centenario della morte*, 27–40. Belluno: Provincia di Belluno Editore, 2002.

Canosa, Romano. *Il velo e il cappuccio: Monacazioni forzate e sessualità nei conventi femminili in Italia tra Quattrocento e Settecento*. Rome: Sapere, 1991.

Carmignani, Marina. *Ricami e merletti nelle chiese e nei monasteri di Prato dal XVI al XIX secolo, "la tediosissima fatica": Prato, Palazzo Pretorio 9 marzo 8 aprile 1985*. Nova zincografica fiorentina, 1985.

Casola, Pietro. *Viaggio a Gerusalemme*. Edited by Anna Paoletti. Alessandria: Edizioni dell'Orso, 2001.

Cecchetti, Bartolomeo. *La Repubblica di Venezia e la corte di Roma nei rapporti della religione*. Venice: Prem. Stabilim. Tipog. di P. Naratovich, 1874. 1:197–211; 2:79–179.

———. *La vita dei Veneziani nel 1300, Le vesti*. Venezia: Tipografia Emiliana, 1885–86.

Chojnacki, Stanley. *Women and Men in Renaissance Venice: Twelve Essays on Patrician Society*. Baltimore: John Hopkins University Press, 2000.

———. "Gender and the Early Renaissance State." In Stanley Chojnacki, *Women and Men in Renaissance Venice: Twelve Essays on Patrician Society*, 27–52. Baltimore: John Hopkins University Press, 2000.

———. "Introduction: Family and State, Women and Men." In Stanley Chojnacki, *Women and Men in Renaissance Venice: Twelve Essays on Patrician Society*, 1–24. Baltimore: John Hopkins University Press, 2000.

———. "Subaltern Patriarchs: Patrician Bachelors." In Stanley Chojnacki, *Women and Men in Renaissance Venice: Twelve Essays on Patrician Society*, 244–256. Baltimore: John Hopkins University Press, 2000.

Cicogna, Emanuele Antonio. *Delle inscrizioni veneziane*. Bologna: Forni, 1969.

"Ci vuole pazienza": Lettere di Elena Mocenigo Querini, 1733–1788. Edited by Antonio Fancello and Madile Gambier. Venice: Fondazione Querini Stampalia, 2008.

Cipriani, Renata. *Codici minati dell'Ambrosiana*. Vicenza: Neri Pozza, 1968.

Clare of Assisi, Saint. *Lettere ad Agnese: La visione dello specchio*. Edited by Giovanni Pozzi and Beatrice Rima. Milan: Adelphi, 1999.

Corner, Flaminio. *Notizie storiche delle chiese e monasteri di Venezia e Torcello*. Bologna: Forni, 1990, anastatic reprint.

Coronelli, Vincenzo Maria. *Ordinum religiosorum in ecclesia militanti catalogus, eorumque indumenta, iconibus expressa, auctus, nec non moderatus posteriori hac editione, anni 1707 . . . a p. generali Coronelli consecratus.* Venice: 1707.

Cortese, Isabella. *I Secreti.* Venice: G. Fornetti, 1584.

Cortesi Bosco, Francesca. *Gli affreschi dell'Oratorio Suardi: Lorenzo Lotto nella crisi della riforma.* Bergamo: Bolis, 1980.

Coryat, Thomas. *Coryat Crudities: Hastily Gobled Up in Five Months of Travels.* Glasgow: J. MacLehose and Sons, 1905.

Cowan, Alexander. "Rich and Poor among the Patriciate in Early Modern Venice." In *Studi Veneziani,* n.s., 6 (1982): 147–160.

Davanzo Poli, Doretta. *Abiti antichi e moderni dei Veneziani.* Venice: Neri Pozza editore, 2001.

———. "Le cortigiane e la moda." In *Le Cortigiane di Venezia dal Trecento al Settecento,* 99–103. Milano: Berenice 1990.

———. "Dalle origini alla caduta della Repubblica." In *Le stoffe dei veneziani,* by Doretta Davanzo Poli and Stefania Moronato. Venice: Albrizzi, 1994.

———. "Il merletto: Un'arte tutta veneziana." In *Merletti: Esposizione di una selezione di antichi merletti veneziani dalle collezioni IRE,* by Doretta Davanzo Poli and Silvia Lunardon. Venice: IRE, 2001.

———. "Merletto ad ago e a fuselli." In *Storia di Venezia: Temi: L'arte,* 2:985–1003. Rome: Istituto della Enciclopedia Italiana, 1995.

———. *Il merletto veneziano.* Novara: Istituto Geografico De Agostini, 1998.

———. *I mestieri della moda a Venezia, Documenti.* Venice: Edizioni del Gazzettino, 1984–86.

———. "La moda nella Venezia del Palladio." In *Architettura e Utopia,* edited by Lionello Puppi, 291–234. Milan: Electa, 1981.

Davanzo Poli, Doretta, and Silvia Lunardon. *Merletti: Esposizione di una selezione di antichi merletti veneziani dalle collezioni IRE.* Venice: IRE, 2001.

Davanzo Poli, Doretta, and Stefania Moronato. *Le stoffe dei veneziani.* Venice: Albrizzi, 1994.

Da Varagine, Jacopo. *Legenda Aurea.* Florence: Libreria Editrice Fiorentina, 1976.

Davis, James C. *A Venetian Family and its Fortune, 1500–1900: The Donà and the Conservation of Wealth.* Philadelphia: American Philosophical Society, 1975.

Del Basso, Giovanni Maria. "Il sigillo delle monache: autorità e modello." In *Donna, disciplina creanza cristiana dal XV al XVII secolo: Studi e testi a stampa,* edited by Gabriella Zarri, 347–366. Rome: Edizioni di storia e letteratura, 1996.

Dizionario degli Istituti di perfezione. Edited by Guerrino Pelliccia and Giancarlo Rocca. Milan: Paoline, 1975.

Dolce, Lodovico. *Dialogo della institution delle donne.* Venice: Gabriel Goito de' Ferrari, 1547.

Economopoulos, Harula. "Considerazioni sui ruoli dimenticati: Gli 'Amanti' di Paris Bordon e la figura del compare dell'anello." *Venezia Cinquecento* 2, no. 3 (1992): 99–123.

Ellero, Giuseppe. *L'archivio IRE: Inventari dei fondi antichi degli ospedali e luoghi pii di Venezia*. Venice: IRE, 1987.

Evangelisti, Silvia. *Nuns: A History of Convent Life, 1450–1780*. Oxford: Oxford University Press, 2007.

Fees, Irmgard. *Le monache di San Zaccaria a Venezia nei secoli 12. e 13.* Venice: Centro tedesco di studi veneziani, 1998.

Ferrara, Daniele. "Il ritratto del Doge Leonardo Loredan: Strategie dell'abito tra politica e religione." *Venezia Cinquecento* 1, no. 2 (1991): 89–108.

Ferraro, Joanne M. *Marriage Wars in Late Renaissance Venice*. New York: Oxford University Press, 2001.

Flugel, Johan C. *Psicologia dell'abbigliamento*. Milan: F. Angeli, 1987.

Fortini Brown, Patricia. *Venetian Narrative Painting in the Age of Carpaccio*. New Haven, CT: Yale University Press, 1988.

———. *Private Lives in Renaissance Venice: Art, Architecture, and the Family*. New Haven, CT: Yale University Press, 2004.

Fonte, Moderata. *Il merito delle donne ove chiaramente si scopre quanto siano elle degne e più perfette de gli uomini*. Edited by Adriana Chemello. Venice: Eidos, 1988.

Franco, Giacomo. *Habiti delle donne veneziane intagliate in rame, nuovamente da Giacomo Franco*. Edited by Lina Urban. 1610; Venice: Centro Internazionale della Grafica, 1990.

Fulin, Rinaldo. *Studi nell'archivio degli Inquisitori di Stato*. Venice: Visentini, 1868.

Geron, Gastone. *Carlo Goldoni, cronista mondano*. Venezia: Filippi, 1972.

Giuliani, Innocenzo. "Genesi e primo secolo di vita del Magistrato sopra monasteri, Venice 1519–1620." *Le Venezie Francescane* 28 (1961): 42–68, 106–69.

Goffen, Rona. *Titian's Women*. New Haven, CT: Yale University Press, 1997.

Grevembroch, Giovanni. *Gli abiti de' Veneziani di quasi ogni età con diligenza raccolti e dipinti nel secolo XVIII*. 4 vols. Edited by Giovanni Mariacher. Venice: Filippi, 1981.

Grimani, Antonio. *Constitutioni, et decreti approvati nella sinodo diocesana sopra la retta disciplina monacale sotto L'illustrissimo, Reverendissimo Monsignor Antonio Grimani Vescovo di Torcello. L'anno della Natività del Nostro Signore, 1592. Il giorno 7. 8. & 9 d'Aprile*. Venice, 1592.

Hélyot, Pierre. *Storia degli ordini monastici, religiosi, e militari, e delle congregazioni secolari dell'uno, e l'altro sesso, fino al presente istituite, con le vite de' loro fondatori, e riformatori*. 8 vols. Lucca: per Giuseppe Salani e Vincenzo Giuntini, 1737–39.

Hills, Paul. *Colore veneziano: Pittura, marmo, mosaico e vetro dal 1200 al 1550*. Milan: Rizzoli, 1999.

Hughes, Diane Owen. "Sumptuary Law and Social Relations in Renaissance Italy." In *Disputes and Settlements: Law and Human Relations in the West*, edited by John Bossy, 68–99. Cambridge: Cambridge University Press, 1983.

King, Margaret L. *Le donne nel Rinascimento*. Rome: Laterza, 1991.

Kovesi Killbery, Catherine "Heralds of a Well-Instructed Mind: Niccolosa Sanuti's Defence of Women and Their Clothes." *Renaissance Studies* 13, no. 3 (1999): 99–120.

Labalme, Patricia. "Venetian Women on Venetian Women: Three Early Modern Feminists." *Archivio Veneto* 5, no. 117 (1981): 81–109.

Labalme, Patricia, Laura Sanguineti White, and Linda Carroll. "How to (and How Not to) Get Married in Sixteenth Century Venice (Selections from the Diaries of Marin Sanudo)." *Renaissance Quarterly* 52, no. 1 (Spring 1999): 43–72.

La sostanza dell'effimero: Gli abiti degli Ordini religiosi in Occidente. Exhibition catalogue. Edited by Giancarlo Rocca. Rome: Edizioni Paoline, 2000.

Laven, Mary. *Virgins of Venice: Enclosed Lives and Broken Vows in the Renaissance Convent*. London: Viking, 2002.

Levi Pisetzky, Rosita. *Il costume e la moda nella società italiana*. Turin: Einaudi, 1978.

———. *Storia del Costume in Italia*. Milan: Istituto Editoriale Italiano, 1964–69.

Limojon de Saint-Didier, Alexandre Toussaint. *De la ville et la Republique de Venise*. Paris: chez Guillaume de Luyne, 1680.

Lorenzi, G. *Leggi e memorie venete sulla prostituzione*. Venice, 1870–72.

Lowe, Kate J. P. "Secular Brides and Convent Brides: Wedding Ceremonies in Italy during the Renaissance and Counter-Reformation." In *Marriage in Italy, 1300–1650*, edited by Trevor Dean and Kate J. P. Lowe, 41–65. Cambridge: Cambridge University Press, 1998.

———. *Nuns' Chronicles and Convent Culture in Renaissance and Counter-Reformation Italy*. Cambridge: Cambridge University Press, 2004.

———. "Power and Institutional Identity in Renaissance Venice: The Female Convents of S. M. delle Vergini and S. Zaccaria." In *The Trouble with Ribs: Women, Men, and Gender in Early Modern Europe*, edited by Anu Korhonen and Kate J. P. Lowe, 128–152. Helsinki: Helsinki Collegium for Advanced Studies, 2007.

Lunardon, Silvia. "Le Zitelle alla Giudecca." In *Le Zitelle: Architettura, Arte e Storia di un'Istituzione Veneziana*, edited by Lionello Puppi. Venice: Albrizzi, 1992.

Luzzatto, Lia, and Renata Pompas. *I colori del Vestire: Variazione: Ritorni, persistenze*. Milan: Hoepli, 1997.

Makowski, Ekizabeth. *Canon Law and Cloistered Women: Periculoso and Its*

Commentators 1298–1545. Washington DC: Catholic University of America Press, 1997.

Malpezzi Price, Paola. *Moderata Fonte: Women and Life in Sixteenth-Century Venice*. Madison, NJ: Fairleigh Dickinson University Press; London: Associated University Press, 2003.

Mariacher, Giovanni. *Il merletto veneziano*. Venice, 1974.

Mason Rinaldi, Stefania. "Jacopo Palma il Giovane e la decorazione dell'Oratorio dei Crociferi." In *Hospitale S. Marieae Cruciferorum: L'ospizio dei Crociferi di Venezia*, edited by Silvia Lunardon, 87–148. Venice: IRE, 1984.

———. *Jacopo Palma il Giovane: Opera completa*. Milan: Electa, 1984.

Mayo, Janet. *History of Ecclesiastical Dress*. New York: Holmes & Meier, 1984.

Medioli, Francesca. *L'Inferno monacale di Arcangela Tarabotti*. Turin: Rosemberg & Sellier, 1990.

Menetto, Luciano, and Giuseppe Zennaro. *Storia del malcostume a Venezia nei secoli XV e XVI*. Abano Terme: Piovan, 1987.

Molà, Luca. "Le donne nell'industria serica veneziana del Rinascimento." In *La seta in Italia dal Medioevo al Seicento: Dal baco al drappo*, edited by Luca Molà, Reinhold C. Mueller, and Claudio Zanier. Venice: Marsilio, 2000.

Molmenti, Pompeo. *Storia di Venezia nella vita privata*. 3 vols. Trieste: Lind, 1973.

Monaca, moglie, serva e cortigiana: Vita e immagine delle donne tra rinascimento e controriforma, edited by Sara F. Matthews-Grieco and Sabina Berveglieri. Florence: Morgana edizioni, 2001.

Monasteri benedettini nella laguna veneziana. Exhibition catalogue. Edited by Gabriele Mazzucco. Venice: Arsenale, 1983.

Moschetti, Andrea. "Il Gobbo di Rialto e le sue relazioni con Pasquino." *Archivio Veneto* 5 (1893): 5–85.

Mottola Molfino, Alessandra, and Maria Teresa Binaghi Olivari. *I pizzi: Moda e simbolo*. Milan: Electa, 1977.

Musatti, Eugenio. *La donna in Venezia*. Bologna: Forni, 1975.

Mutinelli, Fabio. *Del costume veneziano fino al secolo Decimosettimo*. Venice: Filippi, 1984. Anastatic reprint.

Newton, Stella M. *The Dress of the Venetians, 1495–1525*. Aldershot: Scolar Press, 1988.

Nicoletti, G. *Intorno alla acconciatura del capo e calzature delle donne veneziane, sec. XV e XVI, per nozze Allegri*. Venice: G. Cecchini, 1884.

Odorisio Conti, Ginevra. *Donna e società nel Seicento: Lucrezia Marinelli e Arcangela Tarabotti*. Rome: Bulzoni, 1979.

Ospedaletto: La Sala della Musica. Edited by Tiziana Favaro, Silvia Lunardon, and Emanuela Zucchetta. Venice: IRE, 1991.

Pastoreau, Michel. *La stoffa del diavolo: Una storia delle righe e dei tessuti rigati*. Genoa: Il melangolo, 1993.

Paschini, Pio. "I monasteri femminili in Italia nel '500." In *Problemi di vita religiosa in Italia nel Cinquecento*, 40–53. Padua: Antenore, 1960.

Pazzi, Piero. *Il corno ducale o sia contributi alla conoscenza della Corona Ducale di Venezia volgarmente chiamata Corno*. Treviso: Trivellari, 1996.

Pedani, Maria Pia. "Monasteri di Agostiniane a Venezia." *Archivio Veneto*, 5th ser., 125 (1985): 35–78.

———. "L'osservanza imposta: I monasteri conventuali femminili a Venezia nei primi anni del Cinquecento." *Archivio Veneto* 5th ser., 144 (1995): 113–125.

Perini, Giovanna. "Meyer Schapiro: Incunaboli di una lettura semiotica dell'arte figurativa." In *Per una semiotica del linguaggio visivo*, by Meyer Schapiro. Rome: Meltemi, 2002.

Piana, Mario, and Wolfgang Wolters, eds. *Santa Maria dei Miracoli a Venezia: La storia, la fabbrica, i restauri*. Venice: Istituto Veneto di Scienze, Lettere ed Arti, 2003.

Piccolo Paci, Sara. *Le vesti del peccato: Eva, Salomè e Maria Maddalena nell'arte*. Milan: Ancora, 2003.

Pilot, Antonio. "Una capatina in alcuni monasteri veneziani del '500." *Rivista d' Italia* 13 (1910): 49–72.

Pizzichi, Federico. "Viaggio per l'alta Italia del Serenissimo principe di Toscana, poi granduca Cosimo II." In *Storia arcana ed aneddotica d'Italia raccontata dai Veneti ambasciatori*, edited by Fabio Mutinelli. Venice: Pietro Naratovich, 1858.

Polacco, Giorgio. *Antidoto spirituale per le monache, cioe della colpa, & della pena, che incorrono, tanto i secolari, quanto gli ecclesiastici nel parlar con monache senza la legittima facolta. Allegazione in iure di D. Giorgio Polacco veneziano . . . All'Illustrissimo, & Reuerendissimo signore il sig. cardinale Vendramino*. Venice: appresso Barezzo Barezzi, 1618.

Primhak, Victoria. "Women in Religious Communities: The Benedictine Convents of Venice, 1400–1500." PhD diss., University of London, 1991.

———. "Benedictine Communities in Venetian Society." In *Women in Italian Renaissance Culture and Society*, edited by Letizia Panizza, 92–104. Oxford: European Humanities Research Centre, 2000.

Priuli, Girolamo. *I Diarii*. Edited by Arturo Segre. Città di Castello: 1912.

Queller, Donald E. *Il patriziato veneziano: La realtà contro il mito*. Rome: Il Veltro, 1987.

Queller, Donald E., and Thomas F. Madden. "Father of the Bride: Fathers, Daughters, and Dowries in Late Medieval and Early Renaissance Venice." *Renaissance Quarterly* 46, no. 4 (Winter 1993): 685–711.

Renier Michiel, Giustina. *Origine delle feste veneziane*. Milano, 1829.

———. *Origine delle feste veneziane*. Venezia: Tip. di Alvisopoli, 1852.

———. *Origine delle feste veneziane*. Milano: Editori Annali Universali delle Scienze e dell'Industria, 1859.

Riccoboni, Sister Bartolomea. *Life and Death in a Venetian Convent: The Chronicle and Necrology of Corpus Domini, 1395–1436.* Edited and translated by Daniel Bornstein. Chicago: University of Chicago Press, 2000.

Ridolfi, Carlo. *Delle meraviglie e dell'arte: Ovvero le vite degli illustri pittori veneti e dello stato.* Venice: G. B. Sgava, 1648.

Roach-Higgins, Mary E., and Joanne B. Eicher. "Dress and Identity." *Clothing and Textile Research Journal* 10, no. 4 (1992): 1–8.

Roche, Daniel. *Il linguaggio della moda.* Turin: Einaudi, 1991.

Romanelli, Giandomenico. "Gli abiti dei Veneziani: Mille mestieri di una città di moda." In *I Mestieri della moda a Venezia*, 719–744. Venice: Il Cavallino, 1988.

Rossetti, Giovanventura. *Notandissimi secreti de l'Arte profumatoria.* Venice: F. Rampazzetto, 1560.

Ruggeri, Guido. *The Boundaries of Eros: Sex Crimes and Sexuality in Renaissance Venice.* New York: Oxford University Press, 1985.

Sansovino, Francesco. *Venetia Città Nobilissima et Singolare Descritta in XIII Libri da M. Francesco Sansovino.* Venetia: appresso Iacomo Sansovino, 1581.

Sanudo, Marin. *Diarii, 1496–1533.* From the original in BNM, Cl. It., VII, codd. 419–477. Venice: Auspice la R. Deputazione Veneta di Storia Patria, 1879–1903.

———. *De origine, situ et magistratibus urbis Venetae overo la città di Venetia.* Edited by Angela Caracciolo Aricò. Milan: Cisalpino-La goliardica, 1980.

Saussure, Ferdinand de. *Corso di linguistica generale.* Bari: Laterza, 1966.

Savio, Rosa, and Luigi Savio. "L'organizzazione del lavoro femminile a Venezia nelle antiche istituzioni di Ricovero e di Educazione." In *I pizzi: Moda e simbolo*, edited by Alessandra Mottola Molfino and Maria Teresa Binaghi Olivari, 39–42. Milan: Electa: 1977.

Schapiro, Meyer. *Per una semiotica del linguaggio visivo.* Rome: Meltemi, 2002.

La sostanza dell'effimero: Gli abiti religiosi in Occidente. Exhibition catalogue. Edited by Giancarlo Rocca. Roma: Edizioni Paoline, 2000.

Sperling, Jutta G. *Convents and the Body Politic in Late Renaissance Venice.* Chicago: University of Chicago Press, 1999.

Spinelli, Giovanni. "I religiosi e le religiose." In *La Chiesa di Venezia nel Seicento*, edited by Bruno Bertoli, 173–209. Venice: Studium, 1992.

Tarabotti, Arcangela. *Antisatira in risposta al "Lusso donnesco" satira menippea del Sig. Francesco Buoninsegni.* Siena: 1660.

———. *Lettere.* Venice: Guerigli, 1650.

———. *Lettere familiari e di complimento.* Edited by Meredith Ray and Lynn Westwater. Turin: Rosemberg & Sellier, 1995.

———. *Paradiso monacale libri tre.* Venice, 1643.

———. *Paternal Tyranny*. Edited and translated by Letizia Panizza. Chicago: University of Chicago Press, 2004.

Tassini, Giuseppe. *Curiosità veneziane*. Venice: Filippi, 1970.

———. *Feste, spettacoli divertimenti e piaceri degli antichi veneziani*. Venice: Filippi, 1971.

Tre monasteri scomparsi a Venezia, sestiere di Castello: S. Daniele, S. Maria delle Vergini, S. Anna. Edited by Odilla Battiston. Venice: Filippi, 1993.

Urban, Lina. *Processioni e feste dogali*. Vicenza: Neri Pozza, 1998.

Urbani de Gheltof, Giuseppe M. *Di una singolare calzatura già usata dalle donne veneziane*.Venice: tip. Fontana, 1882.

Vecellio, Cesare. *De gli habiti antichi, et moderni di diverse parti del mondo libri due, fatti da Cesare Vecellio, & con discorsi da lui dichiarati*. Venetia: presso Damian Zenaro, 1590.

———. *De gli habiti antichi, et moderni di diverse parti del mondo libri due, fatti da Cesare Vecellio, & con discorsi da lui dichiarati*. Venetia: appresso i Sessa, 1598.

Vico, Enea. *Diversarium gentium aetatis*. Venice, 1558.

Vigorelli, Giancarlo, ed. *Vita e processo di Suor Virginia Maria de Leyva monaca di Monza*. Milan: Garzanti, 1985.

Vitali, Achille. *La moda a Venezia attraverso i secoli*. Venice: Filippi, 1992.

Visconti, Alessandro. *L'Italia nell'epoca della controriforma*. Milan: Mondadori, 1958.

Warr, Cordelia. "Religious Dress in Italy in the Late Middle Ages." In *Defining Dress: Dress as Object, Meaning, and Identity*, edited by Amy de la Hoye and Elizabeth Wilson, 79–92. Manchester: Manchester University Press, 1999.

———. "The Striped Mantle of the Poor Clares: Image and Text in Italy in the Later Middle Ages." *Arte Cristiana* 86 (1998): 415–30.

Weaver, Elissa B. *Convent Theatre in Early Modern Italy: Spiritual Fun and Learning for Women*. Cambridge: Cambridge University Press, 2002.

Wotton, Henry. *Life and Letters*. Edited by Linda Pearsall Smith. Oxford: Clarendon Press, 1907.

Zanette, Emilio. "Una monaca femminista del Seicento." In *Atti del reale Istituto Veneto di Scienze, Lettere e Arti*, CII, p. ii. Venice: 1943, 483–496.

———. *Suor Arcangela: Monaca del Seicento veneziano*. Venice-Rome: Istituto per la collaborazione culturale, 1960.

Zanetti, Anton Maria. *Della Pittura Veneziana e delle opere pubbliche de' Veneziani Maestri Libri V*. Venice: nella stamperia di Giambatista Albrizzi a S. Benedetto, 1771.

Zarri, Gabriella. *Recinti, donne, clausura e matrimonio nella prima età moderna*. Bologna: Il Mulino, 1997.

———. "La vita religiosa tra rinascimento e controriforma: Sponsa Christi:

Nozze mistiche e professione monastica." In *Monaca, moglie, serva, cortigiana: Vita e immagine delle donne tra Rinascimento e Controriforma*, edited by Sara F. Matthews Grieco and Sabina Berveglieri, 118–121. Florence: Morgana edizioni, 2001.

Zorzi, Alvise. *Venezia scomparsa*. Milan: Electa, 1984.

Zuffi, Stefano. *Dettagli di stile: Moda, costume e società nella pittura italiana*. Milan: Mondadori, 2004.

Index

Page numbers in italic refer to illustrations.

Barbaro Gritti, Cornelia (Aurisbe Tarsense), 47
Barbaro, Ermolao, 13
Barbaro, Marina, 75
Barbarossa, Federico, emperor, 34
bareta da vesta, 36
bechetto, 36. *See becho*
becho, 36. *See bechetto*
Bella, Gabriel, 26, 31, 45, 170nn24–25, 175n71
bellacosa, 139, 199
Bellini, Gentile, 108
Bellini, Giovanni, 169n5, 182n46
Bembo, Pietro, daughter of, 115, 186n106
beretin, 109, 199. *See beretino*
beretino, 53, 109. *See beretin*
Bianchi, Betta, 59
bionde, 86, 89, 90
boccassini, 41, 173n62, 173–74n63, 199
Bonanni, Filippo, 54, 186n98, 187nn120–121; habit of San Lorenzo, 82–84; habit of San Zaccaria, 78; habit of the Vergini, 75
Boniface VIII, pope, 62
borzacchini, 69
bottana, 99, 182n180, 199
bozzoladi, 148, 150
braccio, 116, 169n9. *See brazzo*
brazzo, 42, 47, 133, 135, 150, 154, 175nn83–84, 199; Laura Acerbi's conventual trousseau, 145–47; San Zaccaria dress allowances, 55–56, 116. *See braccio*
Bridget, Saint, clothing of, 48
brocatelle, 135
Burano, 59, 91, 92, 116, 190nn159–60, 190n162
busti, 63–64, 181n43, 187n117

Ca' d'Oro, Venice, palace, 117
Caesalpinia brasiliensis, 86
calcagnini, 68
Caliari, Benedetto, 103, 105
Cambrai, city, 201
Cambrai, League of, 164n36, 167–68n50
camerlenghe, 150
camisa, 63, 158n4, 173n57, 183n39, 183n42
Canonicae saeculares, 71, 185n84. *See Canonissae*
Canonissae, 71. *See Canonicae saeculares*
Capitolare de sartoribus, 169n9
Caravella, Laura, 105
Carmelitani scalzi, 53. *See Descalced Carmelites*
Carnival, 9, 29, 51; concerts and plays, 96–97, 99; nuns' costumes, 91
Carpaccio, Vittore, 65
Casanova, Giacomo, 122
Casola, Pietro, fra', 64, 67, 68, 73, 76, 85, 183n57, 186n101
Casoli, Timoteo, fra', 22
cassi, 63–64, 181n39, 181n41, 192n180
Catecumeni, Hospitale, 103
Catherine of Alexandria, saint, Mystical marriage of, 24, 31–33
ceruse, 86
ciambellotto, 26, 169n8
Clara, *suor*, 91
Clarisse, 53, 178n7. *See Poor Clares*
Clothing, 37, 37–38, 42–44, 52; hair cutting, 48–50; poetic compositions in honour of, 171–72n41
Codice Cicogna, 170n22, 172n47, 179n20, 180n21, 182n47, 184n79, 190n156
colana in sbara, 27. *See paternostro*
Colombina, *suor*, 91, 92

About the Author

Isabella Campagnol, a dress, textile, and decorative arts historian, is the co-editor of *Rubelli: A Story of Venetian Silk*. She has lectured on the topics of Venice and Venetian textiles in Italy and Europe and the United States. She lives between Murano and Rome.